FOODSERVICE MANAGEMENT

FOODSERVICE MANAGEMENT

Third Edition

CHARLES E. ESHBACH

A CBI Book
Published by Van Nostrand Reinhold Company
New York

A CBI Book
(CBI is an imprint of Van Nostrand Reinhold Company Inc.)
Copyright © 1979 by CBI Publishing Company, Inc.

Library of Congress Catalog Card Number
ISBN 0-8436-2176-1

Printed in the United States of America

Published by Van Nostrand Reinhold Company Inc.
115 Fifth Avenue
New York, New York 10003

Van Nostrand Reinhold Company Limited
Molly Millars Lane
Wokingham, Berkshire RG11 2PY, England

Van Nostrand Reinhold
480 La Trobe Street
Melbourne, Victoria 3000, Australia

Macmillan of Canada
Division of Canada Publishing Corporation
164 Commander Boulevard
Agincourt, Ontario M1S 3C7, Canada

16 15 14 13 12 11 10 9 8 7 6 5 4

Library of Congress Cataloging in Publication Data

Eshbach, Charles E. 1914-
    Foodservice management.

    Includes index.
    1. Foodservice management. I. Title.
TX943.E82   1979   642.'5   79-20378
ISBN 0-8436-2176-1

Contents

	Preface	vii
1	Receiving Food in Foodservice Establishments	1
2	Food Storage Management	17
3	The Cyclical Menu	34
4	Frozen Foods in Foodservice Establishments	43
5	Bacterial Food Poisoning	61
6	Care and Handling of Prepared Frozen Foods	71
7	Principles of Planning Kitchen Layout	78
8	Using Storage Controls to Simplify Determination of Food Costs	90
9	Using Financial Statements	99
10	Operating Budgets	119
11	Using Break-Even Analysis	140
12	Employee Training	158
13	Purchasing Food	167

14   Purchasing Beef   187

15   Purchasing Canned Fruits and Vegetables   221

16   Purchasing Eggs   242

17   Purchasing Dairy Products   259

18   Effective Communication   285

19   Foodservice and the Computer   300

     Appendix A   311

     Index   313

Preface

Many and varied problems confront operators of foodservice establishments in the day-to-day management of their operations. These problems are common to all kinds of foodservices, although they may occur in somewhat different form in different kinds of establishments.

This book is concerned with identifying, solving, and preventing such problems, which can range from purchasing to sanitation, including receiving, storing, menus, frozen foods, kitchen layout, controls, training of employees, and communication. It brings together in one volume information, suggestions, and recommendations.

Each subject is considered in easy-to-read and easy-to-understand language; and the book is ideal for use in educational institutions and in industry training programs.

Much of the material in this book is based on published reports of the Cooperative Extension Service Foodservice Program, Department of Hotel, Restaurant, and Travel Administration, University of Massachusetts at Amherst. These reports have been widely acclaimed for their usefulness and value.

A number of present and former faculty members of the University of Massachusetts made valuable contributions to the preparation of the original reports. They included Ernest M. Buck, Norman G. Cournoyer, H. M. El-Bisi, Robert M. Grover, Kirby M. Hayes, Robert T. Lukowski, A. T. Miller, Frank E. Potter, R. Miles Sawyer, and Albert L. Wrisley. Their contributions, and especially those of Dr. Wrisley and Professor Lukowski, are gratefully acknowledged. Also greatly appreciated is the assistance provided by Kenneth H. Dean of the University of Massachusetts faculty.

This edition of the book has been updated, and new material has been added, including questions at the end of each chapter, providing much value to foodservice people at a time when many of the basic problem areas are requiring more attention if foodservice operations are to be operated effectively and profitably.

1

Receiving Food in Foodservice Establishments

It is difficult enough to make profits from any business. It is certainly a lot harder if inefficient operation increases costs and reduces the amount of money that remains after all the bills are paid. Combined with rising costs and increasing competition, such a situation can only spell trouble.

Foodservice establishments are especially vulnerable to loss of profits; one area in which this can easily happen is receiving. In many operations, profits are being thrown away by owners, managers, and supervisors who tolerate bad receiving practices.

Management could profitably take a critical look at how food deliveries are being received. It might reveal leaks that could be plugged, and so ensure receiving full value on what is being paid for, and adding more profits.

The efficiency of the receiving operation is just as important in subsidized institutional eating places, where good receiving practices can result in smaller losses and a reduction in the foodservice subsidy.

Proper Receiving Is Essential

Often, foodservice operators are inclined to feel that receiving will take care of itself. Or they assume that *any* employee can take care of it in his spare time. Nothing could be farther from the truth, if the goal is to have an efficient operation. This particular part of foodservice is one of the most critical. It is a vulnerable point for waste, for stealing, and for lost profits.

It is the place where what is gained from using good purchasing practices can be lost day after day. It is the place where detailed purchase specifications and careful buying are nullified. No profitable serving of meals can result if the food does not arrive, if it is short in weight, or if it is in poor condition. Deficiencies will go undetected unless checks are made to discover the true situation. Both the quantity and the quality need careful checking.

Stated another way, the receiving of deliveries is one part of the foodservice operation where strict controls are needed. It so happens that it is also a place where controls can be applied with good results. But all too often, receiving is overlooked, or it is not given the amount of attention it needs.

How receiving is performed varies considerably among foodservice establishments—it depends on the size of the establishment, the facilities available, and the policies of management. However, there are certain principles that apply everywhere. The basic processes of receiving in a foodservice establishment are to:

Receive the merchandise.

Check that the merchandise agrees with the invoice.

Check that the merchandise agrees with the specifications.

List all items received on the receiving clerk's daily report.

Deliver the merchandise to the storeroom or kitchen.

This quick quiz could help evaluate receiving practices in a foodservice establishment.

Do I know each time an order arrives that I am getting what I ordered?

Am I paying just for what I ordered?

Is the quality of what arrived exactly what I ordered?

Is the weight exactly what it should be?

Is the count exactly what it should be?

Does what I receive go into the storeroom for use in the establishment and not out the door for someone else's use?

If the answer to any of these questions is No, the receiving practices could be improved.

Invoice Does Not Tell Entire Story

It is not enough to glance at the invoice or delivery ticket when supplies arrive. The invoice that comes with the merchandise does not give a complete picture of what is being received. All items must be checked for quantity, quality, and price.

Quantity must be checked to assure that the amount ordered has been received.

Quality must be evaluated. Merchandise must be inspected for any damage. It must be of the type and variety ordered and must conform to the specifications of the establishment.

Price must be checked for accuracy. In many foodservice establishments the receiving clerk is responsible for checking prices of merchandise received. In other service establishments the purchasing or the accounting department is solely responsible for checking prices.

Careful verification is not a reflection on the integrity of the supplier—it is good business practice on the part of management. Mistakes may be made by employees of the supplier and by employees of the foodservice establishment. Careful checking will prevent or correct such errors.

The invoice is the supplier's bill or charge against the foodservice establishment for merchandise delivered. It is based on the purchase order and should follow it in detail. How it is handled varies greatly with the policies of management. Often it follows this general routine:

The receiving clerk dates the received invoice and routes it to the purchasing department.

The purchasing department compares the invoice with the original purchase order and submits the invoice to the accounting department.

The accounting department records the invoice, compares it with the receiving clerk's daily report, and forwards the invoice to the main office together with a voucher for final payment.

If the receiving clerk receives a delivery ticket in place of an invoice, the delivery ticket follows the same route as the invoice. Variations of this procedure also depend on the policies of management.

Methods of Receiving

Foodservice establishments generally use one of three principal methods to control the receiving of food.

Invoice Receiving Being quick and economical, this method is the most frequently used. The receiving clerk checks the items on the invoice against the purchase order or telephone order, and notes any discrepancies. The clerk can easily check quality and quantity against the specifications.

3

The clerk should not check from the invoice only but should compare with purchase order or telephone order.

Blind Check Receiving   The clerk is given a blank invoice or purchase order listing incoming merchandise. Quantities, weights, and prices are omitted. The supplier's invoice is mailed to the main office; but if sent with the merchandise, prices and quantities are omitted.

Partial Blind Receiving   This method is a combination of the other two. The clerk is furnished with itemized purchase orders or invoices with quantities and prices omitted. He records the quantity and price of each item as he checks the merchandise. This method is more accurate than invoice receiving, but it takes more time; it is not as accurate as complete blind receiving, but is faster and less costly.

Responsibility of Receiving

The person in charge of receiving, whether called the receiving clerk or by some other name, is one of the most important people in the entire foodservice operation. It is an important position with major responsibilities. The receiving clerk must know the job thoroughly and must be able to work effectively with other employees.

In large operations, one person may be assigned full time to the job of receiving. But in many places the work involved in receiving deliveries is not that great. The person who is assigned to receiving may have other jobs as well. One frequently found combination is receiving and storeroom management.

Regardless of whether the receiving clerk devotes full time or just part time to receiving, he needs to know the job. Explain the job's duties and exactly what the clerk is expected to do. Describe how responsible the position is. The proper introduction to the job and ample training will pay good dividends. It can mean the difference between profit and loss, since the effectiveness of the receiving clerk determines how well the controls function.

Duties of the Receiving Clerk

The specific jobs and responsibilities of the receiving clerk vary according to the policy, the size, and the available facilities of the foodservice establishment. Of the many duties, the most important are:

Check incoming deliveries for quantity and weight.

Inspect for quality.

Record deliveries in a daily report.

Deliver merchandise to its proper place for storage or use.

Additional duties that are of much significance in effective control, but often are not considered very important, include:

storing food

ordering staples

taking inventory

Store foods in the proper area and in accordance with their frequency of use—use the *first-in, first-out* method. Mark or tag all items received with the date of receipt. Store new merchandise in back of present stock. Store the most frequently used items in the front of the storeroom.

In some foodservice establishments the clerk orders staple items when the supply reaches the reorder point set by management Avoid small lot ordering. Be sure that such orders are not placed too frequently. Frequent and small orders are costly.

Monthly inventories are necessary for preparing monthly financial statements. Since most foodservice establishments do not maintain a perpetual inventory system, it is important that inventories be recorded carefully so that they are accurate. An accurate inventory is necessary to determine the monthly food cost.

The Receiving Area

The location of the receiving area and the amount of space allocated to the receiving department affect the handling of deliveries. An efficient layout of the receiving area:

facilitates the handling of merchandise

reduces handling to a minimum

promotes an effective use of labor

conserves space and provides comfort in doing the work

Location   The receiving department should be located between the service entrance and the storeroom. This type of layout controls the flow of deliveries coming into the establishment. It prevents the mislaying of merchandise between the service entrance and the storeroom. If this type of layout is not possible, receiving and checking should be done as close to the storeroom as possible.

Space Required   There is no definite rule for the amount of space required in the receiving area. The amount depends on how often and how large the deliveries are. Each establishment should determine the area needed for efficient handling of incoming deliveries. As a general rule, sufficient space should be provided to:

> accommodate the receiving equipment
>
> prevent orders from piling up and disrupting normal operations
>
> facilitate the smooth movement of merchandise on trucks

Types of Receiving Scales

The receiving clerk, like any worker, needs the proper equipment to do an efficient job. Since weighing of foods as they are received is of prime importance, a set of accurate scales is essential. Keep in mind that a set of scales is only a tool for measuring weight. Receiving scales need to be in balance and carefully handled if they are to record correct weights.

Various types of platform scales are available. Platform scales built into the floor are more expensive, but this feature saves time and expedites the handling of deliveries. The type of scale used will vary according to the size of the foodservice establishment.

Automatic Indicating Scale   This type of scale is expensive, but it indicates an accurate zero when in balance. It is springless and has a glass-enclosed dial face. Weights are recorded immediately on the dial face in clear view of all concerned. This feature saves time and avoids disputes in case of shortages.

Beam-Type Scale   This scale is usually a satisfactory weighing device when used by a competent receiving clerk. While it is less expensive than the automatic indicating scale, it is not always accurate. It frequently becomes out of balance to the extent of 2 or 3 pounds without the receiving clerk knowing it. But, in most establishments, an ordinary beam-type, portable floor model should be sufficient.

Recording Scale   This type of scale stamps the weight of the merchandise on the invoice or delivery ticket. It is very expensive and usually is found only in establishments with very large volume.

Other Equipment

Several other items of equipment are needed for efficient receiving operations. These include:

Desk   A desk, preferably a stand-up desk, is needed in the receiving area for checking invoices or delivery tickets.

Table   A table in the receiving area is useful for checking and sorting merchandise before it is transferred to the storeroom.

Trucks   A 2-wheel or a 4-wheel hand truck is useful in moving merchandise from the dock to the receiving area and to the storeroom. A 4-wheel truck can accommodate about three or four times as much weight and bulk as the 2-wheel hand truck.

Thermometer   A thermometer is a useful tool in the hands of a competent receiving clerk. It can be used to determine if the proper temperatures of frozen foods and perishables have been maintained in the process of delivery.

Wire Baskets   The use of wire baskets for storing produce will help the receiving clerk check quality. Transferring produce from the original container into a wire basket reveals the quality of all the produce in the container. Produce sorted into wire baskets is properly aerated in storage. The basket serves as a convenient unit of issue.

Receiving Procedures

The largest single cost of operation for many foodservice establishments is the expenditure for food. Since food cost takes such a large percentage of the sales dollar, efficient receiving procedures help keep the food cost percentage in line.

For example, if the food cost of a foodservice establishment is 45 percent, this means that 45 cents of the sales dollar is spent for food to resell. If the 45 cents is increased to 47 cents by poor receiving procedures, and other expenses remain unchanged, then profits must decrease 2 cents per dollar of sales or the selling price must be increased.

Good receiving procedures are necessary to keep food costs in line, as well as to reduce handling costs, handling times, and the chance of spoilage. There are a number of practices which are essential to good receiving procedures:

Be Ready for the Delivery   The establishment, the customer, and the quality of the food, especially that of perishables, will all benefit if the receiving clerk is ready to receive the merchandise.

Check the Merchandise   Check all merchandise on arrival to determine whether it meets the purchase order price, count, and weight. Open items ordered in cases, if the case is damaged or discolored. Date canned goods before storing. Dating them as they are placed on the shelf helps ensure first-in, first-out use. Many systems have been devised for checking the quality of produce, but the best practice is to inspect the produce when it is delivered. Select

7

a typical fruit or vegetable and cut it in half to check for juice content, rust, or taste.

Weigh Each Item Separately   When receiving bulk items, remove excess paper, cheesecloth, or ice. A scale weighs anything and everything placed on it. Excessive wrapping or ice gives the merchandise added weight. It is not always practicable to unpack heavily iced items at delivery to obtain the net weight. A good practice in checking the net weight of items packed in ice is to weigh them before preparing, but frequently items being received should be unpacked to be checked for net weight.

Weigh Meat Orders Separately   Never weigh meat orders together. Meat is the most costly of all items received by a foodservice establishment. Weighing meats separately may make the difference between an acceptable food cost and one that is out of line. Ten pounds of tenderloin missing in an order will not be offset by 10 pounds of flank steak.

Tag Meats on Delivery   This practice prevents disputes over weights with the supplier, the kitchen staff, or the butcher. Tagging meats also reduces the chance of spoilage or excess weight loss, as the tag can be dated for first-in, first-out use.

Check for Quality   Checking for quality is often neglected by the receiving clerk. It is important to see that the grade and quality of the merchandise agree with what is shown on the invoice. Remember that there are grades within grades.

Because of large orders received or other duties, the receiving clerk does not always have the time to make a complete quality check. Under such circumstances, he should inspect merchandise for quality by selecting random samples. For example, if thirty cases of lettuce are received, the receiving clerk could inspect every fifth case for quality. If this system of inspecting for quality is to be effective, the receiving clerk *must* know quality as well as whether the quality meets the specifications of the establishment.

Store Items Promptly   Check and store perishable items first. Exposure to high room temperature can mean quality loss or spoilage. The quicker all merchandise is stored, the less chance it has of spoiling or becoming mislaid.

Receiving Specifications

Detailed specifications should be prepared for all merchandise received. These specifications must be the same as the specifications set up for purchasing. A statement such as—"tomatoes, fresh, 30 pounds to the lug, 75 tomatoes to the lug"—immediately tells the receiving clerk the weight of the tomatoes and the number of tomatoes in the lug. This knowledge helps him do a good job of checking merchandise received.

Charts should be prepared showing the average weights of all merchandise usually received. The use of these charts can prevent the loss that sometimes results, for example, from the occasional case of eggs that may be one layer short.

The person in charge of receiving should have access to the specifications and weight charts for easy reference. Probably the most convenient place to post these charts is near the receiving clerk's desk.

Proper use of specifications and weight charts:

eliminates guess work by the receiving personnel

ensures receiving a product that meets the standards of the establishment

gives the manager a tool to control quality from the time food is received until it is served

Receiving Manual

Much of the information needed by the receiving personnel can be put into a manual. This information will then be available for use in receiving, and also for training personnel.

This manual need not be an elaborate book, but simply a place to put together such data as the purchasing specifications, the average weight charts, copies of the forms used in receiving with explanations of the receiver's responsibilities for them, the procedure for receiving, the procedure for rejecting items that are being delivered, lists of the things to look for in checking the quality of various products, and information on which products go to which storage area.

Receiving Forms

Recording all incoming deliveries is as important as checking for quantity and quality. The form or style of recording is of secondary importance and may be designed to suit the needs of the establishment. The fact that an accurate record is made of all incoming deliveries *is* important.

Too often the receiving record is considered by both management and receiving personnel as a copybook for posting food bills. A receiving record is not a copybook. The purpose and function of a receiving record is to record all incoming food deliveries. Each delivery should be accurately recorded as to date of delivery, quantity, price, and amount of each item received. If this is done properly, the receiving record becomes a useful tool for management to study and compare the day-to-day purchases. This is necessary if food cost is figured on a daily basis.

The record of merchandise received should be in a form suitable for checking against the supplier's invoice. It is usually in the form of a receiving clerk's daily report. The receiving record shown in Figure 1-2 is in wide use by medium-sized hotels and foodservice establishments. Such a record should show:

> date of receipts
>
> invoice or purchase order number
>
> supplier's name
>
> description of merchandise
>
> quantity received
>
> unit in which merchandise came
>
> unit price
>
> total amount of extension
>
> distribution of deliveries

The number of copies of each receiving report to be made up and distributed depends on the practices or policies established by management but at least two copies of the receiving clerk's daily report should be made. One copy goes to the office for verification. The other copy remains in the receiving clerk's file.

Receiving forms (Figures 1-2 and 1-3) may be purchased, or they may be designed by the foodservice establishment. The simple receiving sheet (Figure 1-3) shows invoice number, from whom purchased, unit, amount, article, unit price, total amount, and where stored. This can be mimeographed on a sheet of paper 8½-by 11-inch.

Distribution of Deliveries

Deliveries are divided into two main categories: *food direct* and *food stores*. The category, sundries, refers to non-food items that go to another storage area. Purchases sent directly to the kitchen for use the same day or the next are classified as food direct and become part of the daily food cost. Purchases that are sent to the storeroom (including the meat and produce box) for further storage are classified as food stores on the receiving sheet and become part of storeroom control.

If the receiving record is used as a consolidation of each day's purchases, the total amount column must equal the amount of all invoices for the day plus the total of the food direct column and the food stores column.

Other forms for recording merchandise are *memorandum invoices* or *substitution invoices* (Figure 1-1).

Figure 1-1   Invoice

SUBSTITUTE INVOICE

FROM: ___Quality Meat Company___   DATE: 9/16/

QUANTITY	UNIT	DESCRIPTION	AMOUNT
25	lbs.	Ground Round @ $.84	21 00

RECEIVED BY: ___John Black___

Figure 1-2 Daily Report

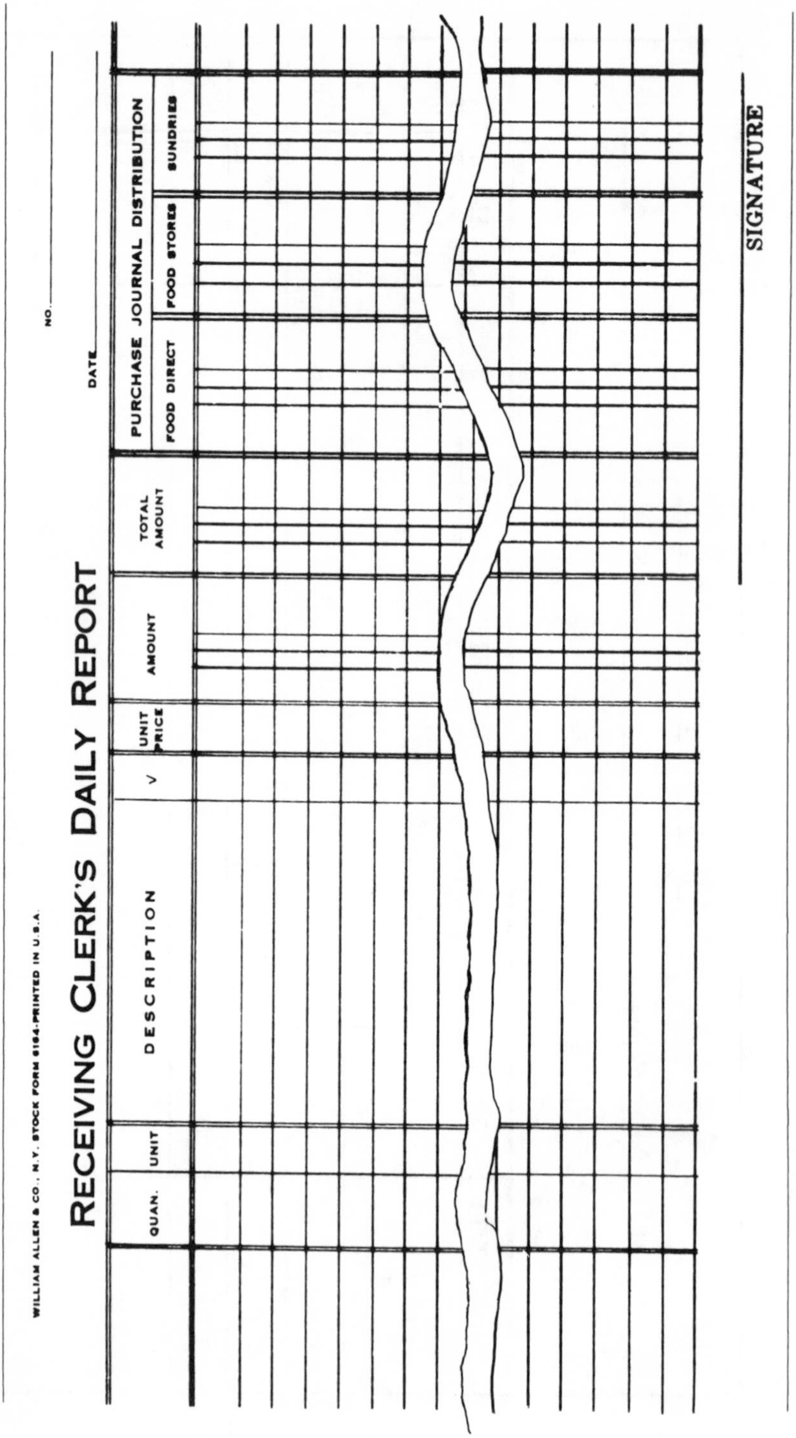
WILLIAM ALLEN & CO., N.Y. STOCK FORM 6164-PRINTED IN U.S.A.

NO. ____

DATE ____

RECEIVING CLERK'S DAILY REPORT

QUAN.	UNIT	DESCRIPTION	√	UNIT PRICE	AMOUNT	TOTAL AMOUNT	PURCHASE JOURNAL DISTRIBUTION		
							FOOD DIRECT	FOOD STORES	SUNDRIES

SIGNATURE ____

Figure 1-3   Receiving Clerk's Daily Report

Invoice No.	From Whom Purchased	Unit	Amt.	Article	Unit Price	Total Amt.	Food Direct	Food Stores
16981	Barnes Meat Co.	lb.	75	Beef, round choice	1.63	122.25		122.25
16981	Barnes Meat Co.	lb.	32	Rib of Beef, choice	2.65	84.80		84.80
3967	Arbuckle Dairy	gal.	30	Milk	1.40	42.00	5.30	36.70
3967	Arbuckle Dairy	½ pt.	150	Milk	.10	15.00	15.00	
3967	Arbuckle Dairy	gal.	16	Ice Cream	2.17	34.72		34.72
986	Interstate Corp.	lf	25	Bread, white	.39	9.75	9.75	
986	Interstate Corp.	lf	12	Bread, dark	.45	5.40	5.40	
21067	Angelo Produce Co.	hd	48	Lettuce, head, 24/crate	.21	10.08	5.04	5.04
21067	Angelo Produce Co.	lb.	15	Carrots	.19	2.85	2.85	
				Total Food Received 2/20		326.85	43.34	283.51

Signature

These forms are used primarily when merchandise arrives without an invoice. They contain practically the same information as the receiving record. The memorandum invoice or substitution invoice is sent to the office for verification and approval when the invoice arrives. One of these forms must be used when an establishment keeps a daily food cost.

Purchase Invoice Stamp

In larger foodservice establishments an invoice stamp is used on all incoming invoices. The receiving clerk stamps and dates the invoice. He also signs or initials his name on the Quantity O.K. line indicating that the correct amount has been received. The invoice is routed to purchasing for approval of prices, and next to accounting where it is compared with the receiving clerk's daily report. The invoice is then approved for final payment.

A purchase invoice stamp may be designed to suit the needs of the establishment. Figure 1-4 shows purchase invoice stamps that are widely used in the foodservice industry.

Returning Unsatisfactory Merchandise

If there are shortages in the quantity of the merchandise received, or if the quality does not conform to specifications, a credit memorandum must be made out in duplicate and sent to the office. One copy must be sent to the supplier. All correspondence concerning adjustment by the supplier should be handled by the purchasing department or the buyer.

If a credit memorandum is requested because of unsatisfactory merchandise, the following should be done:

Figure 1-4   Purchase Invoice Stamps

Order No.   Rec'g No.

Date Rec'd

Quantity O.K._____

Quality & Price O.K._____

Ext. & Footing O.K._____

Entered_____

O.K. for Payment_____

DATE REC'D_____

QUANTITY O.K._____

PRICES O.K._____

EXTENSIONS O.K._____

APPROVED BY_____

Make out a credit memorandum.

Return the merchandise immediately.

Note on invoice the reason for returning the merchandise.

Notify the manager so that the menu may be changed if necessary.

A good practice is to have the delivery person sign any invoice that covers merchandise that is deficient in quality or quantity. This can save further explanation and telephone calls.

Periodic Receiving Tests

Safeguards are needed to ensure that the controls established by management remain effective. Personnel have a tendency to become lax in their duties if they are not periodically checked. Periodic receiving tests made at frequent intervals, but in no fixed pattern of time, will help reduce indifference or carelessness of receiving personnel. The manager or assistant manager should verify receiving procedures at least once a week.

Keys to Good Receiving

Basic requirements for receiving procedures to ensure maximum control are as follows:

Have adequate equipment and a convenient place for unloading and checking deliveries.

Assign the responsibility of receiving to a competent person.

Check the receiving procedures frequently—at least once a week.

Post specifications and average weight charts for easy reference.

Have the receiving clerk call a superior when in doubt about the quality of an item.

To control receiving procedures:

Record all incoming deliveries for price, weight, count, and quality.

Keep complete and accurate records—analyze daily.

Make receiving records in duplicate.

Make sure scales are accurate—test them frequently.

Weigh all items separately.

Tag meats on delivery.

Double-check damaged containers and cartons.

Check perishables for appearance and irregularities.

Store all items promptly.

Finally, make sure that you receive what you ordered—the right quantity, in good condition, and at the correct price.

Summary

Good receiving practices are essential in a foodservice establishment but are often not given necessary attention. Incoming food must be checked for quality, price, weight, and number.

Invoice receiving, blind check receiving, and partial blind check receiving are the three principal methods to control receiving of food. Responsibility for receiving should be delegated to a competent person and should not be a "hit or miss" proposition.

The receiving area and space allocated to it should be the best possible for reducing handling, getting better use of labor, and conserving space. An adequate scale for weighing incoming food, and other necessary equipment should be provided.

Good receiving procedures should insure that all is ready for deliveries, the merchandise is checked and weighed, quality is determined, and items go to storage quickly. Specifications and weight charts should be available. Receiving forms should be used. Unsatisfactory merchandise should be returned, and periodic receiving tests should be made to ensure that receiving personnel are performing efficiently.

Questions

1.   Describe the possible results of assuming that the receiving of incoming food will take care of itself with no one person in particular responsible.

2.   List the steps in the procedure for receiving in a foodservice establishment.

3.   Describe three of the principal methods of controlling the receiving of food.

4.   Describe the duties of the receiving clerk in a foodservice establishment.

5.   List the equipment needed for a good receiving room and operation.

6.   Outline a set of receiving procedures essential for effective receiving of food.

7.   What is the purpose and function of the receiving record?

2

Food Storage Management

A lot of money is lost regularly in the food storages of food-service operations; and much of this dollar loss could be prevented rather easily. Foodservice people often do not recognize what a vital part of the foodservice operation the storage really is. Most operators could profit by giving this part of the system more consideration—by ensuring that adequate and proper storage is available and is operated correctly.

Storage deserves this attention for a number of reasons, all of which are related very closely to the success of the foodservice operation. Storage is the link between receiving and preparation. In the same way that effective receiving is essential if the values from good purchasing are to be realized, so is good storage if the food received from suppliers is to be available in the right condition for the preparation of meals.

Storage performs a holding function, but it is also an excellent control point. It is a location in the business where management can exert control effectively without adding much in terms of either time or personnel.

Good storage management can contribute a great deal to keeping the costs of operation down. Opportunities for increasing profits are greater when there is effective control of shrinkage, pilferage, and the unnecessary handling of food.

Every foodservice establishment should have storage space that is adequate, efficiently arranged, and well managed. The particular operation, its location, and the kind of business conducted have much to do with the exact kind and amount of storage facilities needed. Generally, however, the storage should:

> provide space to hold the food until it is used
>
> keep loss of quality in the food to a minimum
>
> be convenient for the employees who handle the food
>
> function as a major control point for management

To conduct an effective storage function, there should be a storeroom for semi-perishable foods, a frozen storage for frozen foods, a refrigerated storage for meats, a refrigerated room for fresh fruits and vegetables, and refrigerated space for dairy products. These are essentials. In many foodservice operations, additional non-refrigerated and refrigerated storage space is necessary at locations in the preparation area and in the service area.

General Storage Requirements

The perishability of food and the different types of operations in a foodservice establishment require that storage facilities provide specific conditions for holding food. How well the storage facilities do this can influence the success or failure of the business. Also, how well the storage facilities are used and managed affects the efficiency of operation. The location, layout, equipment, and internal arrangement of the storages all greatly affect the efficiency of the storage operation. They also affect how much and how well management can exert control.

Generally, the ideal location for storage facilities is near the receiving area and adjacent to the preparation area. Such a location is not always available, and seldom will there be remodeling to provide it. In most foodservice establishments, the storage facilities are already present and cannot be altered without considerable expense. Usually, however, improvements can be made in the management of the storage facilities that will make it possible to reduce costs. For example, equipment can be arranged and the routes of travel planned, so that workers save steps and time. Time represents money, and time that is lost through cross-travel and backtracking cannot be recovered. It becomes added cost.

Three Factors Affect Layout

There are three factors that need special consideration as far as the layout of storage is concerned.

Frequency of Use   The items that are used most often should be stored nearest the place where they are used. This saves time in handling and locating merchandise and in taking inventories.

Space Requirements   The turnover and frequency of deliveries are important in determining how large the storage should be and what types of storage facilities are needed. If the food is received and used daily, space requirements for storage will not be great. If deliveries are made only weekly or biweekly, more storage space is needed.

Characteristics of the Items   The size, weight, shape, perishability, and ease with which items can be misplaced or stolen have an influence on how the storage should be arranged and operated.

Equipment

Adequate and suitable equipment is needed for good use of storage facilities. Portable equipment is necessary for handling foods. This may include handtrucks, semi-live skids, or platforms with dollies.

Auxiliary equipment, such as ladders, a heavy-duty work table, racks for floor storage, thermometers and other special equipment for refrigerated storages, and materials for record keeping, is needed to help personnel store food properly and efficiently.

Generally, the kinds and volumes of foods to be handled and the storage space available will determine the types of equipment that should be used.

Care of Food in Storage

Maintaining the quality of the foods while they are in storage is one of the major things that the storage facilities must do effectively. All foods are perishable—some more than others. All food items should be handled so as to minimize the loss of quality. Even when foods are held under optimum storage conditions, there is some loss of quality. Good storage conditions keep the loss at a slow rate; poor conditions greatly speed up the rate.

As food loses quality, its appearance, texture, and flavor are affected. Customers are dissatisfied with menu items made from foods that have lost substantial amounts of quality. If more quality is lost, the food can easily become unfit for eating and, in some cases, it can cause food poisoning. Poor handling and storage practices can mean fewer sales, increased food costs, and loss of profit. So, proper care of food in storage rates a high priority in any foodservice establishment.

Controlling the loss of quality in food is a matter of controlling the action of bacteria, yeasts, and molds. Yeasts and molds are not generally considered harmful to humans and perform some helpful functions. For example, in the aging of beef, enzymes provide a desirable flavor. But, other yeasts and molds produce undesirable flavor, odors, and appearance in foods. Bacteria also perform some desirable functions, such as the action that produces cheese, yogurt, and sour cream. But, many bacteria make food unfit for use, and some can cause food poisoning. In general, a foodservice operator needs to handle and store foods in such a way that growth and action of bacteria, yeasts, and molds are kept to a minimum.

Semi-Perishable and Perishable Foods

While all foods are perishable, some lose quality at a slow enough rate that they are often called semi-perishables to distinguish them from perishables, the foods that lose quality at a rapid rate. Storage conditions for semi-perishables are much different from those for perishables. Most foodservice establishments need storage facilities for both classes of foods.

Semi-perishables, as a rule, do not require refrigeration. They do, however, need to be protected from excessive heat, dampness, insects, and rodents. Coffee, tea, flour, rice, and other dry bulk products are likely to cake, lose flavor, and become infested by insects, if they are not stored properly.

Contrary to common belief, canned goods do not last forever. Most canned foods can be stored satisfactorily for a year under the best storage conditions. Under improper storage conditions, they lose flavor, texture, and nutritional values. It is a good idea to specify "current pack only" when buying canned fruits and vegetables. The usual recommendation is to store canned foods for no more than six months. After that, they begin to lose their original quality, and their value decreases.

All perishable foods require refrigerated storage of one type or another, since temperature is a vital factor in the length of time these foods retain their quality. Refrigeration slows the growth of bacteria, which occurs most rapidly between 70° and 90°F. Refrigeration reduces the temperature to levels where bacterial growth progresses only slowly.

The Storeroom

A good storeroom, where groceries and other foods not requiring refrigeration can be stored, is essential for an efficient foodservice establishment. The storeroom should be as conveniently located as possible. It should be large enough to take care of the storage needs dictated by the volume of business and the frequency of food deliveries.

The storeroom should be cool, dry, and well ventilated. Hot water and steam pipes should be well insulated. If the windows allow direct sunlight into the storeroom, they should be painted. Direct rays of the sun can damage food in glass jars. Direct sunlight can also increase the storeroom temperature to a point where it affects the quality of canned foods. Temperature and humidity need to be within the ranges that cause the least loss in quality.

In addition to the equipment used for all storage activities, the storeroom should have metal containers with tight-fitting covers on can dollies. These are practicable and sanitary for storing such items as flour, rice, and sugar. A grocer's scoop is needed for dispensing food stored in containers. There should also be a large scale which can weigh up to 200 pounds, and a small scale for weighing such items as beans, sugar, salt, and spices.

Shelf Construction   Storeroom shelves in foodservice establishments can be made of wood or metal. Wood shelving has these advantages:

> can be made from ordinary lumber that is easy to obtain
>
> can be adapted easily to unusual storeroom layout
>
> provides greater protection for glass containers because of its softer surface

Metal shelving has these advantages:

> easy to assemble and take apart
>
> comes in standard forms and sizes
>
> is durable, easy to clean, and vermin-proof
>
> provides more space for storage
>
> is not a fire hazard

A combination of wood and metal shelving may be used to gain some of the advantages that each material offers.

Shelves should be arranged in the storeroom to provide maximum storage capacity and flexibility. The lowest shelf should be at least 30 inches above the floor. The space underneath can be used to store flour, rice, sugar, and other foods that can be placed on skids or in galvanized cans. Maximum practicable height for shelving is about 7½ feet. Install shelves so that the height of the shelves may be adjusted to take two layers of Number 10 cans, or three layers of Number 2 or Number 2½ cans. The bottom shelf may be 24 to 30 inches deep. Other shelves should be at least 20 inches deep.

Table 2-1 provides measurements of cans and cartons. These can be used to estimate the shelf capacity and vertical clearance needed for storing cans and cartons in the storeroom. The shelves should be strong enough to support the weight of the canned goods and other items being stored. See that the supports are placed so they prevent buckling.

Many storerooms have little or no shelving; goods are held in cases on skids.

Temperature   Temperatures of 50° to 70°F. are recommended for the storeroom. A temperature of 50°F. is considered ideal, but it isn't possible to have *that* low a temperature in many storerooms. Temperatures higher than 70°F. are likely to cause caking of some foods, encourage the

21

Table 2-1   Approximate Measurements of Cans and Cartons

Size of Can	Approximate Diameter of Can (Inches)	Clear Height Per Tier (Inches)	Cans Per Carton (Number)	Size of Carton
Number 2	3½	5	24	14 x 10½ x 9¼
Number 2½	4	5	24	17 x 12¾ x 10¼
Number 3 (Cylinder)	4¼	7½	12	17½ x 13½ x 7¾
Number 10	6¼	7½	6	19 x 12¾ x 7¼

growth of bacteria, and affect the quality of canned foods. A good thermometer to measure degrees in Fahrenheit should be kept in the storeroom so the operator can maintain the temperatures that will help retain quality.

Humidity   Humidity is an important factor in storeroom conditions that is often overlooked or not given sufficient attention. A relative humidity of 50 to 60 percent is considered satisfactory for most products. It should not exceed 70 percent for best storage conditions. Humidity that is too high can result in rusting of cans, caking of dry and dehydrated products, growth of bacteria and mold, and infestation of insects in the storeroom. Humidity can be measured by a device known as a psychrometer or hygrometer.

Ventilation   Ventilation is an important factor in the control of temperature and humidity. Good ventilation provides clean, fresh air at the required temperature and humidity. It can be provided by natural or mechanical means. Mechanical refrigeration requires intake and exhaust fans. Natural ventilation can be obtained by locating openings near the floor level and near the ceiling to get circulation of air. Generally, the air in a storeroom should change six times per hour for adequate ventilation.

Refrigerated Storages

Two main kinds of refrigerated storage are used in foodservice establishments:

Normal refrigeration—in which temperatures are maintained from $32°$ to $45°$F., depending on the type of food being stored.

Frozen refrigeration—in which the temperature is maintained at $0°$F. or lower.

Refrigerated storage space should be convenient to both the receiving area and the preparation area. This arrangement is generally found in most foodservice establishments. Usually, some refrigerated storage space is located where most of the food is received, and additional refrigerated space is provided where the food is prepared. There is a trend toward placing more refrigerated storage nearer to the point of food use. This reduces the amount of waste motion, speeds up service, and gives better control of food quality.

Refrigerated storage conditions can be obtained with both walk-in and reach-in types of storage boxes. Usually, the walk-in types of refrigerated storage are located in the storage area; the reach-in types are nearer the place where the food is prepared. The exact location depends on the size and type of establishment.

The layout of the refrigerated storage space is influenced greatly by activity of the personnel, the requirements for refrigerated storage, and the characteristics of the food that is stored.

There is quite a variation in the capacity of refrigerated storages and also in the combinations of refrigerated storage facilities found in foodservice establishments. The type and size of establishment, volume of business done, purchasing practices (especially as they affect frequency of delivery), and the policy of management are major factors in determining just what size and combination of refrigerated storage facilities are necessary.

Equipment   Portable equipment used in receiving dry food supplies can also be used for handling foods that go into refrigerated storage. However, the most important item of equipment used in a refrigerated storage is the thermometer. Reliable thermometers are essential to ensure that proper temperatures are maintained within the refrigerated storages. A dial thermometer outside the refrigerator, which indicates the temperature inside, is recommended. Readings should be taken daily at regular intervals, since high temperatures quickly affect the quality of perishable foods.

The temperature varies somewhat within refrigerators. It does not go as low in some spots as it does in others. These "warm" spots can be located by putting thermometers in different areas and taking the readings each hour for three or four hours. When the warmest area is located, install a thermometer there and adjust the thermostat so that the storage temperature on that thermometer is at the recommended level.

Temperature   Temperatures in refrigerated storage range between $32°$ and $45°F$. But, different kinds of perishable products require different storage temperatures, if they are to retain quality. As a result, different refrigerated storages are used for different classes of foods.

Meat Boxes   It is recommended that the meat box be maintined at a temperature of $32°$ to $36°F$.

23

Fruits and Vegetables   Vegetables vary in their temperature requirements, but most fruits and vegetables are kept in a storage where a higher temperature range of 32° to 45°F. is maintained.

Dairy Products   Dairy products and eggs require storage temperature similar to many fruits and vegetables. But they need a separate storage because they readily absorb odors and flavors from other foods.

Table 2-2 indicates the temperature, humidity, length of storage period, and highest freezing points for a selected list of fruits and vegetables commonly used in foodservice establishments. *These are optimum figures for commercial storage of fresh fruits and vegetables and are the result of research conducted under controlled laboratory conditions.*

Optimum conditions are seldom available in foodservice establishments. Sufficient different storages are not available for holding products at many different temperature ranges. Most items are held in storage for only short periods of time. As a result, many of these specific temperature recommendations would not be practicable in foodservice operations. Table 2-3 provides a general guide for vegetable storage for foodservice operators. It indicates temperature ranges for both temporary storage and holding storage within which fresh fruits and vegetables may be held where there is a rapid turnover.

Humidity   The humidity of the air in refrigerated storage has an effect on shrinkage and spoilage of the foods stored in the box. As with temperature, different products require different levels of humidity.

Meat Boxes   In meat storages, the humidity should be kept between 75 percent and 85 percent. If the humidity goes too low, the dry air will absorb moisture from the meat, and there will be shrinkage and loss of flavor. If there is too much moisture in the air, the meat becomes wet. This speeds up the growth of bacteria and the meat starts to spoil much sooner.

Fruit and Vegetable   For most fruits and vegetables, a relative humidity of 85 percent to 90 percent gives the best results in a foodservice establishment. Leafy vegetables and root vegetables keep better at 90 percent to 95 percent relative humidity.

With the rapid turnover of food in a foodservice establishment, a relative humidity of 85 percent to 90 percent is adequate.

If produce must be kept in storage longer than three or four days, take care to ensure enough moisture. The produce can be covered with wet cloths. Do not wet the floor to increase humidity, as this is dangerous. Do not set pans of water in refrigerators to increase humidity—the water may encourage growth of bacteria.

Exact control of humidity is rather difficult in some foodservice establishments. However, as new refrigerators are designed and old ones are remodeled, more accurate methods of controlling humidity become available.

Shelving   Shelves in refrigerated storages should be made of metal. The shelving can be either stationary or portable. Portable shelving is preferred as it makes it much easier to move equipment for cleaning. When door sills are flush with the floor, portable tray racks are recommended. They can be loaded with food at the preparation area and stored in walk-in boxes until serving time.

Frozen Food Storage

Need for frozen food storage space has increased steadily as more frozen foods are used in foodservice establishments. Use of frozen foods makes it possible to use less labor per meal. During slack periods, many foods can be prepared in advance, preportioned, and frozen until needed. Thus, adequate frozen storage makes it possible to eliminate many steps in food handling and preparation. However, frozen food storage requires lower temperature conditions than the other types of storage.

There are two basic types of freezers—walk-in and reach-in. The type to use depends on the size and volume of the foodservice establishment. The reach-in freezer is generally available in two styles—the upright or vertical type with removable or adjustable shelves, and the chest-type freezer. The upright or vertical type is preferred in many foodservice establishments, since it requires less floor space and less bending and stooping by workers.

Regardless of size or classification, frozen food holding cabinets must provide storage space at 0° to -10°F. or lower at all times. They should be large enough to store frozen foods with maximum efficiency. It is important that the freezer compressor unit have enough capacity so that it does not overload during the warm months.

It's now generally accepted that frozen food holding cabinets cannot be used successfully for processing. Where on-premise freezing is to be scheduled, separate freezing equipment is called for to provide the necessary subzero temperature. Equipment designed to do the actual freezing job is referred to as a food freezer or a processing freezer or, sometimes, as a blast freezer, plate freezer, tunnel freezer. This equipment operates below -20°F.

Location of the Freezer   The size and volume of business influence the type of freezer for use in a foodservice establishment. Walk-in freezers are stationary and their location cannot be changed without excessive cost. Cost of operation of a reach-in freezer is influenced by where it is located. If it is in a warm area, operating costs will be higher, as frequent opening of the door admits much warm air. At the same time, if the reach-in freezer is far from the point of use, employees will have to spend additional time traveling back and forth between the preparation area and the freezer.

Regardless of the type of refrigerator or freezer used, a regular service

25

Table 2-2   Recommended Temperature, Relative
Humidity, Approximate Length of Storage
Life, and Highest Freezing Points for a Selected
List of Commercially Stored Fruits and
Vegetables

Commodity	Temperature Degrees Fahrenheit	Relative Humidity Percent	Approximate Length of Storage Period	Highest Freezing Point Degrees Fahrenheit
Fresh Fruits:				
Apples	30 to 40*	90	3 to 8 months	29.3
Avocados	40 to 55*	85 to 90	2 to 4 weeks*	31.5
Bananas	56 to 58*	90 to 95*	*	30.6
Grapefruit				
Calif. & Arizona	58 to 60	85 to 90	4 to 6 weeks	
Florida & Texas	50*	85 to 90	4 to 6 weeks	30.0
Lemons	*	85 to 90	1 to 6 months*	29.4
Oranges				
Calif. & Arizona	38 to 48*	85 to 90	3 to 8 weeks*	29.7
Florida & Texas	32	85 to 90	8 to 12 weeks	30.6
Peaches	31 to 32	90	2 to 4 weeks*	30.3
Nectarines	31 to 32	90	2 to 4 weeks	30.4
Pears	29 to 31	90 to 95	2 to 7 months*	29.2
Pineapples	45 to 55*	85 to 90	2 to 4 weeks*	30.0
Strawberries	32	90 to 95	5 to 7 days	30.6
Fresh Vegetables:				
Asparagus	32 to 36*	95	2 to 3 weeks	30.9
Beans				
Green or Snap	40 to 45*	90 to 95	7 to 10 days	30.7
Lima	32 to 40*	90	1 to 2 weeks*	31.0
Broccoli, sprouting	32	90 to 95	10 to 14 days	30.9
Brussels Sprouts	32	90 to 95	3 to 5 weeks	30.5
Cabbage				
Early	32	90 to 95	3 to 6 weeks	30.4
Late	32	90 to 95	3 to 4 months	30.4
Carrots (topped)				
Mature	32	90 to 95	4 to 5 months	29.5
Immature	32	90 to 95	4 to 6 weeks	29.5
Cauliflower	32	90 to 95	2 to 4 weeks	30.6
Celery	32	90 to 95	2 to 3 months	31.1
Cucumbers	45 to 50	90 to 95	10 to 14 days	31.1

schedule for compressors, condensers, and motors should be set up and followed. This maintenance should be done by a competent refrigeration mechanic.

Storage of Fresh Meats

Beef is the most important item in most foodservice establishments, and many eating places are judged on the quality of the beef they serve. So, it is of more-than-usual importance that beef be stored under proper conditions.

Table 2-2   Continued

Commodity	Temperature Degrees Fahrenheit	Relative Humidity Percent	Approximate Length of Storage Period	Highest Freezing Point Degrees Fahrenheit
Lettuce	32	95	2 to 3 weeks	31.7
Melons				
Cantaloup, 3/4 slip	36 to 40	85 to 90	15 days	29.9
Cantaloup, full slip	32 to 35	85 to 90	5 to 14 days	29.9
Casaba	45 to 50	85 to 90	4 to 6 weeks	30.1
Crenshaw	45 to 50	85 to 90	2 weeks	30.1
Honey Dew	45 to 50	85 to 90	3 to 4 weeks	30.3
Persian	45 to 50	85 to 90	2 weeks	30.5
Watermelon	40 to 50*	80 to 85	2 to 3 weeks	31.3
Mushrooms	32	90	3 to 4 days	30.4
Onions				
Dry	32	65 to 70	1 to 8 months*	30.6
Green	32	90 to 95		30.4
Potatoes				
Early Crop	40 to 50*	90*	*	30.9
Late Crop	40 to 50*	90*	*	30.9
Radishes				
Spring	32	90 to 95	3 to 4 weeks	30.7
Winter	32	90 to 95	2 to 4 months	
Spinach	32	90 to 95	10 to 14 days	31.5
Squashes				
Winter	50 to 55	50 to 75*	*	30.5
Summer	32 to 50	90	5 to 14 days	31.1
Sweetpotatoes	55 to 60*	85 to 90	4 to 6 months	29.7
Tomatoes				
Mature green	55 to 70*	85 to 90	1 to 3 weeks	31.0
Firm ripe	45 to 50	85 to 90	4 to 7 days	31.1

*See Agricultural Handbook No. 66 for further information. There are variations from the stated figures for varieties and when the product is being used for certain purposes.
Source: *The Commercial Storage of Fruits, Vegetables and Florist and Nursery Stocks*, Agricultural Handbook Number 66, United States Department of Agriculture, 1968.

Beef should be refrigerated immediately upon delivery. If aged beef is purchased, it should not be held in storage for more than five days. If held longer, it will need extra trimming. Use lower grades of beef immediately, as they do not have the fat covering that is found on the better grades. Beef that has only a small amount of fat covering dries out quickly.

Use fresh lamb, mutton, pork, and veal as soon as possible after they are delivered. Unlike beef, these meats do not improve with aging.

Variety meats, such as livers, kidneys, brains, hearts, and sweetbreads, should not be stored longer than one week. Take these meats from the con-

Table 2-3   Temperature and Humidity Guide

Foods	Temporary Storage	Holding Storage	Relative Humidity %
Meats	32°F.–36°F.	30°F.–34°F.	75–85
Fish	30°F.–34°F.	28°F.–32°F.*	75–85
Dairy Products	35°F.–45°F.	35°F.–40°F.	75–85
Fruits & Vegetables	36°F.–45°F.	32°F.–36°F.**	85–95
Frozen Foods	–10°F.–0°F.	–10°F.–0°F.	

*Fresh fish should be used within 24 hours. If fish must be kept longer, it should be packed in ice at this temperature.

**Fruits and vegetables such as avocados, bananas, cucumbers, eggplants, onions, peppers, potatoes, and winter squash should not be stored at these temperatures. Store dry onions at room temperature or slightly cooler. Keep green onions in plastic bags in the refrigerator. Store potatoes in a dark, dry place with good ventilation and temperatures in the 55° to 60°F. range. Store sweet potatoes, hard-rind squash, eggplant and rutabagas at cool room temperatures of around 60°F. Store bananas at room temperature. Store ripe avocados in the refrigerator, and unripe avocados in open air at room temperatures to ripen. Peppers and cucumbers should go in the refrigerator.

tainers in which they are delivered and put them into pans. Take care to keep the pans drained of juices, since these juices will sour if allowed to accumulate. Smoked meats generally should be given the same attention as fresh meats.

Storage of Fresh Fish

Whenever possible, use fresh fish within 24 hours of the time it is purchased and keep it under refrigeration until it is used. Use within 24 hours requires daily purchases of fresh fish, but in many areas marketing facilities do not make such frequent purchases possible.

When fish is bought once or twice a week, give it special storage care and do not hold it longer than three days. Surround the fish with cracked ice to keep its temperature from going higher than 32°F. If a fish box in which to store the fish in cracked ice is not available, take care that other foods do not absorb the fish odor.

Keep fish that is purchased in frozen form at 0° to –10°F. until it is defrosted for use. The way the defrosting is done is important. Put the frozen fish in a chill box or refrigerator after it is taken out of frozen storage and let it defrost there. *Do not defrost fish in water.*

Storage of Fresh Fruits and Vegetables

Fruits and vegetables continue to live after being harvested. They continue a process similar to the breathing of humans. During this process, energy is released in the form of heat. Gases are released and the product loses water. This release of heat causes a change in the quality and appearance of fresh fruits and vegetables; special handling practices are essential to prevent excessive loss in fresh produce.

In many foodservice establishments, the storage care of fresh fruits and vegetables is a major problem. It could be a much less serious problem if several facts about produce were kept in mind.

Low temperatures extend the life of produce. Fruits and vegetables need moisture to maintain quality. They also need fresh air and ventilation. They need to be handled with care, and certain items need to be kept where they do not impart odors or flavors to others. Here are some suggestions on each of those points:

Refrigerate Immediately High temperatures shorten the life of fruits and vegetables. Refrigeration preserves their color, flavor, texture, and nutritive value. Fruits and vegetables should be stored at temperatures in the $32°$ to $45°$F. range.

Keep Fresh Fruits and Vegetables Moist Moisture plays an important role in maintaining the quality of fresh fruits and vegetables. It is essential for slowing down the loss of water in the breathing process of the produce and retarding wilting. But the humidity cannot be too high or it will speed up the development of decay, especially in refrigerators where there is considerable variation in temperature. Generally, a relative humidity of 85 percent to 90 percent will provide enough moisture for most fresh fruits and vegetables.

Keep Fresh Produce Well Ventilated Fresh fruits and vegetables need fresh air and ventilation to slow down ripening and to retard spoilage. Store produce so that the air can circulate around the containers, but not at too rapid a rate. If the air is moving too rapidly, the loss of water speeds up and the produce wilts.

Handle with Care Fruits and vegetables need careful handling. Even the so-called hardware items, such as potatoes and onions, need to be handled carefully. The skin on fruits and vegetables is a covering that protects the product. If the skin is broken through careless handling, there is an opening for quality loss and decay. Examine fresh produce items for ripeness when they are delivered and before putting them into storage. Use the ripe items immediately.

Keep Produce Free from Odors Some fruits and vegetables will impart odors and flavors to others. Avoid storing apples with celery, cabbage, potatoes, onions, citrus fruits, and other vegetables with a strong scent. Incidentally, eggs and dairy products readily absorb odors from apples and citrus fruits. (See Table 2-4.)

Table 2-4   Foods That Give Off and Absorb Odors

Food	Give Off Odors	Absorb Odors
Apples, Fresh	Yes	Yes
Butter	No	Yes
Cabbage	Yes	No
Eggs, Fresh Shell	No	Yes
Milk	No	Yes
Onions	Yes	No
Peaches, Fresh	Yes	No
Potatoes	Yes	No
Turnips	Yes	No

Storage of Eggs and Dairy Products

Eggs, milk, cheese, and butter should be put into refrigeration immediately upon delivery. Prompt and continual refrigeration is essential for maintaining the quality of these foods.

Eggs   Store eggs between $32°$ and $40°F$., but do not let them freeze, as freezing spoils shell eggs. Cross-stack the egg crates so there is circulation of air, but avoid too much movement of air.

It is well to avoid needless handling of eggs as careless handling can break down the air cell and the yolk. Do not store eggs next to products that have a pronounced odor, as the eggs will readily absorb the odor.

Milk   Keep milk cold and covered. Proper refrigeration preserves the fresh flavor, and the covering prevents the milk from absorbing odors and flavors from other foods. Normally, milk should be stored at $40°F$.

Cheese   Tightly wrap cheese that has been cut and keep it at a relatively high humidity, since the cut surface will dry out and crack.

Store cheese at temperatures from $38°$ to $40°F$. Generally, avoid freezing cheese, since freezing may damage the body and texture of the cheese and cause it to become mealy and crumbly.

Certain cheeses in pieces of a pound or less, that are not over 1 inch thick, may be stored at $0°F$. or lower for as long as six months. The cheese must be tightly wrapped in freezer foil or other moisture-proof freezer wrap, which should be pressed closely against the surface of the cheese to force out air. The cheese should be frozen immediately. Varieties of cheese that can be frozen successfully in this way include: brick, cheddar, edam, gouda, muenster, Port du Salut, swiss, provolone, mozzarella, and camembert.

Butter   Butter loses flavor more rapidly than any other product. So, special care is needed to protect it from foods with strong odors.

Store butter in its original carton to protect it from exposure to light and air, which speed up the development of rancidity. It is well to use within two weeks to ensure fresh flavor. Butter should be stored at temperatures of 50°F. or below.

Storage Recommendations

All employees of a foodservice establishment need to recognize the importance of storing food correctly. Improper storage practices cause waste and increase food costs. Efficient methods save space and make the food easier to handle, and, together with adequate storage facilities to protect quality, they reduce or eliminate waste and hold food costs to a minimum. They also result in more customer satisfaction and can be a key to added profits.

Here are some general recommendations regarding storage practices:

Dry Storage

Store items used frequently where they can be reached most easily. Stock foods of a kind together.

Date boxes and cartons when they are received. Use the first-in, first-out method. Always move the older stock to the front of the shelves and put the new stock in back.

Cross-stack items such as potatoes and flour in alternating patterns on skids or racks.

Store food away from the wall and off the floor.

Stack food as high as ease of handling and safety permit. Store heavier items close to the floor and put the lighter items higher.

Provide separate storage space for items such as waxes and soaps that give off fumes.

Do not allow wearing apparel to hang in the storeroom.

Refrigerated Storage

Refrigerate all perishables as soon as they are delivered. It is well to mark the date of delivery on the container.

Examine fresh fruits and vegetables before putting them into storage. Check for ripeness. Use the very ripe items immediately.

Leave the paper wrappings on fruits to keep them clean and to reduce the loss of moisture.

Examine vegetables for wilted leaves, removing them before putting the vegetables into storage.

Store foods that absorb odors away from foods the give off odors.

Maintain a regular service schedule for compressors, condensers, and motors. Have servicing done by a competent refrigeration mechanic.

Frozen Storage

Keep freezer at $0°$F. or below.

Store frozen foods in original cartons.

Wrap damaged cartons in moisture-proof paper.

Do not refreeze frozen food that has been thawed. Refrigerate and use within 24 hours, if the food is in good condition.

Sanitation in Storage

Keeping the storage facilities clean is a job that must be performed continually. Take measures to prevent infestation by insects and rodents and to prevent accumulation of dust and rubbish.

Sanitation does not become a problem if a regular program to ensure cleanliness is carried out. Here are some general rules to ensure good storage sanitation:

Inspect the storage areas regularly. Check all food supplies. Infestation and spoilage can occur even under ideal storage conditions.

Check all food frequently for signs of spoilage and remove any spoiled food immediately.

Sweep the floors daily. Mop the floors after storing foods.

Wash walls and equipment regularly.

Scrub and wash refrigerators and storerooms at least once a week. Wash shelves, trays, meat hooks, and similar equipment with hot water and soap. Rinse with hot water and baking soda.

Defrost freezers when the quantity of food in storage is small. Follow the manufacturer's directions for best results in defrosting.

Summary

Adequate storage, of the right type, used efficiently can save many dollars that would otherwise be wasted. The storage space should be large enough, provide the correct holding temperatures for the kinds of food, be convenient in location, and function as a control point for management.

Foodservice people responsible for management of storages should know how and why foods lose quality, and the precautions to take to reduce or prevent quality loss. Temperature and humidity are major factors that need control. Foods can be grouped into classes that have similar holding requirements. Fresh meats, fish, fruits, vegetables, and frozen foods need special attention.

Dry storage, refrigerated storage, and frozen storage are the three major types of storage required. Each has a set of practices that produces the best storage holding of foods. Sanitation is a major concern in storage and steps should be taken on a regular basis to ensure freedom from infestation, rodents, dirt, and rubbish.

Questions

1.   Explain how frequency of use, space requirements, and the characteristics of the item to be stored affect the layout of a storage in a foodservice establishment.

2.   How can the loss of quality of food in storage be controlled by controlling the activity of bacteria, yeast, and molds?

3.   Some foods are classified as perishable, and others are classified as semi-perishable. Describe the differences in storage conditions for these two classes of foods.

4.   A good nonrefrigerated storeroom is essential for an effective foodservice operation. Describe the characteristics of such a storeroom.

5.   What are the advantages of wood shelving and the advantages of metal shelving in storerooms?

6.   What are the likely results when temperatures and humidity get too high in a foodservice storeroom?

7.   What are the recommended refrigerated storage temperatures for: (a) meat; (b) fruits and vegetables; and (c) dairy products and eggs?

8.   List five foods that give off odors in storage.

3

The Cyclical Menu

Attractive, appealing, exciting—these are the adjectives that people who prepare and serve meals like to hear from those who eat the meals. But with mealtime three times a day, seven days a week, every week of the year, keeping what is on the menu attractive, appealing, and exciting can be difficult. Too often, the customer reaction may be quite the opposite.

For many foodservice people, especially those in institutional feeding, keeping meals from seeming just like those that came before can be a never-ending problem; providing variety and appeal in each meal can be a challenging task. Foodservice people in schools, hospitals, homes, prisons, and other institutions find it an especially difficult task, since choice is limited and, in many cases, the clientele is the same over extended periods of time. But, the problem also exists in restaurants and other kinds of foodservice operations, where it is important that the changing items on the menu provide the variety that is not provided by the permanent daily specials.

There Is an Answer in Cyclical Menus

Foodservice people take several different approaches to solving the problem of lack of variety and repetition of the same menu items. In some places, much time and work goes into trying to develop new recipes and dishes.

In other places, slight changes and a different name on the menu are used to make a particular food *seem* different.

One good method is to make use of cyclical menus, and to use them in such a way that the time of repetition of specific items eliminates the monotony of the same old thing on the same day each week. In wise use of the cyclical menu, the pattern to be followed is established far in advance and a cycle is set up that prevents a given menu from repeating itself on the same day in consecutive weeks. This makes a big contribution to variety; and it helps to avoid complaints of regular customers about the sameness of the menu.

So, a cyclical menu is not a menu in which items reappear at regular and identical days of the week—week after week after week. It is a menu pattern specifically designed to prevent just that monotony.

Additional Advantages

The cyclical menu has more to offer than the avoidance of monotony in menu planning. It has a positive effect on menu making, forecasting, purchasing, production, service, and training; and it does much to make the operation of the foodservice more effective.

Menu Making   In foodservice menu-making, there are all too often frantic last-minute decisions on which items to include, where they should be placed on the menu, and at what price they should be listed. Preparing a cyclical menu well in advance of the time that it is to be used helps avoid those situations. It allows time to prepare menus that are balanced, that give due consideration to price and to employee and equipment workloads, as well as providing the nutritionally balanced combinations required especially in institutional feeding.

Forecasting   The number of persons expected and how much of each item to prepare are two factors in forecasting that must be determined in order to have an efficient foodservice operation. Using a cyclical menu can contribute much to the forecast of how much of each item to prepare. Inasmuch as the menu items appear in the same grouping each time they are produced, the relative popularity of each item can be determined quite easily.

Production   Use of standardized recipes is one of the keys to maintaining tight control and good management of a foodservice operation; but these recipes must be followed exactly, if they are to be effective for this purpose.

Even well-trained cooks may have trouble with new or strange recipes; and cooks will do a better job with repetition in the production of a specific item. It is here that the use of a cyclical menu can make another valuable contribution. This is especially important with new employees, and is of great value to the seasonal foodservice operator who has a short season and only limited time to break in a new crew.

Service   Service people also become more efficient with repeated appearances of certain menu items. The dishes that need niceties of service or special handling will be presented to the customers with greater flair than if the service person were unfamiliar with them. This can be seen especially in plate service in the way that food is arranged on the plate so that it presents the most attractive appearance.

The use of a cyclical menu also enables the service people to become more familiar with the correct garnishes to go with certain dishes, and the correct use of china or glassware to set off the food.

Training   Use of a cyclical menu makes it much easier to train employees in all these departments to handle food well. In the course of a year, many different items may be served following a cyclical menu plan, but new employees will have time to become proficient in handling an item before a new cycle is introduced. This is especially valuable in a seasonal business where training must be compressed into a relatively short time.

Eliminates Crisis and Chaos   In general, to use a cyclical menu pattern is really to put the menu operations on a businesslike basis. It is organizing that part of the foodservice operation according to a plan, and it eliminates the operation-by-crisis chaos that many times is found in foodservice establishments.

The cyclical menu provides the variety needed in meal patterns, and at the same time gains the advantages of using standardized recipes. It simplifies the foodservice operation, makes it easier for management to do long-range planning and to purchase larger quantities at a time. Substitution is easier. In total, the results are better satisfied customers, patients, workers, students, or whoever makes up the clientele of the establishment.

A Cyclical Menu Pattern

Many patterns can be used for a cyclical menu. One good pattern includes:

> 18 daily Menus
>
> 4 Friday Menus
>
> 4 Sunday Menus

The daily menus can be numbered D-1 through D-18; the Friday menus, F-1 through F-4; and the Sunday menus, S-1 through S-4. The daily menus can be set up for an 18-week period, the cycle including Monday, Tuesday, Wednesday, Thursday, and Saturday. A separate cycle of 4 menus is arranged for Fridays and another for Sundays.

The question of whether there should be separate menu cycles for particular days of the week depends to a great extent on the type of foodservice for which the cycle is being designed.

Some foodservice establishments may want a special menu cycle for Saturdays. An example is a small restaurant in a city, which is not open on Sundays. On the six-days-a-week basis, there could be a menu cycle for Monday, Tuesday, Wednesday, and Thursday, a menu cycle for Friday, and still another for Saturday. For institutions and hospitals, the Sunday menu could be a continuous one.

13-Week and 18-Week Cycles   The menu cycle could be used for 13 weeks instead of the 18 weeks shown here; and it would provide one quarter of the year's menus. Three other 13-week cycles could be worked out, using the same pattern; and then there would be a separate menu cycle for each of the four seasons of the year. This would make seasonal variations easy, while at the same time the same cycle is being retained.

Table 3-1 shows the 18-week cycle pattern with daily menus for Monday, Tuesday, Wednesday, Thursday, and Saturday. The Friday and Sunday patterns are shown in Table 3-2; and the combined daily, Friday, and Sunday cycles are brought together in Table 3-3. The dividing line for transforming the pattern into a 13-week cycle is also shown.

Note in this menu cycle chart that the daily menu D-1 appears on:

Monday—First week

Thursday—Fourth week

Tuesday—Eighth week

Saturday—Eleventh week

Wednesday—Fifteenth week

Thus, in the entire 18 weeks of the cycle, the same menu appears only five times and then at three-week intervals. When it does appear, it is on a different day of the week each time, well separated from the day of the week on which it appeared the previous time.

In this pattern, a special Friday cycle is included because of the importance of fish in meals in some areas of the country, including New England. The Friday menus in this special Friday cycle are more limited in number. The F-1 menus appear on:

Friday—First week

Friday—Fifth week

37

Table 3-1   The Daily Menu Cycle for 13 Weeks or 18 Weeks

Wks.	Mon.	Tues.	Wed.	Thurs.	Sat.
1st	**D-1**	D-2	D-3	D-4	D-5
2nd	D-6	D-7	D-8	D-9	D-10
3rd	D-11	D-12	D-13	D-14	D-15
4th	D-16	D-17	D-18	**D-1**	D-2
5th	D-3	D-4	D-5	D-6	D-7
6th	D-8	D-9	D-10	D-11	D-12
7th	D-13	D-14	D-15	D-16	D-17
8th	D-18	**D-1**	D-2	D-3	D-4
9th	D-5	D-6	D-7	D-8	D-9
10th	D-10	D-11	D-12	D-13	D-14
11th	D-15	D-16	D-17	D-18	**D-1**
12th	D-2	D-3	D-4	D-5	D-6
13th	D-7	D-8	D-9	D-10	D-11
14th	D-12	D-13	D-14	D-15	D-16
15th	D-17	D-18	**D-1**	D-2	D-3
16th	D-4	D-5	D-6	D-7	D-8
17th	D-9	D-10	D-11	D-12	D-13
18th	D-14	D-15	D-16	D-17	D-18

Table 3-2   Cycles of Menus for Fridays and Sundays

Friday	Sunday
F-1	S-1
F-2	S-2
F-3	S-3
F-4	S-4
F-1	S-1
F-2	S-2
F-3	S-3
F-4	S-4
F-1	S-1
F-2	S-2
F-3	S-3
F-4	S-4
F-1	S-1
F-2	S-2
F-3	S-3
F-4	S-4
F-1	S-1
F-2	S-2

This menu appears on the same day each time around, but it is removed by four weeks from the time it appeared previously. If four Friday menus are not enough variation, it is a simple matter to add additional menus to the Friday cycle, without affecting the pattern of the daily cycle or the pattern of the Sunday cycle.

Table 3-3   The Complete Menu Cycle for 13 Weeks or 18 Weeks

Wks.	Sun.	Mon.	Tues.	Wed.	Thurs.	Fri.	Sat.
1st	S-1	D-1	D-2	D-3	D-4	F-1	D-5
2nd	S-2	D-6	D-7	D-8	D-9	F-2	D-10
3rd	S-3	D-11	D-12	D-13	D-14	F-3	D-15
4th	S-4	D-16	D-17	D-18	D-1	F-4	D-2
5th	S-1	D-3	D-4	D-5	D-6	F-1	D-7
6th	S-2	D-8	D-9	D-10	D-11	F-2	D-12
7th	S-3	D-13	D-14	D-15	D-16	F-3	D-17
8th	S-4	D-18	D-1	D-2	D-3	F-4	D-4
9th	S-1	D-5	D-6	D-7	D-8	F-1	D-9
10th	S-2	D-10	D-11	D-12	D-13	F-2	D-14
11th	S-3	D-15	D-16	D-17	D-18	F-3	D-1
12th	S-4	D-2	D-3	D-4	D-5	F-4	D-6
13th	S-1	D-7	D-8	D-9	D-10	F-1	D-11
14th	S-2	D-12	D-13	D-14	D-15	F-2	D-16
15th	S-3	D-17	D-18	D-1	D-2	F-3	D-3
16th	S-4	D-4	D-5	D-6	D-7	F-4	D-8
17th	S-1	D-9	D-10	D-11	D-12	F-1	D-13
18th	S-2	D-14	D-15	D-16	D-17	F-2	D-18

The Sunday cycle is similar to the Friday cycle. It has a four-week interval between appearances of the same menu. Foods that are usually featured in Sunday meals do not offer as great a problem in regard to repetition and variety, so four menus should be enough for many foodservice operations. Again, however, it is a simple matter to add more menus to the Sunday cycle if that is desired.

Other Variations   There are many other opportunities to introduce variation into the menu cycle. The entree of the menu will appear in the place indicated for it in the cyclical pattern, but there can be much variation in the choice of vegetables and other items to accompany the entree. The pattern illustrated in this chapter could be used for any number of weeks. Both 13-week and 18-week variations are shown, but there could be fewer or more weeks.

The number of menus should be such that it does not equal the number of days in the pattern. For example, the number of daily menus in the pattern shown in Table 3-1, which has menus for five days, can be any number of daily menus that is not divisible by five. This ensures that the particular menu will fall on a different day each time it comes around.

Constructing the Menus

After the menu cycle has been established, the menus for each day in the cycle must be constructed. For the menu cycle illustrated in this chapter it is necessary to construct eighteen daily menus, plus four Friday menus, and four Sunday menus.

The start is made with the entree. Every item that is served in the operation need not be included in the cycle menu. Some foodservice people may prefer to list only the entrees. Other may want to include the vegetables along with the entree. In some cases, it may be desirable to include the complete menu for each menu in the cycle. Regardless of what is to be included in addition to the entree, the start should be with the entree.

When all of the entrees for the entire cycle have been listed, it is a simple matter to determine whether the list shows enough variety, and whether balance has been maintained in the complete cycle. The list should be checked for the following:

> entrees unbalanced as to the type of cooking equipment required
>
> no variety of choices in the type of entree
>
> too much preparation required for certain combinations and not enough for others
>
> not a sufficient range of prices

As for the rest of the job of making out the menus, all the standards of good menu-making apply to the cycle menu, just as they do to other kinds of menus. The advantage of the cycle menu is that the foodservice operator can obtain a better overall picture of the menu mix.

The other menu items can be added, once the entrees have been determined. To what extent the menu is finished is a matter of choice for the foodservice operator. But, there can be considerable savings in time and money in having a complete menu schedule well ahead of the time of use. Such advance preparation provides better control of the operation and eliminates the necessity to substitute less satisfactory items for those that are best for the situation.

There Must Be Flexibility

Once the cycle menu is completed, it should not be forgotten, and it should be considered subject to change. There needs to be flexibility so that the cycle menu responds to changes in the situation.

It is well to have a list of substitute items in the various price ranges that can be used in case there is a change in the situation or there is an emergency. There should be no hesitation in substituting seasonal items as they come on the market when price advantages can be obtained.

A disadvantage of the cycle menu—that the future cannot be accurately foreseen when the menu is made—can be eliminated by maintaining this kind of flexibility.

The Problem of Leftovers

One of the objections sometimes offered by foodservice people to adopting a cyclical menu is that they have all the leftovers that they build their menus around. An efficient operation does not have a great amount of leftovers. But, this problem can be solved in a number of ways where a cycle menu is being utilized.

In a restaurant operation, the leftover item can be sold as a flyer or rider item.

Preparation methods can be refined so that smaller batches are made at one time, and the chance of large amounts of leftovers is reduced.

Improved forecasting procedures can provide better production estimates and so reduce the amount of leftovers.

Full use of certain items can be attained by freezing some for use the next time the items appear in the cycle.

The time saved by the operator because he is using cyclical menus should provide him more time for planning and improving his forecasting.

Summary

There are menus available from food publications and from some of the institutional manufacturers, which can serve as guides to the foodservice operator interested in developing cycle menus for his establishment. The menu should be tailored to the particular operation, with attention to all of the things that make a particular operation different from others of a similar type.

The cyclical menu offers many advantages in addition to providing a way to eliminate the problems resulting from a lack of variety in meals. The cyclical menu simplifies the planning of menus, allows better long-range planning and quantity purchasing, and makes possible effective use of standardization of recipes, portions, and production methods. It can be the way to attain greater variety, more efficient purchasing, and better control of costs in foodservice operations.

Questions

1.   What is the cyclical menu, and what advantages does it have for the foodservice operator?

2.   Describe a typical cyclical menu pattern.

3.   With which meal item is the start made in constructing a cyclical menu?

4.   Why is it important that the number of menus in the cycle menu not equal the number of days in the cycle menu pattern?

5.   In evaluating a listing of cycle menu items, what factors should be checked to see if the cycle menu is in balance and provides sufficient variety?

6.   How can the problem of leftovers be solved when there is a cycle menu pattern being followed?

7.   How can use of a cyclical menu provide the foodservice operator better control of costs?

4

Frozen Foods
in Foodservice
Establishments

Frozen foods have a major place in modern foodservice operations. In spite of doubts and even opposition expressed toward these products by people who do not like change, and by the advocates of "everything from scratch," frozen food products have expanded greatly in use and in variety of items available.

There is still some customer opposition to frozen foods, which is being gradually overcome. This opposition is more to the fact that frozen foods are being offered than to any negative result of customer evaluation of those frozen foods. But, the trend to more and more use in more and more ways continues. Frozen foods deserve regular and expanding use in increasing numbers of foodservice establishments.

The use of frozen foods in restaurants, hotels, institutions, and other eating places requires changes in food preparation and cooking methods. These changes make it possible to gain the many advantages of frozen foods while at the same time providing the procedures that minimize the disadvantages. Effective use of frozen foods requires the use of appropriate ordering, handling, storing, preparation, and cooking procedures. Also needed is a good knowledge of the advantages and the disadvantages of this form of food. This chapter suggests ways in which foodservice operators can utilize frozen foods to the best advantage.

Advantages and Disadvantages

When frozen foods are used correctly, they offer some valuable advantages:

more variety

year-round availability

many sources of supply

little or no waste

less preparation time

low labor costs for preparation

long storage life

more accurate cost accounting

On the other hand, frozen foods do have some disadvantages. These include:

storage requirement of $0°$F. or below

quality loss at temperatures above $0°$F.

need for careful prior planning to allow time for thawing

lack of some foods in frozen form

refreezing not recommended in certain situations

Responsibility for Frozen Foods

Good food control is an essential to the efficient operation of an eating place; and with frozen foods it is even more important. The manager should delegate the responsibility for frozen foods to a capable employee, but should also see that the proper procedures are enforced.

Each foodservice unit should follow a standard operating procedure (S.O.P.) for the control of frozen foods. The responsibility for controlling the ordering, receiving, handling, storing, and issuing of frozen foods should be in one person such as the steward or storekeeper. Without such close control in the hands of one person, the value of frozen foods can easily be lowered or lost. The person responsible for frozen food control needs to have a good working knowledge of the subject. He should also have authority to control the entire frozen food operation within the foodservice establishment.

Vital in the effective use of frozen foods are correct ordering, handling, and receiving procedures. Many losses can occur at each of these points unless good practices are followed.

Ordering Procedures

Control starts with the ordering of the frozen foods needed. This ordering needs to be coordinated closely with the master menu (if one is used), with orders placed previously that have not yet been delivered, with accurate inventories of stock on hand, and with expected needs. If these factors are controlled closely, the frozen foods buyer can maintain strict control over costs.

The fact that frozen foods are highly perishable requires much care in ordering, since there can easily be large losses in both quality and dollars if the ordering is not done correctly. Major factors in good ordering procedures are quality, quantity, grades, and size of units. Each deserves attention.

Quality   In frozen foods, quality generally refers to the color, flavor, texture, appearance, and nutritive value of the product. In foodservice operations, quality can mean what is best described as "eatability." Does the product appeal to the customer? Normally, if it does and the food is eaten, then the product quality is right.

Quality can be easily lost if there is lack of care in handling and transporting. To guard against losses, the buyer needs to check frequently the over-all quality of the product.

Quantity   How much frozen food to order depends on a number of factors, including available freezer space, inventory on hand, immediate and long-range needs, frequency of delivery, availability of the product, time of year, and price. The buyer should have general knowledge of the significance of inventories and the turnover rate that is best for the operation. But, the advice of the distributor can also help guide the buyer when final decisions are made.

Modest inventories with rapid turnover usually result in higher quality products than would be the case when a large supply is maintained over a long period of time. Experience and facilities will dictate what quantities to buy at any given time. In some foodservice establishments, the turnover rate is twenty to thirty times a year.

Grades   The U.S. Department of Agriculture has established official standards and grades for many frozen fruits, vegetables, juices, and poultry. The Department of the Interior has established similar standards and grades for certain frozen fish items. These standards and grades are designed to serve as a basis for establishing quality control, and for determining the value of the frozen foods being purchased.

A Guide To Grades   Here is a general guide to grades. There are variations for some products, but these grades generally indicate the quality of products described.

Grade A   Excellent quality. Products are very uniform in size and color, are practically free from blemishes, and have the proper degree of maturity or tenderness, flavor and odor, and conformation.

Grade B   Good quality. Such products may not be as uniform in size or color or as tender and free from blemishes as Grade A products. They are of reasonably uniform tenderness and texture, and have practically normal conformation.

Grade C   Fairly good quality. Products within this classification (omitted for some foods) are as wholesome and nutritious as the higher grades but are less uniform in their adherence to the grading factors.

Generally, Grade A products are best used in dishes where appearance is important. The lower grades may be used for such dishes also, but are probably best used where the product is combined with other foods or where it loses its original appearance.

Brands   Brand names can be of assistance to the buyer in ordering frozen foods. The brand name often indicates a quality range, and through experience may provide a standard or grade that meets the buyer's need. Changing brands for reason of price may result in variable quality. If brand names are used as a guide, it is necessary to know the difference between quality brand names and price brand names before ordering large quantities.

Size of Unit   Unit size for frozen foods varies with the product. Frozen vegetables are normally available in a variety of sizes, including ½-lb., 1-lb., 2-lb., 2½-lb., 3-lb., and 5-lb. packages. Preference seems to be for the 2-lb. and 2½-lb. sizes.

Frozen fruits are available in 10-oz. containers, and in up to 30-lb. tins. The larger sizes, from 10 to 30 lbs., are popular.

There is a wide variety of sizes of units for meats, poultry, and seafoods, depending on whether or not the product is purchased in portion-control form. Sizes range from 1-lb. to 30-lb. units, with the 4-lb. to 6-lb. sizes most widely used, and increasing use of the 10-lb. size for some items.

Correlate the size of the unit with the size of operation. An evaluation of the foodservice operation can yield information that will enable the buyer to select the size of unit best suited. In this evaluation, consider such items as the number of meals served within a given period, the method of service, the size of portions, the kitchen equipment, and the portion cost. Remember that many too-small packages take more labor than can be justified.

Checking the Ordering Procedure

Check your ordering procedure. Ask yourself these questions:

Is ordering done in a haphazard manner with little planning?

Is ordering done so that, frequently, too much inventory is on hand?

Are you considering only price and neglecting quality, brands, grades, and other factors?

If you answer "yes" to any of those questions, you need to improve your ordering procedures.

Receiving Is Critical

The advantages of good ordering procedures will be lost unless receiving practices are also good. There is no profit in buying good quality products and then losing that quality because the products are not handled correctly after they are delivered. Certain procedures should be followed to ensure that the receiving function is performed effectively.

One member of the staff should be responsible for frozen foods. He should have definite authority to direct the ordering, receiving, handling, storage, and dispensing of frozen foods. This does not have to be a full-time job. He may have other duties as well, but his responsibility for frozen foods should be a primary concern.

The time and the frequency of delivery of frozen foods is an important factor in proper receiving. When frozen foods can be delivered only infrequently, special attention must be given to rotating the stock and other procedures that maintain quality.

The deliveries should be at times when it is most convenient for the food-service operator, although this cannot always be done. If you know the approximate delivery time in advance, you have the advantage of your personnel being ready for the delivery. They can get the storage freezer ready and they can clear the area where the foods are to be received. Sufficient help can be on hand to transfer the frozen foods to the storage freezer quickly. This greatly reduces the amount of time that the storage door will be open while the food is being received.

Checking the Deliveries

When frozen foods are received they need to be checked for three things—quality, weight, and amount. Check the bill against what was ordered. Check the prices at which the order was made and the prices that are stated on the bill. Check the weights. To do the latter it is necessary that accurate scales be available.

While unloading frozen foods, *check for signs of thawing and any physical damage to the package.* There may be damaged merchandise that has to be returned or destroyed. Note it on the invoice and indicate the reasons why. After the order is unloaded, *check the item, type, and count* and compare with the invoice. *Enter the amounts received* on the inventory card when the food is put into the freezer.

Checking Temperature

Check several packages from different places in the stock that is being delivered to see if the temperature at delivery time is 0°F. or lower. You can measure the temperature with an unbreakable stainless steel thermometer. The temperature may be checked by two different methods.

> Open the case and remove the top corner package. Use an ice pick to make a hole through the case from the inside, level with the second layer of product. Insert the thermometer stem into the hole about three inches into the case. Replace the package, close the case, and weight down with several additional cases to ensure good contact. Read the temperature after five minutes.

> Cut a flap opening in the case near the middle corner-package. Bend the flap back and insert the thermometer stem between the package layers. Close the flap, weight down with additional cases. Read the temperature after five minutes.

Firm contact between the package and the thermometer stem is needed to give accurate readings. Additional care in checking readings may be required with some products, such as concentrates and tray-packed items.

The thermometer should be checked for accuracy by testing it in a bath of melting ice. After five minutes, the temperature should read 32°F. Any temperature deviation can then be taken into account when temperatures are checked.

Criteria in Storing

Several types of freezing facilities can be used for the storage of frozen foods. A walk-in box, a home freezer, or an across-the-top freezer refrigerator can be used, depending on the location and the amount of food to be stored. Generally, freezers can be divided into walk-in and reach-in types.

Usually, reach-in units have less storage space than walk-in units. Also, more time and more work are required to handle and police the frozen food stored in the reach-in unit. In general, walk-in freezer units offer more efficient use of storage space and easier handling of the stored food.

In checking the storage of frozen foods in a foodservice establishment, several points must be considered:

> Are similar items being put in the same general location, so that there is order in the arrangement of what is in the freezer?

> Are there locks on the freezer?

Is the temperature in the freezer the correct temperature for the food that is being stored?

Is there an emergency alarm system on the freezer?

If you can answer yes to those four questions, your storage procedures are likely to be effective. If your answer is no, then you need to improve your storing procedures.

Efficiency in Use of Freezers

Among the practices that help to increase the efficiency of freezer use, the more important are:

Unloading   Moving the loaded cart right into the freezer reduces handling time and protects the frozen food from exposure to temperatures above $0°F$. If the cart cannot be moved into the freezer, put it as close to the freezer door as possible for unloading.

Segregation   Segregate frozen foods by groups of commodities. Arrange them so that the labels can be seen, or mark the ends of the cartons so that the foods can be identified quickly. This reduces handling time and helps keep the contents of the freezer arranged in an orderly manner.

Rotation   Mark newly received frozen foods to show the date received, and put them behind or under the older stock to make rotation easier and more certain.

Temperature Check   Install a thermometer to measure temperature within the freezer box, and put it where it can be easily seen. Locate the thermometer, or the sensing element of the thermometer, where it will measure the *average* temperature of the freezer, and not be affected by the opening of the door, the cooling coils, or by direct air from the cooling unit. Such a location should be in the upper third of the distance between the ceiling and the floor.

For walk-in boxes, use the kind of thermometer that can be attached to the outside. For reach-in types, have the thermometer mounted inside the door.

Check the temperature of the freezer at least three times a day to make sure that the $0°F.$ temperature level is being maintained.

Occasionally, measure the temperature of the products with a calibrated dial-type hand thermometer to check the accuracy of the freezer thermostat.

Air Circulation   Walk-in freezers need air circulation. Avoid stacking frozen foods against the walls, ceiling, and floors, so as to minimize the transfer of heat to the frozen food by conduction and to prevent interference with the circulation of cold air. Slatted hardwood floor racks can be used to keep the frozen foods off the floor and allow circulation of air under them. Keep frozen foods out of a constant draft or direct flow of air.

Defrosting   Defrost freezers regularly to prevent excessive ice formation. This helps to reduce operating costs, labor, and possible damage to the food and the packaging material. It increases refrigeration efficiency.

Protect the products in the freezer from dripping water while defrosting the freezer. Cover them with some water-proof material, such as plastic or canvas. In some cases it may be possible to move the products out of the area of dripping.

Sanitation   Keep the freezer clean, orderly, and well organized. Schedule daily examination and clean-up. Following such a practice can mean savings in labor and reduction in damage to the frozen foods.

Maintenance   Set up a regular service schedule and see that it is followed. This should be done regardless of the type of freezer.

Issuing and Accountability

The issuing of frozen foods to those who are to use them is a function that needs strict control. Be sure there is accountability for the frozen foods. No employee should be allowed to help himself to frozen foods without some form of accountability. A sign-out form, which the employee signs when frozen foods are issued, provides a record of accountability and a means of control.

Much quality is often lost between the time frozen foods are issued and the time they are used. So, attention to how they are held in this interval is vital. If the foods are going to be used within four to six hours of the time they are issued, they can be held in ordinary refrigeration. If they are issued the night before for use the following day, there should be freezer storage for holding them at the place where they are to be used.

Of much importance in issuing is to move out the foods that were received first, not those which were received last. In this way, packages will not get lost and stay in the freezer too long with resulting loss in quality. The first in, first out principle applies in all storage of food.

Preparation and Cooking of Frozen Foods

Special preparation and cooking practices are necessary with frozen foods. Certain frozen foods need thawing before use, while others are cooked from the frozen state. Usually directions on the package or container provide information on thawing and cooking. Unless you have found other methods to be better, it is advisable to follow the directions on the package.

Frozen foods are thawed in foodservice establishments in three major ways:

Slow Method   In the refrigerator.

Medium Method   At room temperature.

Fast Methods   In ice water or in cool running water (keeping the product in its original waterproof package), at room temperature with a fan, or in a warming oven. Hot water should not be used for thawing.

The water temperature in cold running water for thawing frozen foods should be below 50°F. It is kept running so there is no build-up of heat. In general, potentially hazardous foods should be thawed at refrigerator temperatures of 45°F. or below, or under cold running water. But unless defrosting is absolutely necessary, it is better to cook the food from the frozen state. Also, holding defrosted items under refrigeration for more than a day is not recommended, as this can result in bacteria building up in numbers.

Thawing Guide

While equipment, working space, and time will to a large extent determine the method of defrosting, the following guide provides thawing information for various food groups:

Frozen Vegetables   These vegetables do not have to be thawed. The exception to this is corn-on-the-cob.

Frozen Fruits   These fruits should either be thawed in the refrigerator or in running water.

Frozen Juices   Need not be thawed.

Frozen Meats

Large Cuts   Thaw in refrigerator, or in cold running water, keeping the product in a waterproof package. Allow ample time for thawing.

Small Cuts   May be thawed either in refrigerator or in cold running water keeping the product in a waterproof package, or may be cooked without thawing.

Frozen Poultry

Large Birds   Thaw in refrigerator.

51

Small Birds or Parts   Thaw in the refrigerator, or in cold running water keeping the product in a water-proof package. Can be cooked from the frozen state. If the parts are to be breaded or batter-dipped, they must be thawed.

Frozen Fish   Fillets or steaks may be cooked either frozen or thawed. Any thawing should be done in the refrigerator. Blocks may be thawed in cold running water. If fish is to be breaded or batter-dipped, it must be thawed.

Frozen Shellfish   Thaw in refrigerator. Batter-dipped products must be completely thawed. Thaw clams, scallops, and shrimp enough for separation and then cook.

Frozen Prepared Foods   Thaw or cook in the frozen state according to the manufacturer's directions.

Thawing at room temperature with a fan is done in foodservice operations, but it is not recommended because of possibility of bacterial contamination.

Portion and Cost Control

How much frozen food is served varies considerably with the type of foodservice operation. However, it is possible with frozen foods to determine the number of servings per package, as well as the cost per portion. This is especially so with frozen fruits and vegetables.

Although foodservice operations vary, with the information on the number of servings per unit package of frozen foods, and based on past experience, the manager can thaw or thaw and cook a pre-determined amount.

Using portion-control meats, fish, and poultry can increase efficiency in accounting for cost and at the same time can reduce kitchen expenses. But, when using bulk products, such as 30-lb. units of fruit or large packages of fish, the use of leftovers for each package must be included in the planning, as well as the cost per serving and number of servings per unit.

Charts with information on servings and the cost per serving obtained from various size packages are a big help in this planning. This material can be obtained easily from such organizations as the American Hospital Association, packers, distributors, food guides, foodservice textbooks, and from the educational institutions with programs in the foodservice area. Good planning can help a great deal to reduce such waste as that involved in buying or opening too large containers. Careful selection of unit size is one good way of controlling waste.

Even more care in planning is necessary with frozen foods that must be defrosted for use than would be the case with many other foods. Defrosting only enough to meet the needs is the goal with, of course, some provision for variations that can be expected in the demand for the item. Avoid defrosting too much just on general principles.

Cooking Methods for Frozen Foods

The method of cooking frozen foods is related to the personnel and the equipment available. How well personnel are trained and the cooking methods they use affects the quality of the frozen food as it is judged by the customer. Some suggestions on cooking methods to use and the needed equipment are included in the Cooking Guide.

Cooking Guide

Frozen Vegetables

Boiling   Whether in pots or steam-jacketed kettles, vegetables should be cooked from the frozen state, except when it is necessary to thaw partially to break up large blocks. Use as little water as possible and bring the water to a boil before the vegetable is added. Bring the water and vegetable back to a boil as quickly as possible and start counting the cooking time as soon as the boiling starts. If the item is to be held on the steam table, make allowance for the additional cooking it will receive. After the cooking time has been completed, serve the vegetables as soon as possible; or move them to the serving area to prevent overcooking and loss of flavor and color.

Pressure   There are various types of equipment for pressure-cooking vegetables. Some require the addition of water while others do not. Follow the manufacturer's recommendation closely. Steam pressure equipment allows the foodservice operator to prepare small amounts quickly and reduce waste.

Caution   Regardless of the method of cooking used, it is better to prepare small amounts than to cook single large batches. Nutritive value is lost due to long exposure to heat, and quality is lowered. Constant efforts should be made to shorten the time between cooking and serving.

Frozen Meats   The method of cooking frozen meats depends on the type and amounts to be cooked, the available equipment, the personnel, and the type of foodservice operation. Generally, small cuts of meat such as steaks, chops, and patties can be cooked from the frozen state. Large cuts such as roasts are thawed or partially thawed before cooking. Large cuts can be cooked from the frozen form, but additional time (up to twice that of thawed) must be allowed for cooking.

Less weight loss takes place when meat is cooked without being thawed than when it is defrosted before cooking. However, cooking time and fuel costs may be increased.

Frozen Poultry   Normally, thaw frozen poultry before cooking to make it easier to handle and to enable the kitchen personnel to carry out additional preparation.

Frozen Fish and Shellfish   For best results, thaw fish and shellfish prior to cooking. Cooking should be done at recommended temperatures as soon as the products have been thawed.

Frozen Prepared Foods   Cook according to the directions on the package.

Holding Cooked Frozen Foods

Hold cooked frozen foods on steam tables and in warming ovens for as short a time as possible. Holding for a long period of time lowers the quality of the product by producing changes in color, flavor, and texture. This affects acceptance by customers.

Any need for long standing can be eliminated by preparing smaller amounts frequently. Also, it is well to allow in the cooking time for any additional cooking that is likely to take place after the food is put on the steam table.

It is recommended that food not be held more than four hours, and preferably no longer than two hours. The effect of holding is influenced by the fact that the warm periods are cumulative; and the hours should be figured on the basis of the total. A temperature of 140°F. is essential to prevent rapid growth of bacteria.

The so-called danger zone for food, as described by the U.S. Public Health Service and other people who have studied effects of temperature on bacteria growth, is 45° to 140°F. Some states have now set 150°F. as the upper figure. In Massachusetts, for example, the zone is 45°F. to 150°F., compared with the federal 45° to 140°F.

In this book, 40°F. is recommended as the lower figure instead of 45°F. for a number of reasons. Inaccurate temperature measuring devices, ease of remembering, equipment that is not accurate in temperature are several. Also, 150° is suggested as the upper limit.

The 45°F. figure is considered acceptable by most people for short storage, since bacterial growth is very slow at temperatures at or below 45°F. However, the 40° to 140°F. range, with 100° between the limits is suggested as a good recommendation for foodservice people to follow.

Refreezing Frozen Foods

Foodservice people ask many questions about refreezing frozen foods. It is difficult to provide an answer to these questions without knowing about the specific circumstances. However, there are some general rules based on what happens to frozen food when exposed to temperatures that are too high.

To maintain their quality, frozen foods should be held at 0°F. or lower until it is time to use them. Under certain conditions frozen foods that have been thawed may be safely refrozen.

54

Consider frozen foods that have been thawed as perishable products. When frozen foods are allowed to thaw, microorganisms in the food are going to cause spoilage if conditions are right.

The critical factors on whether or not a food should be refrozen are the length of time it is in the thawed state and the temperature that it reaches. If frozen foods are at too high a temperature for too long, the safety as well as the quality of the food may be affected by the growth of bacteria. This is especially so for pre-cooked or prepared items. An appreciable amount of bacteria growth can occur at the usual temperatures found in kitchens and in serving areas.

There is a guide that is used. If food has thawed for reasons that are known (such as being left overnight in the refrigerator instead of in the freezer, or because of a power failure in the freezer), the food may be safely refrozen if it still feels cold and contains ice crystals, and you know that it has been thawed only a brief time. There will be some loss of quality due to the thawing and refreezing. If, however, there is any question about the safety of the food, do not risk food poisoning. It is better to throw it away.

Effect of Time and Temperature on Frozen Foods*

Maintaining quality of frozen foods is related to time and temperature. Much care is needed in handling and holding these foods because of the effects that time and temperature have on them. Several points regarding time and temperature as related to frozen foods should be understood by all personnel involved with this type of foods.

Low Temperature Is Necessary   Just as fresh foods lose color, flavor, texture, and nutritional value at high temperatures, so frozen foods lose these qualities if the temperature is not kept at $0°F.$ or lower. In addition to losing flavor, foods may develop off-flavors under adverse time and temperature conditions.

Slightly Below Freezing Is Not Enough   A package of frozen food may be cold and hard, but if the temperature at which it is held is not low enough, the quality of that food cannot be maintained.

As storage temperature increases from $0°F.$, the rate at which frozen food loses quality increases. At $15°F.$, these deteriorating changes take place several times as rapidly as they do at $0°F.$ At $25°$ to $30°F.$, the changes take place several times as rapidly as they do at $15°F.$ A 5-to 10-degree increase in temperature in the range between $0°$ and $30°F.$ speeds up the loss of quality from two to five times as rapidly as when the food is stored at $0°F.$

Most products will be cold and hard when held at $20°$ to $25°F.$, so the fact that food is frozen hard and cold is no sign that the quality of that food has

---

*Many of the suggestions in this chapter are based on result of research at the Western Utilization Research and Development Laboratory of the United States Department of Agriculture, and research at the University of Massachusetts in Amherst.

been maintained. Allowing the temperature of a frozen food to rise from 25°F. to 30°F. for even one day can cause much more damage to its edibility and its nutritional value than holding it at 0°F. for a whole year.

Temperature Damage Cannot Be Corrected   Once damage to frozen food occurs from too high a temperature, reducing the temperature in the freezer or holding compartment will not correct the damaged condition. Temperature damage stays with food. Even small changes in flavor or color that occur early in the life of frozen foods will remain, regardless of how well the food is handled afterwards.

Damage to Quality Accumulates   The damage done to quality in frozen foods adds up. There may be severe damage to such foods from accumulations of mild damage, or from a single occasion of greater damage. It is not the highest temperature to which frozen foods have been subjected that determines the amount of damage. It is the combination of high temperatures and the length of time the food has been at the high temperature.

Freezing Is Not a Cure-All   Freezing is only a way of maintaining quality of food for limited periods of time. It will not improve food quality, and it will not serve as a cure-all for the product's deficiencies.

Effects of Temperature on Frozen Foods

The signs of temperature damage in frozen foods vary with the product, and foodservice people should be able to recognize the evidences of such damage. Here are some of the things that happen to different products when they suffer damage from too high temperature.

Frozen Fruits   Most fruits are damaged quickly by high storage temperatures. Changes include browning of peaches, loss of flavor in strawberries, loss of color in raspberries, darkening and toughening of the skin in cherries, and the loss of vitamin C. When the frozen fruits are held at 30°F., some of these changes can take place in several days. At 20°F., they can occur in two weeks. But if fruits are stored at 0°F. or below, they will stay in good condition for a year or more.

Frozen Concentrated Juices   As the temperature rises, quality loss in frozen juices, especially orange juice, increases. The most marked change is indicated by separation into thick and thin parts when the juice is mixed with water. Another change resulting from too high temperature is loss of flavor. Storage of the frozen concentrated juices at 0°F. or below keeps these changes to a minimum.

Frozen Vegetables   When frozen vegetables are subjected to temperatures above 0°F., they show loss of quality first through color change and then in loss of flavor. For example, green snap beans can change color from bright green to a brownish green after three days at 30°F. Peas will change to a grayish green in three weeks when held at 20°F.

Frozen Poultry Products   In frozen poultry, the loss of flavor doubles for each rise of 10 degrees in temperature. But if the poultry is packaged properly and held at 0°F. or below, it will have a storage life of up to one year. Off-flavors may develop in poultry products when they are held at temperatures above 0°F.

Quality loss occurs more rapidly in turkeys than it does in chickens, and it occurs more rapidly in cut-up poultry than in whole birds. Allowing frozen turkeys to stand at 10° to 25°F. for a short time can cause the skin to darken. Holding the turkeys at 0°F. or below minimizes or prevents this damage.

Other Frozen Products   Other types of frozen foods such as baked goods, prepared foods, meats, fish, and shellfish lose quality when subjected to temperatures above 0°F.

The flavor change that is first detected in cooked poultry meat is the loss of the "freshly cooked" flavor. This is followed eventually by staleness and finally by distinct rancidity.

At 20°F., flavor changes can be detected in fried chicken in less than two weeks. Staleness or rancidity develops within six weeks to three months. Mold occurs on pies held for nine months.

At 10°F. and lower, the stability of flavor is affected greatly by the exposure of meat to the air. The sauce or gravy in pies protects the meat. So, dinners, pies, creamed products, and a la king foods are protected against serious flavor damage for as long as six to twelve months at 10°F. or lower. Fried chicken suffers damage twice as quickly at those temperatures.

Separation of liquid, curdling, and loss of smoothness can develop in desserts, puddings, and gravies after they are thawed. When held at temperatures above 0°F., foods provide more problems of this kind.

While the storage life of the different products varies, it can be stated generally that for each rise of 10 degrees in temperature the storage life of the product is cut in half.

Length of Time Foods Maintain Quality

The table on the following pages is based on the results of research work conducted in many parts of the United States. The table shows the length of time that frozen foods may be stored without noticeable loss of quality. The times shown in the table apply only when the foods are stored at

Table 4-1   Approximate Storage Life
of Various Foods at Zero
Degrees Fahrenheit

Fruit	*Number of Months at 0°F.*
Apricots	12
Peaches	12
Raspberries	12
Strawberries	12

Vegetable	*Number of Months at 0°F.*
Asparagus	8 to 12
Beans, Snap	8 to 12
Beans, Lima	12
Broccoli	12
Brussels Sprouts	8 to 12
Cauliflower	12
Corn on the Cob	8 to 12
Corn, Cut	12
Carrots	12
Mushrooms	8 to 12
Peas	12
Spinach	12
Squash	12

Meat	*Number of Months at 0°F.*
Beef	
Roasts, Steaks	12
Ground	8
Cubed, Pieces	10 to 12
Veal	
Roasts, Chops	10 to 12
Cutlets, Cubes	8 to 10
Lamb	
Roasts, Chops	12
Pork	
Roasts, Chops	6 to 8
Ground, Sausage	4
Pork or Ham, Smoked	5 to 7
Bacon	3
Variety Meats	Up to 4
Poultry	6 to 12

Fish	*Number of Months at 0°F.*
Fatty Fish	
(Mackerel, Salmon, Swordfish, etc.)	3
Lean Fish	
(Haddock, Cod, Ocean Perch, etc.)	6

Table 4-1   Continued

Shellfish	Number of Months at 0°F.
Lobsters and Crabs	2
Shrimp	6
Oysters	3 to 4
Scallops	3 to 4
Clams	3 to 4

Precooked Foods	Number of Months at 0°F.
Bread	
Quick	2 to 4
Yeast	6 to 12
Rolls	2 to 4
Cake	
Angel	4 to 6
Gingerbread	4 to 6
Sponge	4 to 6
Chiffon	4 to 6
Cheese	4 to 6
Fruit	12
Cookies	4 to 6
Combination Dishes	4 to 8
Pies	
Fruit	12
Mince	4 to 8
Chiffon	1
Pumpkin	1
Potatoes	
French Fries	4 to 8
Scalloped	1
Soups	4 to 6
Sandwiches	2

0°F. Foods that are stored at 10°F. have about one-fourth to one-half of the storage life listed. Foods stored at minus 10°F. retain their quality for periods of time longer than those shown.

Many foods have a storage life of more than twelve months when held at 0°F. or lower. While the table shows storage times up to one year, good management practices in the foodservice industry require more frequent turnover. The times shown in the table are for foods that are of high quality when put into storage.

Summary

Frozen foods have a major place in foodservice operations and offer both advantages and disadvantages. There are problems in determining quality of these products, and they need special care to retain quality. Responsibility for frozen foods should be in a capable person who has a set of procedures to ensure proper ordering, receiving, and storage.

Defrosting methods and cooking procedures are also major factors in getting optimum use and value from frozen foods. Some products must be thawed before use while others may or may not be thawed. Refreezing of frozen foods should be done with special attention to the potential development of microorganisms in thawed foods.

Maintaining frozen food quality is related to time and temperature. Damage to quality is cumulative and good care will not eliminate damage caused by previous improper storage conditions. Storage life varies for different frozen foods.

Questions

1.   What are the advantages and disadvantages of using frozen foods?

2.   List four major factors in good ordering procedure.

3.   Give a brief description of what is represented by a Grade A, a Grade B, and a Grade C frozen food.

4.   What factors in a foodservice operation determine the size of unit of frozen foods that is best suited to the need?

5.   How would you check the temperature of a package of frozen food? Describe two different methods.

6.   State eight practices that help to increase the efficiency of a frozen food storage.

7.   What are the recommended ways in which frozen foods can be thawed?

8.   What is the danger zone for food?

9.   What should determine whether a thawed frozen food should be refrozen or not?

10.   Explain the significance of time and temperature in maintaining the quality of frozen foods.

11.   Why can temperature damage not be corrected?

5

Bacterial
Food Poisoning

Doors locked, shades drawn, dust gathering on the tables and chairs, equipment silent and employees gone, a "For Sale" sign in the window, an owner's reputation shattered, and a business venture at a disastrous end!

That could be a restaurant's fate after an outbreak of food poisoning. Someone was careless, someone neglected to carry out the sanitation program, food was spoiled, or temperatures were at the wrong levels for too long. The result was sick customers, maybe an item in the newspaper, certainly much negative word-of-mouth comment, and the bankruptcy of the business.

Food poisoning does not occur in restaurants, hotels, cafeterias, lunchrooms, institutions, and other foodservice establishments as often as is popularly believed. But, when it does, it gets a great deal of attention, and many people hear about it. Any outbreak of food poisoning can be highly damaging to reputation and profits, and may hazard the continued existence of the eating place.

Food Poisoning Can Be Prevented

Since food poisoning results from incorrect handling or preparation of food, foodservice personnel need to know what bacterial food poisoning is, how it occurs, and how it can be prevented.

The fact that *it can be prevented* is the key to what can be done in a food-service operation to prevent an occurrence of food poisoning. Required are a good knowledge of the subject, a training program for employees, and an effective and well-conducted sanitation program. This chapter offers suggestions on simple but effective measures to ensure sanitation, and on the use of refrigeration and heat to protect foods and minimize dangers.

Most foods are highly perishable and become even more perishable as they are prepared for serving in meals. Some foods, because of their composition, are more likely than others to cause food poisoning if they are not handled and stored correctly. *Low-acid* foods such as meat pies, poultry, poultry dressings, meat, and fish can easily be a source of food poisoning, especially if they are minced and moist and handled a great deal. Special care is needed for such foods as cream-filled and custard-filled pastries, sandwiches, ham (especially tenderized ham), prepared meats, sausages, and meat, chicken, and turkey salads. *Acid* foods such as fruits, juices, and relishes seldom cause food poisoning.

What Is Bacterial Food Poisoning?

Food poisoning is a term used to describe the effects on people of various poisonous agents in food. Practically all outbreaks of food poisoning in eating places result from the growth of harmful bacteria in food that is spoiled, improperly prepared, or incorrectly handled.

Bacterial food poisoning can be either a food infection or a food intoxication. An infection is illness resulting from eating or drinking food which contains harmful bacteria. An intoxication is illness resulting from eating or drinking food in which bacteria have grown previously and developed a toxin (poison).

Symptoms of both kinds of bacterial food poisoning are the same—a quick onset of illness with stomach pains, vomiting, and diarrhea.

Commonly Used Low-Acid Foods that
Could Be Potential Sources of
Bacterial Food Poisoning

Meat pies	Bland sauces
Poultry	Custard-filled pastries
Poultry dressing	Cream toppings and fillings
Ground meats	Chicken and egg salads
Croquettes	Minced hams
Fish dishes	Salad-type sandwiches
Cream pies	Hors d'oeuvres

Kinds of Food Poisoning

Operators of food establishments should be concerned with the food poisonings caused by three bacteria: *Staphylococcus, Salmonella,* and

Streptococcus. The poisoning that each causes is known by the same name as the bacteria. (Staphylococcus is often referred to as "staph," and streptococcus as "strep.") *Salmonella* and *Streptococcus* bacteria produce a food infection type of poisoning. *Staphylococcus* bacteria produce a toxin or poison in food, and that toxin causes a food intoxication form of poisoning.

A less known bacterium, *Clostridium perfringens,* is receiving increased attention as a cause of food poisoning. Bacteria of this kind can produce bacteria forms known as spores, which cause an infection type of food poisoning.

Another type of food poisoning, botulism, caused by *Clostridium botulinum,* often makes the headlines because of its high fatality rate, even though a botulism outbreak is exceptionally rare in a commercial foodservice operation. This type of poisoning is mostly found in improperly processed, low-acid foods, such as green beans that are canned at home. Recent cases resulting from incorrect processing of food in commercial canneries have given botulism more widespread and, to some extent, sensational publicity that may make it seem a greater factor than it is. However, with about 60 or 65 percent of the very small number of cases proving fatal, foodservice people should not discount the danger of botulism.

The agitation against the use of nitrite in the curing process for bacon, ham, frankfurts, and meat sausages also focuses more attention on botulism. Nitrite is used to prevent botulism from developing in those foods, as well as to provide the typical color and flavor of these products. If, as some groups advocate, the use of nitrite is restricted, the botulism potential could become a very significant factor for foodservice people, since nitrite is an effective agent against bacteria such as *Clostridium botulinum.* Whether some new curing material can be developed and become widely used remains to be seen.

Shigella or Shigellosis is another less important food-borne food infection that is sometimes called bacillary dysentery. It is caused by bacteria of the *Shigella* family.

Ptomaine poisoning is an incorrect term that formerly was used for food poisoning.

Staphylococcus   *Staphylococcus* bacteria are probably responsible for most cases of food poisoning. Most people are sensitive to the toxin produced by this bacteria, and serious illness can result if enough of the trouble-causing substance is present in food they eat. *Staphylococcus* bacteria are found in large numbers in air, water, milk, and sewage; but the main sources are the skin and the intestinal and respiratory tracts of animals.

The bacteria can get into food from boils, infected cuts, coughing, and sneezing of people who handle food. As the bacteria grow, some strains develop the toxin which is a poison and causes intestinal disturbance even though the flavor and appearance of the food may not change enough to be noticed. It takes only a few hours at room temperature for these bacteria to produce the toxin and, once it is formed, heat will not affect it. In fact, the food can be heated enough to kill the bacteria but the poisonous substance will still remain in the food.

Symptoms of staphylococcus food poisoning are severe nausea, vomiting, and abdominal cramps, which usually occur within 2 to 12 hours after the infected food is eaten. They disappear quickly after the irritating substance is eliminated from the body. This kind of food poisoning is rarely fatal.

Most outbreaks of staphylococcus food poisoning have been caused by the bacteria in prepared or unheated foods such as custard-filled pastries, cream pies, salads, fish, meat products, sandwiches, and creamed dishes. Ham, especially when tenderized, precooked, or minced, has been a frequent cause. Poultry and poultry products, especially poultry dressing and chicken and turkey salads, are excellent growing places for this type of toxin-producing bacteria. Improperly handled hors d'oeuvres and canapes are other sources of this food poisoning.

Salmonella   In contrast to the *Staphylococcus* bacteria, which develop an irritating substance in the food, the *Salmonella* bacteria cause a food infection type of poisoning when the bacteria are eaten in food.

These bacteria are mainly intestinal parasites of man, animals and birds. When bacteria of this type are eaten in food, acute symptoms result within 12 to 24 hours.

Food can be contaminated with *Salmonella* bacteria from infected animals, or by contact with rodents and humans who are infected. The appearance and taste of food infected by these bacteria may seem all right.

These bacteria generally cause trouble in low-acid foods such as meat, poultry, fish, and eggs, and especially in prepared meats, sausages, meat pies, and custard-filled bakery goods that are lightly cooked and handled a great deal.

Streptococcus   Like *Salmonella* bacteria, *Streptococcus* bacteria produce an infection type of food poisoning when large numbers of the bacteria are eaten in food.

Sources of this type of bacteria are usually of human origin. Symptoms occur from 3 to 18 hours after the infected food is eaten and include nausea, vomiting, colic, and diarrhea.

Outbreaks of streptococcus food poisoning have been traced to such foods as poultry dressings, sausages, beef croquettes, coconut cream pies, and cheese.

Perfringens   Perfringens is not something new, but it has been only in recent years that these bacteria have been cited as the cause of some specific cases of food poisoning. The bacteria cause infection and the spores produced by the bacteria cause intoxication. So, the characteristics of both the infection and the intoxication types of food poisoning are present. *Perfringens* bacteria are almost everywhere, but the main sources are probably the soil, sewage, and the intestinal tracts of people and animals.

Clostridium perfringens bacteria produce spores, which are bacterial forms that have a hard exterior covering and contain very little moisture. Such forms are resistant to heat, dryness, and chemical action. Ordinary cooking with heating up to 165°F. easily destroys actively growing bacterial cells, but the perfringens spores can withstand up to six hours of boiling. Heating actually helps the bacteria come out of their protective spore stage; and once the food they are in has cooled to about 120°F., they become actively growing bacteria. People have to eat large numbers of these growing stages of the bacteria to become ill. But, enough of the organisms can develop after cooking to cause an outbreak, if the foods stay at or near room temperature for several hours.

Foods usually involved are those high in protein, including meat, meat dishes, and meat gravies. Actually, any food that is prepared and kept warm over a long period of time before eating could be the cause of this kind of food poisoning.

Botulism   Botulism, like staphylococcus, is an intoxication type of food poisoning. It is caused by *Clostridium botulinum,* an organism that grows in the absence of oxygen. It is the toxin produced by the *botulinum* organisms that is so deadly to humans.

Symptoms of botulism are nausea, vomiting, stomach pains, and diarrhea, followed by dizziness, fatigue, impaired vision, inability to swallow, and respiratory paralysis.

One good rule is not to use food in cans that are damaged, leak, bulge, or when opened are found to contain food that appears to be spoiled. Do not taste foods that smell or look as if they are spoiled. Remember that it takes only one taste of food contaminated by *botulinum* organisms to cause botulism and its accompanying good chance of death in three to ten days.

Improperly canned or refrigerated low-acid foods are sources of this food poisoning. These include green beans, beets, spinach, corn, tuna, figs, fermented foods of various kinds, and vacuum-packed smoked fish.

Shigella   Shigella, or bacillary dysentery, is an infection type of poisoning sometimes caused by food, but also coming from other sources such as contaminated water and poor sewage disposal. In foodservice operations, the spread of the bacillary bacteria is almost always the result of poor personal habits of humans who thus contaminate food with the bacteria. People who have had dysentery can be carriers of the bacteria for a year or more, and they can pass along the bacteria.

The symptoms of shigella include diarrhea, fever, cramps, chills, headache, and nausea. These symptoms can appear anywhere from one day to a week after exposure to the bacteria, but it is usually in less than four days.

Personal hygiene is often called the Number One Control. However, using uncontaminated sources of food and water; good control of vermin, insects, and rodents; and the correct disposal of sewage are important. It is essential to maintain good practice in the handling of food, all the way from its receipt at

65

the foodservice location; while it is in storage; and through the prepreparation, preparation, and cooking operations; the holding time; and the serving of the food. The right kind of refrigeration is a vital control measure, and protecting food in proper containers contributes much to control of food poisoning.

Control of Food-Poisoning Bacteria

Some knowledge of what happens in the life cycle of these bacteria is useful in planning measures to protect quality and prevent contamination of food.

When bacteria first get into a food, there is no immediate increase in numbers. When the bacteria begin to multiply, they start doing so slowly. Then they grow at a more and more rapid rate until they reach their maximum rate of growth. After a while, conditions in the food become unfavorable for further growth. So, the growth of the bacteria slows down and stops. After that, the bacteria decrease in numbers.

Symptoms of bacterial food poisoning occur anywhere from one to twenty-four hours after the infected food is eaten.

A program to prevent food poisoning must emphasize *sanitation measures* to prevent bacteria contaminating the food, the *use of refrigeration* to prevent bacteria from growing, and the *use of heat* to destroy bacteria in food. Food that is not protected may become contaminated by food-poisoning bacteria, and this contamination is the first stage of what can become an outbreak of food poisoning. So, take every precaution possible to prevent contamination that can result from a lack of sanitation safeguards.

Require medical examinations of your food handling personnel; do not allow people with infections or diseases to handle food.

Provide facilities so that food handlers can wash hands with soap and warm water; insist that hands be washed before employees start work, after each trip to the toilet, after handling contaminated or soiled utensils and equipment, after smoking, and before preparing food.

Keep the establishment clean by having available adequate cleaning materials, establishing regular cleaning schedules, and insisting that cleaning be done well and on schedule.

Carefully clean preparation tables and equipment. Bacteria can exist for long periods of time in cracks and on rough surfaces.

Keep dogs and cats out of areas where food is prepared.

Protect your eating place from insects and rodents.

Handle food rapidly.

> Use containers, covers, and other barriers to prevent food from becoming contaminated.

You need such sanitation measures, not only because humans can carry dangerous bacteria, but also because you cannot depend on the smell, taste, and appearance of the food to determine whether it is good.

In general, prevention of food poisoning must depend a great deal on general hygiene and personal cleanliness, and on the protection of food during its storage and preparation.

Refrigeration Controls Growth of Bacteria

Bacteria grow best in temperatures between 40° and 150°F.* Since foods should be held the least possible time in this danger zone, refrigeration of foods is a necessary control measure. That means having adequate refrigeration facilities and making effective use of them.

> Refrigerate food immediately after it is cooked to check the growth of bacteria. Delaying this refrigeration until the food reaches room temperature allows the bacteria to grow more rapidly.
>
> Refrigerate leftovers as soon as possible.
>
> Chill perishable foods rapidly and hold them at 40°F. or below.
>
> When freezing foods, chill or freeze them so that the center temperature is reduced to 40°F. or below within four hours.

Some people believe that putting hot food into a refrigerator or freezer speeds its spoilage. That is not true unless the cooling unit is overloaded and, as a result, the temperature of the refrigerator or freezer is raised to the level where spoilage starts. If a lot of hot food must be refrigerated, pre-cool it. Putting it in shallow pans placed in cold water speeds the cooling, and brings down the temperature to the point where it will not increase unduly the temperature of the cooler when the food is refrigerated.

Some Foods Need Special Precautions   Temperature is especially important in handling some types of foods, and extra precautions are necessary to ensure that these foods are handled and stored correctly.

> Do not allow turkey or other poultry dressings to stay more

---

*The U.S. Public Health Service recommends 45°F. as the lower limit in this temperature range. Some states, such as Massachusetts, have now set 150°F. as the upper figure in the range.

than a total of four hours at temperatures between 40° and 150°F. Never stuff the birds and then let them stand without refrigeration.

Do not allow leftover poultry meat, dressing, and gravy to remain at room temperatures. Refrigerate them. Before serving again, reheat so that every part of the leftover food reaches 165°F.

Do not let sandwich fillings or prepared salads stand at temperatures between 40° and 150°F. for more than four hours total.

Do not keep bread or sandwiches moist with a damp cloth. Bacteria grow especially well under such conditions.

If cooked hams are placed on steam tables, keep them at 150°F. or higher. Never allow them to remain between 40° and 150°F. for more than four hours total.

Refrigeration Limits

Remember the time that food remains in the danger zone (that is, at temperatures over 40°F. but below 150°F.) is cumulative. It adds up. If something is refrigerated at intervals, the total time it is out of refrigeration at temperatures between 40° and 150°F. should not exceed four hours.

Refrigeration Does Not Kill Bacteria

Food-poisoning bacteria are not killed by holding food at low temperatures, even when the food is frozen. Only their growth is stopped. Special precautions are necessary with frozen foods.

Keep frozen foods refrigerated during thawing. Otherwise, they offer excellent places for bacteria to grow, and they can easily spoil and become unfit for use.

Keep frozen precooked foods at 0°F. When thawed, these foods also provide good places for bacterial growth.

Keep precooked foods that are not frozen at 40°F. or lower.

Refrigeration alone is not the complete answer. Temperatures must be low, and the food must be cooled rapidly and handled in a sanitary way if refrigeration is to be effective in preventing food poisoning.

Proper cooking is the best way to destroy dangerous bacteria in food; to be effective, temperatures of 165° to 170°F. should be reached in the center of the food being cooked. This applies especially to leftovers. Keep foods on steam tables at 150°F. or higher.

Remember adequate cooking will kill bacteria, but it will not destroy the toxin (poison) that some types of bacteria produce in foods.

Summary

Food poisoning, though infrequent, can have serious consequences for a foodservice establishment. Programs to prevent it are well worth the effort put into them. Bacteria can cause food poisoning when people eat food containing live bacteria or food in which bacteria have produced a toxin (poison). By proper handling, preparation, and storage practices, bacteria can be prevented from contaminating food.

Food can be contaminated in several ways. Sources of contamination can include food, food handlers, the practices and procedures used in handling foods, other food materials, and the kitchen tools that are used in food preparation.

People are a major cause of contamination. Some foodservice workers may have an infection and pass this along to other people by contaminating the food with which they work. Some may practice poor habits of personal hygiene and, as a result, cause contamination. Some may handle food in ways that allow it to become contaminated from many sources including humans.

Many times equipment that is unsanitary from not being correctly or adequately cleaned can be the contamination source. Also, customers can contaminate food, as in the case of a salad bar that does not have sneeze guards.

Persons handling food in eating establishments can do much to prevent food poisoning by observing a few simple precautions:

Sanitation cleanliness and good health of workers, and cleanliness of equipment and places where food is prepared are essential.

Refrigeration cold does not kill harmful bacteria, but it controls the rate at which they grow. Temperatures between 40° and 150°F. are the danger zone.

Heat heat kills bacteria, but it does not destroy the toxin produced in food by *Staphylococcus* bacteria. Be sure that temperatures of 165° to 170°F. are reached in the center of food being cooked.

Do not let susceptible foods stay at temperatures in the danger zone any longer than is necessary. Never let them stand at temperatures between 40° and 150°F. for more than a total of four hours.

Sanitation, the correct use of heat, and the proper use of refrigeration, together with an understanding of how bacteria cause food poisoning, can prevent the economic losses that result from an outbreak of food poisoning.

Make these measures standard practice in your foodservice operation.

Questions

1.   What is the difference between food infection and food intoxication?

2.   What are five most important food-poisoning bacteria?

3.   What is the range of temperature (Fahrenheit) within which food can be protected from rapid bacteria growth?

4.   Explain how heat and cold can be used effectively to prevent bacterial food poisoning.

5.   Describe why humans are often called the greatest source of bacterial food poisoning.

6

Care and Handling
of Prepared Frozen Foods

All foods present problems in the development and growth of bacteria, and spoilage. Foods that are not handled correctly have the potential for causing illness and even food poisoning. Precautions are necessary to protect food quality, and in so doing to protect the health of the consumer.

Frozen foods, like all other foods, need attention in processing, handling, storing, and preparation to prevent bacterial contamination. Prepared frozen foods present special difficulties in maintaining quality and in protection against contamination by bacteria. They are more susceptible to bacterial invasion, and they offer a more favorable environment for bacterial growth than many other products.

Most prepared frozen foods are cooked only a minimum amount of time by the processor, since they are going to be cooked again. Minimizing the length of cooking time also minimizes the breakdown of tissue and disruption of cell structure, which is considerable in processing, freezing, storage, and preparation for use. This does not mean that prepared frozen foods are more likely to cause food poisoning than foods preserved by other methods. Actually, they have an excellent public health record. It does mean, however, that they need to be provided the protection against loss of quality that their special characteristics require.

Foodservice people must understand the effects of freezing on foods, since many of the pre-cooked foods are greatly changed by freezing, by being held in frozen storage, and by being reheated for use. They must also understand how microbiological contamination occurs, in order that they may introduce and maintain effective procedures to prevent contamination. An effective program must focus on these two areas of prevention of microbial contamination and maintenance of quality.

Safety Program Is Necessary

Microorganisms are very widely distributed, and their presence in prepared frozen foods is not unusual. Of concern are the kinds of bacteria in the food, and the numbers or count of the bacteria present.

Bacteria are present in the food from which the finished products are prepared. The amount of bacterial contamination in the final product is influenced by the way in which the raw food material is handled and processed. Generally, the more contamination of the raw materials from which the product was made, the more bacteria will be found in the finished product. To prevent bacteria problems requires a constant effort to keep bacteria out of the food and, to the extent possible, to keep bacteria present in the food from multiplying to the point where they can cause trouble.

To maintain quality it is necessary also to ensure correct handling of the products, their storage at the correct temperatures, and their correct preparation for use. Sanitation, time, cold temperatures, and heat all play a part, and are the basic components of an effective program to maintain the quality and safety of prepared frozen foods. The program must be applied all the way from production to consumption—in the processing plant, in storage, in transportation, in handling, and in preparation for use. It is especially important that it be applied in the foodservice establishment where the problems of maintaining good sanitary practices may be much more difficult than in the commercial plant.

Sanitation Practices in Production

Good sanitation practices are essential in the commercial processing plant where the products are produced on a large scale; and also essential in the individual foodservice establishment where foods are produced and frozen for later use, or where leftovers are frozen for use at a later time.

When good sanitation practices are followed, prepared frozen foods can be produced with very low bacteria counts. When sanitation measures are poorly enforced or otherwise ineffective, the foods produced will have high bacterial counts. Use of high quality raw materials for making the frozen foods assists greatly in keeping down the bacterial count.

Low temperatures will not counteract the effects of poor sanitation. Also, if the microorganisms present in food are poisonous, they may have formed toxins in the food; these toxins are not affected by low temperatures. So, freezing and storage should not be expected to destroy bacteria.

Heat Does Not Kill All Bacteria

Similarly, heat will not kill all the bacteria in food, even though most of the microbial contamination in the raw food is destroyed when meats, poultry, vegetables, and other foods are cooked. Some kinds of bacteria are not killed by heat during the processing of food. Also, holding the cooking temperature and duration of cooking time to a minimum in the cooking process to minimize changes in flavor and texture of the final product affects the number of surviving bacteria.

Special care is necessary in food processing to avoid contamination from people. Workers with disease, skin infections, or cuts can easily cause microbial contamination of foods in the preparation for processing and in other handling of the foods. Precautions should be taken so that they do not handle or come in contact with the food.

Chances of recontaminating the food during handling after it has been cooked and before it is frozen are many. Boning, dicing, weighing meat for pies, and similar procedures before the final freezing provide opportunities for recontamination, even though the heat in the preparation process has reduced the number of bacteria that were present in the food.

Freeze without Delay

Since bacteria reproduce at a rapid rate, prepared foods should be frozen without delay after cooking to prevent the bacteria from increasing in number.

There is great variation in the numbers of bacteria found in pre-cooked frozen foods. For example, fish products are likely to show more bacteria than creamed meat and poultry products. Also, unbaked frozen meat pies offer more favorable conditions for the growth of many types of microorganisms than other foods. Types of bacteria that cause food poisoning have been found in many kinds of commercially prepared pre-cooked frozen foods. Included are chicken á la king, cream and custard dessert pies, breaded shrimp, poultry and beef pies, and poultry dressing.

Low Temperature Effects on Microorganisms

Once the foods are prepared at the production plant, they are frozen and put into freezing storage. Even though freezing and low temperature storage do much to maintain quality and control development and growth of bacteria, they do have limitations in the extent to which they can control microorganism life and growth.

Freezing does not effectively kill microorganisms as many people believe it does. It does destroy some of the microorganisms that are present in the food, but not all of them; and many of the organisms that can cause food problems can survive freezing conditions, even for extremely long periods in storage.

However, freezing temperatures can slow down or halt growth of many bacteria, if the temperatures are low enough.

Many factors govern how many and what types of bacteria survive in frozen foods. Included are such things as how great the contamination was in the first place, the rate of freezing, the storage temperature, the time in storage, the composition of the food, and the process used to thaw the food before use.

Microorganisms can grow in frozen foods. The frozen foods many seem to be completely frozen when they are cooled to a little below 32°F. But, the foods actually retain water in liquid form until very low temperatures are reached. Even at 5°F., as much as 15 percent of the water may stay unfrozen in some foods. However, growth of the food-poisoning bacteria seldom occurs at temperatures below 40°F.

A great number of nonpoisonous bacteria, which are known as psychrophilic bacteria, can grow at temperatures below 32°F. Even though these bacteria are not poisonous, they do cause food spoilage. They grow at temperatures above 20°F. for the most part, but occasionally are found at temperatures down to 14°F. Rarely are they found growing at temperatures below that level. Generally, then, the chances that frozen foods will spoil increase greatly as the temperatures at which they are stored rises above 20°F.

Care and Handling After Production

Prepared frozen foods may be produced under good sanitation conditions and the products may have high quality and low microbial counts. But this is no guarantee the products will remain in that condition until they are used. A great deal of quality loss can occur between the production line and the point of use in a foodservice establishment.

Commercially prepared frozen foods may be inadequately refrigerated where the products are held before being sent out. The products may be improperly handled in warehouses, order assembly rooms, and delivery trucks, producing conditions which favor growth of the microorganisms that are usually present in these foods. Sometimes, the food is held at temperatures which are too high, and sometimes it is held too long in storage. These same problems are often found in the individual foodservice establishment.

Storage temperature is a major factor in controlling the number of microorganisms in frozen foods. If the holding temperature is correct and is maintained, growth of microorganisms will be prevented, and the original wholesomeness and quality of the food will be retained. It is essential that all frozen foods be stored at 0°F. or below.

When frozen foods are allowed to defrost, bacteria starts to multiply, and decomposition of the food begins. Frozen foods deteriorate in the same general way that fresh foods do, but they may decompose more rapidly. The tissues are likely to be partially softened from the effects of cooking, freezing, and low temperature storage. As a result, they are more vulnerable to invasion of bacteria than are the tissues of fresh foods.

Care and Handling at the Foodservice Establishment

Even if the prepared frozen foods are produced under sanitary conditions and arrive at the foodservice establishment without any appreciable quality loss, they still can be subject to microbial damage before they are eaten.

One common cause of quality loss is storage of the product at too high a temperature for too long a period of time. Another is baking the product for a shorter period of time than is recommended. A third is holding the product after baking without refrigeration.

When Heat Does Not Kill

Potpies prepared from bacterially contaminated raw food materials pose a serious hazard when baked for a short time at a high temperature (500°F.). This quick cooking could produce a browning of the crust before the heat has penetrated the pie sufficiently to kill any dangerous bacteria that might be present. Pay special attention to the heat treatments that are recommended on commercial packages. They are usually adequate and should be followed.

If prepared frozen food is not consumed in a relatively short time, it should be put under refrigeration to prevent the bacteria that survived the cooking process from multiplying.

Frozen foods are probably no more likely to cause food poisoning than foods processed by other methods of preparation. But, the potential is there, and foodservice people need to understand the special requirements for maintaining the quality and safety of the frozen products. They also need to maintain high sanitation levels, and to use good handling methods.

Some Reminders and Precautions

Among the things to be kept in mind and the precautions to be followed are:

Understand the effects on prepared frozen foods of freezing, storage, and reheating for use.

Use good sanitary procedures in the production and handling of precooked frozen foods.

Do not expect low temperatures to cancel out the effects of poor sanitation.

Do not expect freezing and low temperature storage to destroy all the bacteria.

Freeze prepared frozen foods without delay after cooking to prevent bacteria from increasing in number.

See that no employee who has disease, skin infections, or cuts handles or comes in contact with food.

Maintain good control of cooling and storage temperatures to prevent growth of microorganisms.

Store all frozen food products at $0°$F. or lower.

Do not bake prepared frozen foods for less than the recommended time.

Follow the recommendations for heating found on commercial packages of prepared frozen foods.

Summary

Prepared frozen foods require special attention to maintain their quality and protect them from bacterial contamination. Sanitation, time, cold temperatures, and heat are the basic components of a quality and safety program. Neither heat nor cold will kill all bacteria, but both can hold down bacterial development.

Defrosted food deteriorates in the same way as fresh food but at a more rapid rate, due to the effects on the tissues of cooking, freezing, defrosting, and low temperature storage.

Foodservice operators need to understand the effects of freezing, storage, thawing, and reheating on prepared frozen foods; and need to provide the best possible storage and holding conditions. Also, they need to make adjustments in cooking methods.

Questions

1.   Why do prepared frozen foods present special difficulties in maintaining quality and protecting against contamination by bacteria?

2.   Name the basic components of an effective program to maintain the quality and safety of prepared frozen foods.

3.   Explain why heat is not the complete answer for control of bacteria in food.

4.   Indicate some of the ways in which food prepared for freezing can be contaminated before the final freezing.

5.   There is considerable variation in the numbers of bacteria found in pre-cooked, frozen foods. Compare fish products, creamed meat and poultry products, and unbaked frozen pizza in this regard.

6.   List some of the commercially prepared precooked frozen foods in which types of bacteria that cause food poisoning have been found.

7.   How effective is freezing in killing microorganisms present in food?

8.   What are psychrophilic bacteria, and what problems do they cause?

9.   Why are frozen foods likely to decompose more rapidly than fresh
foods?

7

Principles of Planning Kitchen Layout

Major costs in the operation of a foodservice establishment are food and labor, and the trend of both of these operating expenses seems to be ever upward. Since the kitchen is where much of the activity involving food and labor takes place, the kitchen is where inefficiencies can often be found.

High on the list of requirements for an efficient foodservice operation is a well-designed kitchen. If the kitchen is laid out poorly, excessive numbers of personnel and excessive time are required. No matter how capable the employees are, there will be excessive cost, and also confusion and unhappy workers.

Unfortunately, kitchens many times do not get the attention necessary when the eating place is being planned. Many eating places are expansions of smaller operations with little advance planning. In other cases, either through lack of knowledge or an effort to skimp on costs, the kitchen is allocated too little space and the arrangement is poor. The result is frequently a foodservice establishment with an excellent dining room, but with a kitchen that is a hodge-podge of equipment, randomly located. Such an inefficient kitchen can only lead to excessively high costs of handling food, and unchangeable characteristics that make it almost impossible to organize the production facilities on any kind of efficient basis.

However, it may be possible to make some changes, and even though the high level of efficiency desired may not be attained, costs could be held to present levels, or even reduced. Of course, if a new operation is being planned, the inefficiencies can be avoided.

The Objective in Planning the Layout

The goal in kitchen planning involves six elements that must be considered, evaluated, and coordinated to produce the efficient kitchen operation that is desired. Equipment, food, personnel, ease of movement, time, and distance are the factors with which the kitchen planner deals. The objective is to coordinate the equipment, food, and personnel such that, in the given space, food may move through the kitchen and be subjected to the kitchen processes as easily as possible, with a minimum distance between operations, and in the shortest possible time.

If this objective can be met, the work in the kitchen is easier, employees need take fewer steps, and considerable time is saved. That result, of course, can mean reduced costs and a smooth kitchen operation. This is the goal toward which planning efforts should be directed, whether it is a new kitchen that the foodservice operator is planning, or whether it is the remodeling of a kitchen already in operation.

A layout for an efficient kitchen makes the best use of the available space, the structure of the building, and the essential equipment. Much attention needs to be directed to putting the right kind of equipment in the right location, so that the processing of food from raw materials to finished meals can progress efficiently.

There are some complications in foodservice kitchen planning that must be considered. Unlike many businesses where the functions of manufacture, distribution, and selling are performed separately in different places, the foodservice business combines all the functions at the same location, with the kitchen the major focus of activity. Also, there is a special need to maintain quality in preparing food in quantity, and to provide sanitation safeguards. The low profit nature of the foodservice business adds another major consideration, in which the proper use of equipment and the work force depends to quite an extent on the layout and the flow of work.

The contribution to maximum profits resulting from better control of costs and quality of the product, which results from a well-planned kitchen, is considerable in itself. But, a well-planned kitchen layout also contributes a great deal to:

gaining greater customer satisfaction

improving the handling of materials

improving employee working conditions

reducing expenses of operation

reducing or eliminating confusion

improving overall control of the kitchen operation

coordinating the various kitchen operations

Foodservice Operator Should Initiate the Plan

Development of the plan for a kitchen can be done by the operator with assistance from staff members. Or, the job can be turned over to outside people who are experts in the field.

Regardless of whether the planning is done by the operator or by outside assistance, the foodservice operator should make the preliminary plan. Only the operator and the people who work in the establishment know the business and the demands on the kitchen. They understand how production takes place and how they relate it to the other parts of the total foodservice operation. They know the significance of layout features which provide more security, better safety and sanitation, and reduce problems of supervision in their operation.

If the initial planning job is done well before the changes are to be made, the operator and employees might well do much of the planning. But, if immediate changes are needed, the job probably should be turned over to someone else because of the demands of time and because a good foodservice consultant can bring solutions from the outside world that the operator or employees might not be aware could be applied.

Experts Pay for Themselves

Consultants and architects have a place in planning of kitchen layout. In most cases, the operator can benefit from employing a consultant when planning a new kitchen. Foodservice consultants can be utilized on a part-time basis, or the entire job can be turned over to a consultant. Such outside assistance from a reliable and capable foodservice consultant can provide guidance on the layout of the kitchen, the equipment needed and its costs, with a saving in money and time for the operator.

However, many architects lack the needed understanding of the technical problems involved in large-scale food production and their relationship to the kitchen layout. An architect who is familiar with planning foodservice kitchens can provide guidance on selection of the types of construction needed with a considerable savings in cost. He can also provide valuable advice on such vital subjects as compliance with building codes, preparation of building plans and specifications, and making changes in building construction.

It is essential that the consultant and the architect be qualified to deal with problems of foodservice kitchen planning and layout, if the plans that are developed are to meet the needs of the particular operation. So, employment of a consultant and an architect is suggested for kitchen changes of any substantial nature; and plans should be approved by a qualified foodservice consultant and architect.

Preparation of Preliminary Layout

In planning a kitchen, first plan it on paper. Make accurate drawings of the kitchen area. The original construction plans, if available, can provide substantial savings in both cost and time. If they cannot be obtained, a new plan of the kitchen can be drawn to scale, using ¼ inch to represent each foot.

The layout is a plan for placing equipment and locating other elements of the kitchen. It offers a way in which ideas on what should be done in a new or improved kitchen can be developed and changed before the final plans are made. It is a visual translation of those ideas into arrangements of the parts of the kitchen and the kitchen equipment. It offers a picture of the total results of changes in a total kitchen, rather than a view of just parts of the total.

A layout can help determine the most efficient locations for equipment. Models or templates of the equipment can be used to try various combinations to determine which are the most efficient. These arrangements show whether the needed equipment is going to fit into the available space, whether there is enough aisle space, and whether workers in the kitchen can do their jobs without interfering with one another.

Work centers are the basic parts of the layout. Operations that are of the same type are performed in a work center. For example, there can be a work center for mixing operations and another for slicing meat. The work centers that are closely related to one another in terms of the kind of work performed, or the kind of workers who perform the work, are grouped together into sections. Then these sections are linked to each other according to the flow of the work. The flow of work is the sequence of operations that takes place when food materials are processed and the other tasks performed in the kitchen are done.

Use of Templates, Overlays, and Models

The use of templates or models of equipment and fixtures makes kitchen planning easier.

Models provide a three-dimensional effect that makes it easier to visualize the plan. They show the relationships of the equipment and fixtures on a reduced scale, and they provide a chance to see and evaluate the arrangement that is proposed. They add the important concept of height to the consideration. It is possible to detect poor arrangements and to avoid serious mistakes in the final plans. Scale models add to cost, but that cost is more than repaid if the models prevent planning mistakes.

Templates are two-dimensional representations of the equipment. They can be purchased at low cost, or they can be easily made. They, too, offer visual representation of the arrangements which can be made for the equipment. They are not as realistic as models, but they can be of much value in kitchen planning.

Overlays are tracings which are made over the original drawings or plans.

Figure 7-1   Scale Templates of Kitchen Equipment

SCALE TEMPLATES

OF

KITCHEN EQUIPMENT

ELECTRIC COOKING EQUIPMENT

GAS COOKING EQUIPMENT

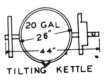

STEAM COOKING EQUIPMENT

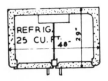
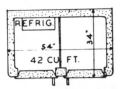
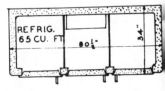

PORTABLE REACH-IN REFRIGERATORS & CABINETS

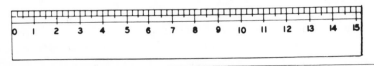

Scale Rule: Each Number Represents One Foot for Templates

Use of overlays will save considerable time and will reduce the possibilities of error in drafting.

The Flow of Food

The sequence of operations in a kitchen is related to food and what is done to it and with it. So, the layout should show the flow of food. Arrows and lines can be drawn on the layout to show in what direction the flow moves. Different color lines can be used to show the movement of different kinds of materials. One color line can show the flow of the raw food materials, and another color line can show the movement of the prepared food.

Determining how the food flows is related to the specific kitchen since kitchen layout differs so much from one foodservice operation to another. The flow that is best in one kitchen may not be at all satisfactory in another.

To determine where the lines and arrows should go on the layout:

List the various kitchen operations.

Use a process chart to show the sequences.

Use flow diagrams to show travel.

Adapt the flow lines to the kitchen plan.

The flow lines integrate people, equipment, food, and the supporting activities. Through this kind of integration, the food can be moved to the various locations necessary in the shortest possible distances between the different operations.

The Layout of the Work Space

Space must get considerable attention in the making of the layout. Wherever a worker performs an operation, there should be enough space to do the job efficiently. It pays to plan carefully the location of tools, materials, and supplies that the worker needs to perform the particular tasks.

When equipment is involved in the operation, other factors must be considered. When a piece of equipment is in a work place, be sure there is sufficient space so that:

The worker can perform all the tasks related to that work space.

The tools the worker uses can be conveniently located.

The worker has ready access to tools, materials, and equipment. All of the materials he needs to do the job should be within easy reaching distances for him.

The finished products can be stored temporarily until they are moved elsewhere.

83

Figure 7-2 The Flow of Food

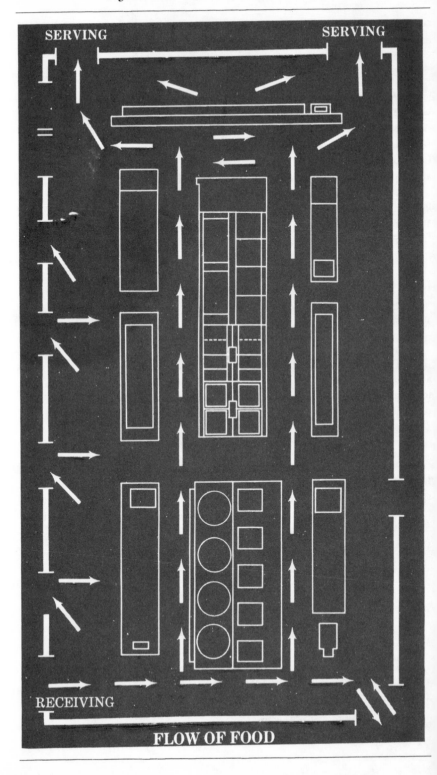

SERVING

SERVING

RECEIVING

FLOW OF FOOD

Figure 7-3   Work Table Areas

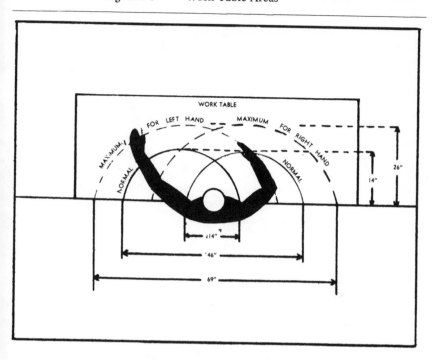

WORK TABLE AREA

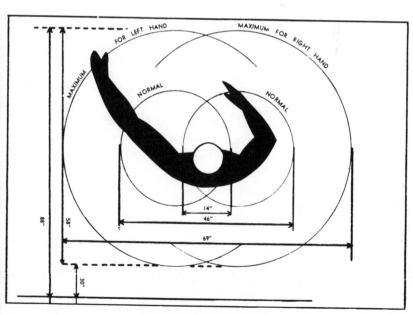

STANDING AREA

Shown in Figure 7-3 are the normal and the maximum work areas for a worker who is seated at a work table and for one who is standing while performing his job. The distances are for a medium-sized man. A medium-sized woman would have about 10 percent less normal work area.

The idea is that workers should not have to reach or travel farther than the maximum work areas; and most of their motions should be within the normal work areas. The work areas are determined by the limitations of the human body.

In making the layout, there is value in drawing the work space to scale and being sure that there is enough space for all that is required in that particular work space. Remember that too much space is as bad as not having enough space. But, be certain that enough space is provided for servicing, cleaning, and loading the equipment, and for the workers themselves.

An Operations Analysis Chart

The operations analysis chart is of value in analyzing the work done by an employee. If the overall operation is to be efficient, the working methods of the individual worker must be efficient. So, observation of those working methods is important. Notice that the chart calls for observation of both hands of the employee. If both hands do equal amounts of work, the total time of the operation can be reduced (Figure 7-4).

The Final Check

When all of the ideas and recommendations have been considered and evaluated, and what will be in the layout is agreed upon, carefully review the materials for the proposed layout to see if it provides all of the objectives that were in mind when the planning started. Also, check at this point to be sure that the proposed layout is justified from the cost point of view. Generally, a new layout results in increased savings, since it eliminates some of the known inefficiencies that were in the old layout. But find out if:

The kitchen as laid out is within the proposed budget.

The anticipated savings in labor and equipment justify the proposed layout.

The capital required and the return on investment justify the new layout.

The over-all profit of the establishment will increase if the new layout is used.

Figure 7-4   Operations Analysis

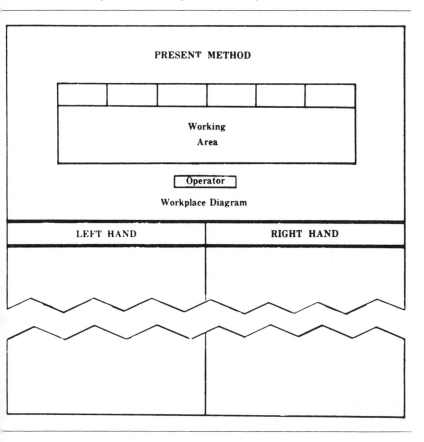

Working with sketches developed in preliminary planning, the architect or the consultant can prepare the final working drawings that show all of the details of the proposed kitchen and the specifications that must be met.

Reminders

Remember that the purpose of preparing a kitchen layout is to provide an efficient arrangement of equipment and workers so that production can be streamlined and the kitchen area can be used most effectively. To attain maximum efficiency in producing a layout and so accomplish the goals, the following basic requirements are essential:

Know the present and future requirements of the foodservice operation.

87

Know the potential for growth of the establishment.

Draw a preliminary plan for the kitchen on paper.

Analyze each operation that occurs in the kitchen.

Relate the various operations and determine the efficient flow of work.

Estimate in detail the cost of the project for which the layout is being made.

Relate the projected changes to the needs and goals and evaluate how well the proposed changes meet those needs and goals.

Have a qualified consultant or architect help develop the final plans and do the final drawings.

Summary

Inefficiencies in the kitchen produce greater operating expenses than necessary, as poor layout requires excessive personnel and time. Improvements can be made that will stabilize or reduce costs in present kitchens, and inefficiencies can be avoided in planning new kitchens.

Equipment, food, personnel, ease of movement, time, and distance must be considered, evaluated, and coordinated for efficient kitchen planning. The foodservice operator can best make the preliminary plan, but might well call on outside expert assistance for the development of those plans. Templates, overlays, and models can be of much assistance in determining the layout of the kitchen and determining the flow of food. People, equipment, food, and supporting activities all are integrated by the flow lines. Adequate space for workers and equipment is essential.

Questions

1. Name the six elements that must be evaluated and coordinated to produce an efficient kitchen operation.

2. What is the objective of the kitchen planner in the coordination of these elements?

3. A well-planned kitchen gives better control of costs and quality of product and so contributes greatly to profit. What other results in the operation of the foodservice establishment can come from a well-planned kitchen?

4. Explain the significance of work centers and flow of work in developing a layout for the kitchen.

5. A worker needs sufficient space to perform his or her job efficiently and that requirement is a part of the layout of work space when equipment is involved in the operation. What other factors should be considered?

6.   What is an operations analysis chart and how is it used?

7.   Describe a step-by-step procedure for getting maximum efficiency in producing a kitchen layout.

8

Using Storage Controls to Simplify Determination of Food Costs

Many foodservice operations find a major problem in obtaining food cost figures quickly enough that the data can signal that problems exist. Management can then do something about those problems immediately. Action can be taken without a month or more elapsing between the time the problems occur and they become known to management.

Even though the computer has greatly reduced time lags in the foodservice industry, many operators still determine food cost figures monthly by using the figures for inventory and for purchases. However, they may find that the information becomes available too late to institute measures to correct something that has gone wrong.

They could check inventories and total purchases at more frequent intervals than once a month, but this involves substantial amounts of time and work by the personnel. However, there is one way to determine food costs daily with a relatively small amount of work and with acceptable accuracy. That way is through the use of storage controls and the information that comes from the storage control records.

There are two essentials for good storage control. One is a capable individual who can assume responsibility for all of the food that moves into and out of the storage. The other essential is a set of forms sufficient to exercise the desired control. The receiving record and the storeroom requisition show what has moved in and what has moved out of the storage.

One Person Responsibility

For good storeroom control, one person should be made responsible. In larger foodservice operations, he may have a full-time assignment to the storeroom. In smaller operations, he may have other assignments in addition to storage control. He may also function as the receiving clerk.

The duties of the storeroom person vary considerably depending on the organization, its size, and its policies; the following primary duties, however, go with a well-run storage operation:

receiving foods that are delivered

checking the foods into storage

maintaining an orderly arranged and clean storage

issuing foods, upon proper requisition

assisting in the taking of inventory

assisting with pricing of foods in storage

reporting foods of which the stock is depleted and needs ordering

notifying the appropriate person of foods that are moving slowly, foods that have been overlooked and are losing quality, and foods that have been ordered but have not been received

Effective performance of these duties by a responsible and efficient person in charge of the storage not only makes it possible to get accurate food cost figures quickly, but also contributes to the overall efficiency of the foodservice establishment.

Storage Forms Necessary for Good Control

Two forms are needed to control and record information on movement of foods into storage and out of storage—the receiving record and the storeroom requisition.

Receiving Record   All incoming deliveries are recorded on the receiving record. This is its purpose and function. If it is used correctly, the receiving record is a useful tool for management since it provides a comparison of day-to-day purchases. This record is also necessary for figuring the daily food cost. A typical receiving form is shown in Figure 8-1.

This form is easy to use. All purchases of food that go directly to the kitchen to be used the same day are listed under the heading, food direct. All purchases that are sent to the storeroom are listed under food stores. These include purchases that go to the meat, freezer, and produce storage boxes to become part of the storage inventory, under the storage clerk's control. All nonfood items such as cleaning supplies are listed under the heading, sundries.

Figure 8-1   Receiving Clerk's Daily Report

No. 325
Date 7/6

Vendor and Invoice Number	Quan.	Unit	Description	Unit Price	Amount	Total Amount	Purchase Journal Distribution		
							Food Direct	Food Stores	Sundries
Atlas Provision 8713	3	can	#10 Pieces Tomatoes	4.95	29 85			29 85	
"	2	can	#10 BL Green Beans	8.15	16 30	46 15		16 30	
Stellar Meats 1967	60	lb	Rib of Beef Choice	1.87	112 20			112 20	
"	25	lb	Loin of Pork Rolled	1.12	28 00	140 20	28 00		
Dairy Crest Co. 3062	30	gal	Milk	1.28	38 40		38 40		
"	150	½ pt	Milk	.10	15 00		15 00		
"	15	gal	Vanilla Ice Cream	2.00	30 00			30 00	
"	15	lb	Butter Patties	.83	12 45	95 85		12 45	
Ace Produce 1653	1	crate	Lettuce - 48 heads	6.90	6 90			6 90	
"	30	lb	Tomatoes	.52	15 60		15 60		
"	1	crate	Val. Oranges - 125's	4.70	4 70			4 70	
"	15	lb	Carrots	.13	1 95	29 15		1 95	
Allison's Inc.	15	lb	Cleaning Materials	1.00	15 00	15 00			15 00
TOTALS					500 60	500 60	150 00	310 00	15 00

The receiving record, and also the summary of daily food costs, can be used to provide a breakdown of food expenditures into such categories as meats, dairy products, and fresh vegetables, by adding columns with appropriate headings.

Storeroom Requisition   To ensure tight control of the issuing of food from storage, requisition forms are necessary. Food will be issued only upon presentations of such a form. A typical requisition form is shown in Figure 8-2. It has space for the date, the department, the amount and weight of

Figure 8-2

FOOD REQUISITION

Date

Department

No.	Unit	Description	Unit Price	Extension

No. 110

Authorized _____   Received By _____

the item, the price, and the signature of the person who is authorized to make out the requisition. There also is space for the signature of the person who receives the food.

The pricing of the requisition may be done by the storeroom clerk, or it may be done by the accounting office. If the storeroom clerk does the pricing, a price book or price card file should be available in the storeroom. New prices should be entered each day from the receiving record or the invoices.

Determining the Daily Food Cost

Maintaining a simplified daily food cost control involves the calculation of only the food that is sent to the kitchen for preparation each day. Two figures are necessary to make this calculation:

> the amount of food that is sent directly to the kitchen when it is delivered
>
> the amount of food that is issued to the kitchen by the storeroom

The daily total for the amount of food sent directly to the kitchen is the total of the food direct column on the daily receiving record (Figure 8-1). The total amount of food that is issued to the kitchen is determined by adding up the storeroom requisitions for the day.

Adding the food direct total to the total for the storeroom requisitions yields the gross cost of food sold for the day.

To find the net cost of food sold, subtract from the gross figure any food that was sent directly to the kitchen or issued to the kitchen from the storeroom that was used for any other purposes than feeding guests or employees. In this category would go such items as lemons and limes that were sent to the bar or any food that is sold directly to employees or other people—transactions that are usually at cost.

Estimated Rather than Actual Cost

Keep in mind that this method of calculating the daily food cost produces an estimated figure rather than the actual cost figure, since the kitchen leftovers have not been included in the figures. This omission does not reduce the value of the cost figure to any appreciable extent for several reasons:

> In most foodservice operations, the amount of leftovers or kitchen inventory runs about the same from day to day. Where that situation exists, the food cost figure is not affected very much by the leftovers or kitchen inventory.

Maintaining a running or "to-date" cost of all daily costs will result in the averaging out of any discrepancy after the first few days of the month.

Poor business or inaccurate forecasting may result in a day of more than the usual amount of leftovers. There will be a high cost figure for such a day. But in the next day or two, when the leftovers are used, there will likely be low cost figures.

An Example

An example will illustrate how the daily food cost can be figured. Following are the daily figures for a foodservice establishment:

Total Food Direct	$150.00 (from Receiving Record)
Total Storeroom Issues	250.00 (from Storeroom Requisitions)
Transferred to Bar	20.00 (from Bar Requisitions)
Steward's Sales to Employees	10.00 (from Steward's Book)
Daily Food Sales	1110.00 (from Record of Sales)

To determine daily food cost—

Add Food Direct		$150.00
and Total Issues		250.00
to get Gross Cost		400.00
Subtract from Gross Cost		400.00
Transfers to the Bar	$20.00	
and Steward's Sales	10.00	
which total		30.00
to get Net Food Cost		370.00

To determine food cost percent—

Divide the Net Cost	$370.00
by Daily Food Sales	$1110.00
to get Food Cost Percent	33 1/3%

Summary of Daily Food Cost Form

Figure 8-3 is an example of a simple form that can be used to record daily food cost. This Summary of Daily Food Cost Form can be printed especially for the foodservice operation, or a 13-column analysis sheet can be used. Such sheets can be obtained from any office supply store.

The first three columns in this form are used for a perpetual storeroom inventory record, and are not used for figuring the food cost. The storeroom inventory at the beginning of the month goes on the first line in column 1. The total of the daily purchases sent to the storeroom is found in the food stores column of the receiving record; it is entered in column 2 of this form. The figures in column 1 and column 2 are added, and this total is entered in column 3. The daily storeroom issues figure, found in column 4, is subtracted from this column 3 total, and the resulting figure is the next day's beginning inventory.

At the end of the month, the final inventory figure is checked against the

Figure 8-3   Summary of Daily Food Cost

1962 DATE		(1) BEGINNING STOREROOM INVENTORY		(2) STOREROOM PURCHASES		(3) TOTAL		(4) STOREROOM ISSUES		(5) DIRECT PURCHASES	
1/1		3500	00	310	00	3810	00	225	00	150	00
1/2		3585	00	400	00	3985	00	185	00	115	00
1/3		3800	00								
					*INFORMATION FOR COLUMN 2 AND COLUMN 5 COMES DIRECTLY FROM THE RECEIVING RECORD					

(7) LESS TRANSFERS		(8) NET COST		(9) SALES		(10) FOOD COST PER CENT	MONTH TO DATE					
							NET COST		SALES		PER CENT	
25	00	350	00	1050	00	33.3	350	00	1050	00	33.3	
10	00	290	00	850	00	34.1	640	00	1900	00	33.7	

actual physical inventory to find out how efficient the storeroom records are. If there are any major differences, each should be checked to determine where control was lost. Measures can then be taken to tighten up control so that the storeroom records can be kept more efficiently.

Columns for Food Cost Data   The other columns on the form, numbers 4 through 13, are used for the data from which the daily food cost and the to-date food cost are figured.

Storeroom issues (column 4) are added to direct purchases (column 5) to provide the figure for gross cost (column 6). Transfers (column 7) are subtracted from the gross cost to provide the figure for net cost (column 8). Dividing this by sales (column 9) provides the daily food cost percent (column 10). To find the month-to-date cost, carry the totals of net cost and sales to columns 11 and 12.

This procedure illustrates the importance to management of storage as a major place for control. It also emphasizes the manner in which storage forms can be used to get good control and, in the process, produce needed figures when they are of most value.

Summary

Storage control records provide foodservice operators with a way of determining daily food cost figures with relatively little work, and enabling them to determine problems quickly. Much of the responsibility for obtaining this information rests on the person in charge of the storeroom.

Receiving records, storeroom requisitions, and summaries of daily food costs are necessary forms for recording needed information. The daily food cost can be controlled through the use of figures on the amount of food sent directly to the kitchen upon delivery and the amount issued to the kitchen from the storeroom. While the results may be estimated rather than actual food cost, it is close enough to be of value. A monthly inventory check will reveal any major differences. These can be checked and controls tightened up to produce an even more accurate storeroom record.

Questions

1.   What is wrong with determining food cost figures once a month by using the figures for inventory and for purchases?

2.   State the two essentials for good storage control.

3.   What are the duties of the person responsible for the storage?

4.   Name two forms needed for control and recording of information on the movement of foods into and out of storage; explain how each form is used.

5.   Does the omission of kitchen leftovers from the figures obtained substantially reduce the value of the daily food cost figure? Why or why not?

9

Using Financial Statements

Financial statements provide an excellent management tool. But many foodservice operators have difficulty in understanding and interpreting these statements, and they make only limited use of them in reaching decisions. This is unfortunate, because it is not difficult to acquire the understanding. An operator does not have to be an accountant to learn the financial statement vocabulary and how to use the statements to help make management decisions.

Basically, the difficulty in understanding and interpreting financial statements is that foodservice people in many cases do not recognize the significance of the relationships between the items found in the balance sheet and those in the profit and loss statement. Many operators seem to direct their attention for the most part to the profit and loss statement as they try to reduce their expenses and increase their profits.

What is needed is to learn the technical terms that accountants use, and then learn how to interpret the data that are found in financial statements. With that knowledge, it is much easier to recognize the relationship between the data that affect operating policies, and so affect the financial condition of the business now and in the future.

Financial statements provide data on how the firm is performing and on its financial position. When these statements are analyzed, management has an interpretation of what they mean. This helps management to determine the position of the business at the present time, and to plan what the needs of the business will be in the future. The budget is the blueprint for the plan and is stated in financial language.

Two Basic Financial Statements

There are two basic financial statements that are prepared in a business. One of these is the balance sheet. The other is the income statement, which is usually referred to as the profit and loss statement.

Additional or supplementary schedules, as they are called, are also prepared in many business establishments. These include the reserves for depreciation schedule, and the retained earnings schedule. Both of these have much significance in a foodservice business. A statement on the source and application of funds is also encountered in some businesses.

It is essential that the foodservice operator give the proper interpretation to the data available in the balance sheet and the profit and loss statement, because these data can help determine:

> the financial resources of the business
>
> the ability to meet the future financial obligations incurred by the business
>
> the proper proportion of assets to capital
>
> how profitable the foodservice establishment is
>
> the past operating results on which to project what results can be expected in the future

The key to successful financial management is in making such an analysis and then using the financial and operating ratios that can be developed in guiding the management decisions which are made. The result is successful financial management of the business, with the needed profits.

Objectives of Financial Management

There are three objectives in the financial management of a foodservice establishment:

> to preserve and maintain the assets of the business as long as it is in existence
>
> to determine what should be an adequate return on investment for the owners
>
> to develop financial controls for checking and maintaining the efficiency of the business operation

To reach these goals requires that management analyze the relationships among the various items found in the financial statements; and that management consider these relationships in relation to change that is taking place, the trends of the industry, and the standards of the industry.

There is much on the balance sheet and the profit and loss statement that provides information about the business and its state, but it is necessary to make comparisons that have even more meaning. So, combinations are made of statement items, and the resulting ratios make it possible to make a more meaningful analysis.

The Balance Sheet

The balance sheet (Figure 9-1) is the basic accounting record that is prepared for a foodservice business. It is where the effect of every accounting transaction that takes place in the establishment appears. The balance sheet shows the financial condition of the business at a given point in time. It lists the assets, liabilities, and net worth of the business. Here is a brief description of the accounts that are found on the balance sheet:

Assets   These are the items owned by the business. For a foodservice establishment, assets usually include cash, accounts receivable, inventories, food, supplies, land, building, and equipment. Usually, foodservice establishments do not have large amounts of money in inventories or in accounts receivable. Most of the money is invested in fixed assets.

Liabilities   These are amounts that the establishment owes to creditors. Liabilities usually include accounts payable, notes payable, accrued expenses, and taxes collected.

Net Worth   This represents the equity of the owners. These are the claims of the owners of the business. In a foodservice establishment, the usual net worth account is the proprietor's account.

It is well to remember in considering the balance sheet that total assets must always equal total liabilities plus net worth.

Many people consider the balance sheet as an annual statement, but there are no such restrictions. It may be prepared at any time. Monthly and quarterly balance sheets are in use in many foodservice establishments, providing data for short-range planning purposes. The annual statements can be used for long-range planning.

More frequent preparation of the balance sheet, or at least parts of it, is highly recommended. This financial statement is used to find weaknesses in the financial condition of the business. So it is important to use it more frequently and analyze it on a regular basis to detect problem areas as soon as possible.

Figure 9-1   Quality Restaurant Balance Sheet as of December 31

Assets
CURRENT ASSETS:

Cash on Hand . . . .$ 900		
On Deposit 7,100		
Total Cash	$ 8,000	
Accounts Receivable	500	
Inventories:		
Food 2,500		
Supplies 900		
Total Inventories	3,400	
Prepaid Expenses	1,000	
Total Current Assets		$12,900

FIXED ASSETS:

Land 26,900		
Building & Improvements 10,000		
Furniture & Equipment 40,000		
Operating Equipment (china,		
glass, and silver) 3,000		
Total Fixed Assets	79,900	
Less Depreciation to Date	15,980	
Total Fixed Assets		63,920
Total Assets:		$76,820

Liabilities and Net Worth
CURRENT LIABILITIES:

Accounts Payable . . . .$ 5,000		
Notes Payable 3,000		
Accrued Expenses 3,500		
Total Current Liabilities:		$11,500

OTHER LIABILITIES:

Equipment Contract		7,200
Mortgage Payable		15,000
Total Liabilities		33,700

NET WORTH:

Owner's Capital (Equity) 26,880		
Profit for Year 16,240		
Net Worth		43,120
Total Liabilities and Net Worth:		$76,820

Some people say it costs too much, but the cost is well worth it since, if the business is to be managed well, management must keep up to date with up-to-date data.

The Profit and Loss Statement

The profit and loss statement (Figure 9-2) summarizes the business transactions during an accounting period. This particular financial statement is also known as the earnings statement, the income statement, or the operating statement. It is the summary of the activities of the business in buying, selling, and operating.

The items that are included in the profit and loss statement can be classified for purposes of analysis as follows:

1. Net sales
2. Cost of food consumed or sold
3. Total payroll and related expenses
4. Operating profit
5. Profit (or loss) before taxes

There are various ways in which the profit and loss statement can be set up. The example in Figure 9-2 is typical of the format used in many foodservice operations. The best guide in determining how to select the best form for the business is to keep in mind that it should be in a form most helpful for the people who are going to use it. These uses included providing management the data needed to make good everyday decisions, serving as a guide in planning for the business, and assisting in projecting future operating results.

Figure 9-2   Quality Restaurant Profit and Loss Statement for Year Ended December 31

	Amount	Percentage of Sales
NET FOOD SALES	$105,138	100.0
Cost of Food Sold	40,688	38.7
Gross Profit on Sales	64,450	61.3
CONTROLLABLE EXPENSES		
Salary and Wages	25,900	24.6
Employees' Meals	1,250	1.2
Payroll Taxes and Related Expenses	2,600	2.5
Total Payroll and Related Expenses	29,750	28.3
Laundry, Linen, and Uniforms	2,370	2.3
China, Glass, and Silver.	1,640	1.6
Cleaning and Other Supplies.	900	.8
Utilities	2,410	2.3
Repairs and Maintenance	1,300	1.2
Legal and Accounting Fees	1,240	1.2
Advertising and Promotion	1,500	1.4
Administrative and General	2,500	2.4
Total Controllable Expenses	43,610	41.5
OPERATING PROFIT BEFORE FIXED EXPENSES	20,840	19.8
Fixed Expenses	4,600	4.4
PROFIT BEFORE TAXES	$ 16,240	15.4

The accounting period usually covered by a profit and loss statement is one month, three months, six months, or a year. The year should be the length of the accounting period, since usually it represents the start of another cycle as far as activities of the business are concerned. The year period of the business is known as the business's fiscal year.

The balance sheet and the profit and loss statement present data that provide a view of the business; but each presents to management a different view of the business. The statements complement each other, and are of vital importance to people who own and people who manage foodservice operations.

The balance sheet shows the assets, liabilities, and net worth or, as it is also known, the proprietorship of the business at a given point in time. It shows management how many dollars are available for use in continuing business operations. It provides this information in summary form.

The profit and loss statement shows the financial activity of the business over a stated period of time, which results in the present situation regarding assets, liabilities, and net worth.

The relationship of the two statements can be described in this way. The operator of the foodservice establishment operates the business so as to increase his proprietorship of that business. The balance sheet shows the amount of this proprietorship as of the date of that balance sheet. Comparing the figure on balance sheets prepared on successive dates indicates if and by how much his proprietorship is increasing or decreasing. *Why* there was an increase or a decrease cannot be determined.

The foodservice operator must be able to find out from time to time the amount and the causes of any gain or loss in income, so decisions on what course to follow can be made. The income or loss is the result of buying and selling—buying materials such as food and selling meals after the food has been processed, in the case of foodservice operations. Reports are needed on sales and on the cost of getting, processing, and selling the products. The difference between those costs is either income or loss. The profit and loss statement does this for the foodservice operator.

Comparison Is Necessary

The effective use of financial statements depends to a great extent on the ability of the statements to provide management information on which comparisons can be based. The data that appear on the forms are of value, but the real value comes in the measurement that can be made by comparison. If the financial statements do not show a comparison of data for the past and for the present period, the analysis of the business cannot be most effective.

The comparative statements more clearly show the changes that have occurred in the business' financial position, the overall profitability of the business, the relative importance of the different expense items, and trends in the operation of the foodservice establishment that are significant.

The comparison can be of a short-run kind or it can provide comparisons over a longer period of time. Generally, comparative statements can be classified into one or the other of two categories.

> those that compare the relationship among the items in a single set of statements for one accounting period
>
> those that compare changes that have occurred in the items on the statements for a number of accounting periods

It takes both kinds of statements and their analyses to obtain the best interpretation of how efficiently the business is operated from the point of view of management performance, how efficient the operations themselves have been, and what the changes have been in the financial position of the business.

If comparative analysis is to be possible, the balance sheet and the profit and loss statement should include the following items:

> total dollar amounts
>
> percentage of totals
>
> increases or decreases in dollar amounts
>
> increases or decreases in percentages

The Comparative Balance Sheet

One place where the comparison between financial statements can be shown is in the comparative balance sheet. The example (Figure 9-3) shows a comparison for the Quality Restaurant as of the last day of two successive years. It shows the increase and the decrease in dollar amounts and in percentages, and these indicate the comparison which shows changes in the financial condition of the business. Management can study these changes and assess operations in terms of how they affect the financial position of the company.

The Comparative Profit and Loss Statement

The same thing can be done with the profit and loss statement. A comparative profit and loss statement enables management to make a more detailed analysis of what has happened regarding the business' sales and costs of operation. It makes it possible for management to determine more precisely the changes that have occurred as a result of operations.

The comparative profit and loss statement (Figure 9-4) offers a good example of the comparisons that are found in such a statement. It compares both the dollar amounts for each item and the percent of net sales for each item for two years. It also shows the increase and decrease in dollar amounts and their percentages over the figures for the prior accounting period.

Figure 9-3   Quality Restaurant Comparative Balance Sheet
as of December 31, Year One and Year Two

Assets	December 31 Year One	December 31 Year Two	Amount of Increase or Decrease Year Two	Percent of Increase or Decrease Year Two
CURRENT ASSETS				
Cash on Hand . . . .$	900	$ 500	−$400	−44
Cash in Bank.	7,100	8,500	1400	20
Accounts Receivable	500	750	250	50
Inventories				
Food	2,500	2,900	400	16
Supplies	900	950	50	6
Prepaid Expenses	1,000	1,500	500	50
TOTAL CURRENT ASSETS	12,900	15,100	2,200	17
FIXED ASSETS				
Land	26,900	26,900		
Building and Improvements	10,000	11,000	1,000	1
Furniture and Equipment	40,000	43,500	3,500	9
China, Glass, and Silver.	3,000	2,500	500	−17
Total Fixed Assets	79,900	83,900	4,000	5
Less Depreciation.	15,980	16,630	650	4
Total Fixed Assets	63,920	67,270	3,350	5
TOTAL ASSETS	76,820	82,370	5,550	7

Liabilities and Net Worth

CURRENT LIABILITIES				
Accounts Payable	5,000	4,500	500	−10
Notes Payable	3,000	3,500	500	17
Accrued Expenses.	3,500	3,800	300	9
Total Current Liabilities . . .	11,500	11,800	300	3
OTHER LIABILITIES				
Equipment Contract	7,200	7,200		
Mortgage Payable	15,000	13,000	2,000	−13
Total Liabilities	33,700	30,300	3,400	−10
NET WORTH				
Owner's Capital	26,880	43,061	16,181	60
Profit for Year.	16,240	9,009	−7,231	−45
Net Worth	43,120	52,070	8,950	21
TOTAL LIABILITIES AND NET WORTH.	.$76,820	$82,370	$5,500	7

Figure 9-4 Quality Restaurant Comparative Profit and Loss Statement as of December 31, Year One and Year Two

	Year One Amount	Year One Percentage of Sales	Year Two Amount	Year Two Percentage of Sales	Increase or Decrease* Amount	Increase or Decrease* Percent
NET FOOD SALES	$105,138	100.0	$123,200	100.0	$18,062	17.2
Cost of Food Sold	40,688	38.7	45,584	37.0	4,896	12.0
Gross Profit on Sales	64,450	61.3	77,616	63.0		
CONTROLLABLE EXPENSES						
Salary and Wages	25,900	24.6	31,293	25.4	5,393	20.8
Employees' Meals	1,250	1.2	1,725	1.4	475	38.0
Payroll Taxes and Rel. Exp.	2,600	2.5	3,240	2.6	640	24.6
Total Payroll and Rel. Exp.	29,750	28.3	36,258	29.4	6,508	21.9
Laundry, Linen, and Uniforms	2,370	2.3	3,573	2.9	1,203	50.8
China, Glass, and Silver	1,640	1.6	3,600	2.9	1,960	119.5
Cleaning and Other Supplies	900	.8	1,200	.9	300	33.3
Utilities	2,410	2.3	3,326	2.7	916	38.0
Repairs and Maintenance	1,300	1.2	5,200	4.2	3,900	300.0
Legal and Accounting Fees	1,240	1.2	4,550	3.7	3,310	266.9
Advertising and Promotion	1,500	1.4	1,700	1.4	200	13.3
Administrative and General	2,500	2.4	3,100	2.5	600	24.0
Total Controllable Expenses	43,610	41.5	62,507	50.6	18,897	43.3
OPERATING PROFIT						
Before Fixed Expenses	20,840	19.8	15,109	12.2	−5,731	27.5
Fixed Expenses	4,600	4.4	5,200	4.2	600	13.0
PROFIT BEFORE TAXES	$ 16,240	15.4	$ 9,909	8.0	−$ 6,331	39.0

*Percent of increase or decrease is computed using Year One dollar figures as the base.

107

While that statement offers an example of a comparison of a year's totals, there is much value in a monthly comparative profit and loss statement. This statement (Figure 9-5) compares dollar amounts and percentages for the current month, the past month, and the total to date. The comparative profit and loss statement should be completed at least monthly.

When the comparative profit and loss statement is compared with a budget, it makes a valuable management analysis tool, since it is comparing performance with a standard. Certain performance standards, such as cost of food and the operating expenses, have been predetermined in terms of percentages by the budget.

Sometimes the percentages are included with the regular statements as in the examples. But they can also be presented in a separate statement which lists just the percentages and omits the dollar amounts. An example (Figure 9-6) shows this type of statement.

Comparative Percentage Analysis

The value of percentages is that they are not affected by changes in the dollar amounts and can show *relative* change. When percentages are computed and recorded over a period of years, they can be used by management to:

> Identify the kind of changing conditions that affect the business, and identify the trends relating to these changing conditions.
>
> Compare the current operations and trends with the average or typical performance by similar operations.

Studying the financial statements really reveals whether the financial position of the company or the operating results are satisfactory or unsatisfactory.

However, to make this effective analysis of the financial statements requires more than the simple analysis of the balance sheet and the profit and loss statement. Not enough of the reasons that certain conditions exist or trends persist can be obtained that way. To obtain that needed information, certain financial and operating ratios are used. Ratios are expressions of relationships between items on the financial statements and are clues to what is happening.

The question of what and how many ratios are of significance to foodservice operators is a difficult one to answer. For many other kinds of business, it would be an easy question, but there has been far less done in the financial management area in the foodservice industry; and the guide for selecting and using ratios is not far advanced.

Too many ratios can be a problem, since the number can complicate

Figure 9-5   Quality Restaurant Comparative Profit and Loss Statement for Period Ending March 31

	March Dollars	March Percent	February Dollars	February Percent	Total to Date Dollars	Total to Date Percent
SECTION I: SALES						
Food	$15,000.00	73.2	$17,000.00	74.1	$39,000.00	68.9
Bar	5,000.00	24.4	5,500.00	24.9	16,000.00	28.3
Other Income	500.00	2.4	450.00	2.0	1,600.00	2.8
Net Sales	20,500.00	100.0	22,950.00	100.0	56,600.00	100.0
SECTION II: COST OF SALES						
Food Cost	5,550.00	37.0	6,630.00	39.0	15,990.00	41.0
Bar Cost	1,750.00	35.0	1,750.00	32.0	4,000.00	25.0
Other Cost	400.00	80.0	400.00	89.0	1,376.00	86.0
Total Cost of Sales	7,700.00	37.6	8,780.00	38.3	21,366.00	37.7
SECTION III: GROSS PROFIT						
Gross Profit	12,800.00	62.4	14,170.00	61.7	35,234.00	62.3
SECTION IV: EXPENSES						
Controllable Salary and Wages*						
Food	4,200.00	28.0	5,100.00	30.0	12,090.00	31.0
Bar	1,100.00	22.0	1,200.00	22.0	3,680.00	23.0
Other	50.00	10.0	50.00	13.0	176.00	11.0
Total Wages	5,350.00	26.1	6,350.00	27.7	15,946.00	28.2
Other Expenses:						
Laundry	250.00	1.2	350.00	1.5	849.00	1.5
China, Glass, Silverware	100.00	.5	150.00	.7	340.00	.6
Repairs and Maintenance	50.00	.3	65.00	.3	226.00	.4
Supplies	250.00	1.2	300.00	1.3	679.00	1.2
Utilities	150.00	.7	165.00	.7	340.00	.6
Total Controllable Expenses	6,150.00	30.0	7,380.00	32.2	18,380.00	32.5
Fixed Expenses	3,600.00	17.6	3,600.00	15.7	10,800.00	19.1
Total All Expenses	9,750.00	47.6	10,980.00	47.8	29,180.00	51.6
SECTION V: NET PROFIT						
Net Profit Before Taxes	$ 3,050.00	14.8	$ 3,190.00	13.9	$ 6,054.00	10.7

*Includes Payroll Tax and Related Expenses.

Figure 9-6   Quality Restaurant
Comparative Percentage Analysis

	Month of May		Five Months Ending May 31	
	Year One	Year Two	Year One	Year Two
EXPENSE RATIO TO SALES:				
Cost of Sales	38.7	37.0	40.1	38.9
Salary and Wages	24.6	25.4	29.2	25.5
Employees' Meals	1.2	1.4	2.5	1.6
Payroll Taxes and Related Expenses	2.5	2.6	2.7	2.5
Total Operating Expenses	41.5	50.7	47.6	46.2
Profit Before Income Taxes	16.2	8.0	8.2	10.7

things to the point where the ratios lose their accuracy and their significance. On the other hand, if not enough ratios are used in analyzing the business progress, the wrong decisions can be made due to lack of sufficient information and the necessary number of ratios to acquire it.

Ratios for the Foodservice Operator

Three kinds of ratios are important to the operator of a foodservice establishment—financial ratios, operating ratios, and interstatement ratios.

Financial Ratios   These are relationships between items on the balance sheet; or relationships between one item on the balance sheet and one item on the profit and loss statement. They provide the data and comparison that show the health of the business.

Operating Ratios   These are relationships between and among items on the profit and loss statement. They are the means of examining expenses incurred in what goes on to produce sales. They are used by foodservice operators to appraise the relationship of their expenses and profit to sales, and to improve the efficiency of their operations.

Interstatement Ratios   These show the relationship between an item on the profit and loss statement and one in the balance sheet statement. This kind of comparison is only valid if the figures used for comparison are for the same period of time. If the profit and loss statement is computed on a quarterly basis, the figures from the balance sheet should be those computed for the same quarter.

There are many other ratios in addition to the ones in these groups that could be computed on a regular basis. How valuable they would be is open to question. Those ratios to be discussed further in this chapter are ones that are commonly used by many foodservice people. They are grouped according to their primary use as tests of liquidity, of solvency, and of business profitability, Figure 9-7. Data from the balance sheet and the profit and loss statement previously discussed (Figures 9-1 and 9-2) will be used to illustrate how each ratio is computed.

Financial Ratios

Three financial ratios concerned with testing the liquidity of the foodservice establishments are listed. These ratios show the ability of the establishment to meet its current obligations.

The Current Ratio   The current ratio expresses the relationship of the total current assets to the total current liabilities. It is one of

Figure 9-7   Financial Ratios

LIQUIDITY

1. Current Assets to Current Liabilities . . . . $\dfrac{\$\ 12,900\ \text{(C. A.)}}{\$\ 11,500\ \text{(C. L.)}}$ = 1.09 Times

2. Liquid Assets to Current Liabilities . . . . $\dfrac{\$\ \ \ 8,500\ \text{(L. A.)}}{\$\ 11,500\ \text{(C. L.)}}$ = .74 Percent

3. Turnover of Net Working Capital* . . . . $\dfrac{\$105,138\ \text{(Sales)}}{\$\ \ \ 1,400\ \text{(W. C.)}}$ = 75 Times

SOLVENCY

1. Current Liabilities to Tangible Net Worth** . . . . $\dfrac{\$\ 11,500\ \text{(C. L.)}}{\$\ 43,120\ \text{(T. N. W.)}}$ = 27 Percent

2. Total Liabilities to Tangible Net Worth . . . . . . $\dfrac{\$\ 33,700\ \text{(T. L.)}}{\$\ 43,120\ \text{(T. N. W.)}}$ = 76 Percent

3. Fixed Assets to Tangible Net Worth . . . . $\dfrac{\$\ 63,920\ \text{(F. A.)}}{\$\ 43,120\ \text{(T. N. W.)}}$ = 1.48 Times

PROFITABILITY

1. Net Profit (before taxes) to Tangible
   Net Worth . . . . $\dfrac{\$\ 16,240\ \text{(N. P. B. T.)}}{\$\ 43,120\ \text{(T. N. W.)}}$ = 37.7 Percent

2. Net Profit (before taxes) to Total Assets . . . . . $\dfrac{\$\ 16,240\ \text{(N. P. B. T.)}}{\$\ 76,820\ \text{(T. A.)}}$ = 21.4 Percent

3. Net Sales to Fixed Assets . . . . $\dfrac{\$105,138\ \text{(N. S.)}}{\$\ 63,920\ \text{(F. A.)}}$ = 1.64 Times

*Net working capital is obtained by subtracting current liabilities from current assets.
**Tangible net worth is the worth of a firm minus any intangible items such as good will, trademarks, etc. In a corporation, the tangible net worth includes all outstanding stock and surplus accounts. In a proprietorship or partnership, the tangible net worth consists of the capital account.

the most widely used indicators of the financial strength of the business. It shows the firm's ability to meet its obligations. It is used as a basis for determining how much margin of protection there is for short-term creditors.

This ratio provides information of much help to management. If the ratio is low, it may mean that the company is not able to pay its bills. If the ratio is high, it could mean that management has not done well, since there would be an excessive amount of cash, or the investment in accounts receivable or inventory might be too high.

The current ratio is determined by dividing the current assets by the current liabilities. In the example used in this chapter, the Quality Restaurant, the current ratio is 1.09 to 1.00, or 1.09 times the current liabilities.

It had generally been considered that a 2 to 1 ratio was acceptable for all kinds of businesses; and many businessmen go on that assumption. But it is more realistic to consider that there is no ideal ratio that applies across the board. What is a good ratio depends a great deal on the kind of business and on make-up of the current assets.

For many foodservices, operations are conducted on a current ratio considerably less than 2 to 1. There are several reasons for this. In the food-service business, the amount of credit extended to customers is very low compared with many other businesses, and so large sums of money are not tied up in accounts receivable. Also, the inventories carried are at minimum levels. Furthermore, there is a steady flow of cash as a result of the rapid turnover of inventories.

There are foodservice operations where the current ratio is above the 2 to 1 ratio. An analysis of these businesses would likely show that the foodservice operator is not keeping enough capital invested profitably in the business, and needs to give attention to this deficiency.

An example will clarify these points. If the balance sheet of a foodservice operation shows that current assets are $40,000 and current liabilities are $10,000, then the current ratio for that establishment would be 4 to 1. Whether this is good or not depends on how it was attained. If this current ratio, which seems to be favorable, were achieved through neglecting to keep the property and the equipment maintained properly, then it could be misleading.

Assume that it would cost $35,000 to renovate the property and bring it up to standard, then the ratio would become .5 to 1. If the renovating job were done, there would be much improvement of the property and the equipment, but there would be a real problem caused by the reduction in the amount of working capital. This lack would limit the firm's ability to pay its bills on time, and its credit rating would go down.

No Ratio Is Ideal   So, neither extreme is desirable. Since there is no ideal ratio, the foodservice operator has to fall back on averages. He can compare his current ratio with his ratios from previous periods. He can also compare his current ratio with average ratios for the foodservice industry.

Averages are never entirely dependable, since an average includes a lot of levels above and below the average figure. But if the current figure deviates from the average, or deviates from the figures for previous accounting periods, it is a signal to look more closely. Management needs to do additional analysis of the items that make up the ratio to determine what has produced the change.

Acid Test or Quick Ratio   While the current ratio is valuable in analysis, it has a serious deficiency. It gives the same liquidity to all the items that make up the numerator of the ratio formula. It disregards the fact that accounts receivable are closer to being converted into cash than is inventory.

Some foodservice operators make use of the quick ratio or, as it is also known, the acid-test ratio, to determine the relationship between current liabilities and the liquid assets that are immediately available for use in meeting current obligations of the business. This ratio measures the immediate debt-paying ability of the firm.

The liquid assets include cash, accounts receivable, and marketable securities. These are added and divided by the total current liabilities to provide the quick ratio. It is a measure of the extent to which these cash and near-cash items cover the current liabilities. These items are sometimes referred to as quick asset items.

The quick asset ratio should be about 1 to 1. Such a ratio indicates the firm can pay off all its current liabilities without making any more sales. A small ratio could mean that the firm does not have enough liquidity to meet its immediate obligations. Most foodservice operators should be concerned about a ratio below 1 to 1. It is a sign of impending trouble, since it indicates financial stress, and the fact that the firm could not pay all of its bills if it had to do so.

Net Working Capital Ratio   The difference between current assets and current liabilities represents the equity that the owner has in the current assets that can be readily converted into operating funds for carrying on the regular activities of the business. This difference is called net working capital.

To compute the net working capital ratio, divide net sales by net working capital as of the close of any given accounting period. For the firm used as an example, the Quality Restaurant, net working capital turned over 75 times during the year. This can be stated as the fact that the working capital was used 75 times during the year to produce the total of sales, which was $105,138.

An ever-increasing ratio of sales to working capital might seem to be good. But too rapid a turnover of working capital could mean that the sales are being produced by a limited amount of working capital. If sales were to drop unexpectedly, this close balance between funds that are coming in and those going out could mean serious trouble for the business.

Again, the other extreme could also be bad. If there is a slow turnover in working capital, it could mean that too much capital has been invested in the business, or that enough sales are not being generated by the amount of capital invested. This means there is idle capital that is not producing anything, and there is a loss of interest that might be realized if that capital were put to more productive uses. Also, when excess working capital is available, sometimes there is too much investment in facilities and equipment that are really unnecessary and the efficiency of operation is lowered.

The number of turnovers of net working capital that is best for a particular firm should be that number which keeps the capital busy but has leeway in case of sudden drops in sales so that the balance is not upset, and does not allow idle nonproductive capital of any appreciable amount. The exact number depends greatly on the particular operation and the conditions under which it is conducted, as well as the firm itself that owns and operates the business.

Tests of Solvency

Tests of solvency are used to analyze the firm's ability to meet its long-term financial obligations; and they are concerned with net worth ratios. These ratios offer a means of comparison of the owner equity with creditor interests, which is of importance since a foodservice establishment's assets are acquired through money provided by the owner and by creditors. These ratios also are valuable in making an analysis of ownership investments in fixed assets.

Current Liabilities to Tangible Net Worth This ratio compares the temporary short-term claims of creditors with the owner's investment. It is a measure of safety for those who have invested in the business, as it relates their investment to that of the owners.

The current liabilities to tangible net worth ratio is computed by dividing current liabilities by tangible net worth. The current liabilities for the Quality Restaurant are 27 percent of the tangible net worth. This indicates the amount of security that the creditors' claims against the firm have.

Total Liabilities to Tangible Net Worth It is not enough to relate current liabilities to tangible net worth. There may be a satisfactory ratio of current liabilities to tangible net worth, but there are so many long term debts that the firm's liability situation is very great. So, it is necessary to consider total liabilities.

The total liabilities ratio is obtained by dividing total liabilities by total net worth. This ratio for the Quality Restaurant is 76 percent. The size of that figure shows that creditors have a larger stake in the business than does the owner, and is an indication to the creditors that they should seek a part in the management of the operation in order to protect their claims against the business.

Fixed Assets to Tangible Net Worth   Another test of solvency is the relationship between fixed assets and tangible net worth. This ratio is obtained by dividing the depreciated fixed assets by the tangible net worth. The ratio shows the relationship between investment in plant and equipment and the owner's capital. In other words, it shows how liquid is the net worth.

The higher the ratio of fixed assets to tangible net worth is, the less the owner's capital is available for use in meeting debts of the business and for use as working capital. In the case of the restaurant used as an example, fixed assets are 1.48 times the tangible net worth.

Tests of Profitability

Foodservice operators are generally greatly interested in the relationship of dollar profits to dollar sales. However, the real test of profitability is the rate of return on investment, not the relationship of profit to sales. Two major groups of ratios that can be used to determine the profitability of a foodservice establishment are:

ratios that measure profitability as a return on investment

ratios that measure profitability in relation to sales

Net Profit Before Taxes to Tangible Net Worth   This ratio offers a means of measuring the return to the owner of the business. It is computed by dividing the net profit before taxes by the tangible net worth. The ratio can be used to appraise the earning power of the owner's investment; and it is of value to people who are interested in investing money.

A foodservice operator has invested his money in the business to make profits and he wants to know how well he is doing. This ratio answers that question.

What is a good return is something that is a judgment, and must be considered along with the other uses to which the money could be put. For example, it could be deposited in a bank and earn interest and be insured by the government. That is an alternate use that the owner could find for his money.

Net Profit Before Taxes to Total Assets   The return as a percent of total assets is another measure of the rate of return. This ratio is computed by dividing the net profit before taxes by the total assets. The total assets acquired by the firm represent the capital provided by the owner, by investors, and by creditors.

This ratio measures how well management is handling the financial aspects of the business, and the ability of management to generate a fair return on the total assets that are used.

Net Sales to Fixed Assets   The net sales to fixed assets ratio is not strictly a profitability ratio, but it is a significant one to use in making management decisions. This ratio determines the dollar amount of sales that is generated for each dollar of assets after the allowance for depreciation has been taken out. In the example of the Quality Restaurant, the ratio of net sales to fixed assets is 1.64 times. This means that for every dollar of assets, $1.64 is produced in sales.

Foodservice operators can use this ratio to determine the feasibility of buying additional equipment, based on the capacity of that equipment to generate additional sales. They can also use it in forecasting and budgeting sales.

Operating Ratios   There is another group of ratios that is used for testing the profitability of a business. These ratios measure profitability in its relationship to sales; they are generally referred to as operating ratios.

In these ratios, each item on the income statement is identified as a percentage of net sales. Three of these ratios are:

$$(1) \qquad \frac{\text{Net Profit Before Taxes}}{\text{Net Sales}} \qquad \frac{\$\ 16{,}240}{\$105{,}138} = 15.4\%$$

$$(2) \qquad \frac{\text{Gross Profit}}{\text{Net Sales}} \qquad \frac{\$\ 64{,}450}{\$105{,}138} = 61.3\%$$

$$(3) \qquad \frac{\text{Operating Profit}}{\text{Net Sales}} \qquad \frac{\$\ 20{,}840}{\$105{,}138} = 19.8\%$$

There are two principal uses for ratios of this type. If they are computed over a period of years, they are valuable for identifying changing conditions and trends in the performance of the business. They also are a tool for comparing the current operations of the firm and the trends that are evident with the operations and trends of the industry.

Not a Substitute for Good Management

Financial and operating ratios and their use should not be considered a substitute for good management. These ratios do not make precise measurements. But they are guides for the operator in analyzing his business. They provide him the means to compare his results of today with results in past accounting periods, and also to compare his results with the averages for the foodservice industry. These comparisons can be of much value in making management decisions. Ratios are general in nature. Like other statistical data, they are only a convenient way of directing attention to certain specific relationships. Further analysis is usually needed. Remember that ratios are computed from accounting records, and that these records are only interim reports, not precise and accurate statements. Also, accounting practices differ among foodservice establishments; and personal judgment is involved in the estimate for many of the items in the statements.

Another limitation is that all items on the financial statements are based on recorded historical information—what has happened in the past. In spite of these limitations, however, the use of financial statements and ratios provides management with data that make possible an intelligent appraisal of the financial activity of the business, and is very valuable in making decisions.

They show the overall profitability, the condition of the business, and significant trends in the operation of the business, and they do it in an adequate manner. When the operator compares his statements and ratios with standard ratios for similar kinds of business operations, he can identify weak areas that will need further investigation, changes, and improvements.

Standards of Comparison

There are numerous standards available against which the foodservice operator can measure his firm's performance. These include:

> ratios and percentages made available by foodservice trade associations
>
> ratios and percentages from accounting firms which provide services to the foodservice industry
>
> ratios and percentages that the operator has developed himself from previous results
>
> ratios and percentages that have been developed for a similar foodservice establishment

These provide the standard with which the ratio from a single statement can be compared. That single standard in itself is not of much significance unless it can be compared with one or more other standards.

However, when comparing financial and operating ratios with the ratios developed by accounting firms and trade organizations, remember that the comparison is being made against averages. Averages, of course, can include the least efficient as well as the most efficient foodservice establishments. To be average is one accomplishment and provides some leeway against failure; but probably most operators want to achieve more than the average.

Selecting ratios for managerial and financial analysis is not easy because there is no one ratio that an operator can use to get a complete financial analysis. It is necessary to select a combination that will do the job for the particular foodservice operation. Some recommendations for making this selection include:

> Determine the particular areas of managerial and financial significance that are going to be appraised.
>
> Select the appropriate ratios for those areas.

Compute these ratios for the present period and also for several past accounting periods.

Use industry or historical standards for making a comparison.

Investigate variations from the standards that are discovered.

Summary

The analysis of financial statements is one of numerous tool that management of a foodservice establishment can use to increase its efficiency in formulating administrative and operating policies. The various basic statements, along with supplementary statements and schedules, provide the information that management needs in order to develop opinions and make decisions

The ratio and percentage analyses are used in judging the financial and operating condition of the business as it is described in the financial statements It is the relationship of the various items listed in the statements that is o significance, and ratios are devised to express those relationships most effec tively. The amount of cash on hand or the amount of money in the bank ar important factors to management. But, they have much more significance whet they are compared with current liabilities, expenses, and total assets.

It is well worth the time and effort of foodservice people to gain an under standing of how to use financial statements most effectively and then to mak their use a standard practice.

Questions

1. What are the two basic financial statements prepared in business?
2. What are the three objectives of financial management?
3. Which accounts are found in the balance sheet?
4. By what other names is the profit and loss statement known?
5. Data appearing in the financial statements are of value, but the rea value for management is in what use of the data?
6. What kind of change is shown by percentages?
7. Name three kinds of ratios that are of importance to the operator of foodservice establishment.
8. What is the acid-test ratio and how is it used?
9. What are the two major groups of ratios used in determining how foodservice establishment is doing?
10. Give three examples of operating ratios. What do they measure?

10

Operating Budgets

The operator of a foodservice business, like all businesspeople, uses material things and people in certain combinations to provide products and/or services that people need, want, and buy. However, supplies of material things and labor are limited, and he must operate his business in a profitable manner if it is to survive. This means that effective use of the available resources is of utmost importance. It means, also, that the operator must establish goals for the business, develop plans that will enable the business to reach those goals, and involve personnel in the purpose and conduct of the business in order to gain their full support in reaching the goals.

The operator must have a way to compare what happens in the conduct of the business with the goals that have been established, in order to know how the business is doing, and to make changes if necessary to keep the business along the desired course.

A means of control is necessary, so that as time goes by the business can be kept on the selected course. When deviations occur, the operator can quickly return to the desired course before the deviations can cause serious problems. The control system must have built-in procedures for obtaining needed information in the forms necessary and at the times needed, so that the control system can work effectively to keep the business on a profitable basis.

Budgets Are Useful Tools

Budgetary accounting provides a plan for financial operation of the business over a period of time. Through the various accounts and summaries that may be made from them, comparisons of the operation may be made with the predetermined plan. Budgetary accounting provides an effective combination of planning and control to guide the future operations of the business.

Many kinds of budgets have a place in profitable business operation. Sales budgets, cash budgets, capital budgets, capital addition budgets, to list few, all serve useful purposes. Which and how many budgets to use depend great deal on the particular operation and whether the addition of one or more would make the profitable operation of the firm more certain.

However, of basic importance to all foodservice operations is the operating budget. It provides an effective device for planning, coordinating, controlling and guiding the course the business will follow. Since the operating budget performs such a fundamental function, what it is and how it can be used should be understood so that it can be developed and utilized in keeping the business profitable. An operating budget is a tool that can be used for both planning and control purposes—planning for the future and control in the present.

More specifically an operating budget is a projection of the goals of the operator for future sales and for costs. It is a plan, stated in dollars and cents for the foodservice operation for a specific future period. This period can be any future period but, for most business operations, the operating budget prepared for a year in advance.

While the operating budget is a plan, it should not be an absolutely fixed one that is not subject to change. Since no foodservice operation stands still and since it is not possible to predict with 100 percent accuracy what the future of the operation will be, the operating budget should be changed as conditions change. It should not be followed exactly, ignoring any changes in conditions under which the business operates.

The operating budget is, in effect, the operator's plan to control business expenses and the profits to be realized from the business, in relation to sales. In that sense, it provides a way to maintain and control profits. It can be the key to increasing the profits from the operation.

Significance of Operating Budgets

As indicated previously, budgeting has as its objectives

providing to management an organized way in which to do planning

a procedure for coordinating the activities of the business so they progress according to the plan

offering a basis on which control measures can be utilized

The three major functions of any manager or team of management people is to plan, to control, and to direct. But too often, management's time and effort are mostly directed to controlling and directing at the expense of planning, in spite of the fact that control cannot be effective unless there is a plan. If control is to be exerted with good results, there must be a way in which the actual performance of the firm can be measured against the performance that was planned and expected.

Setting up operational budgets makes it possible to develop a picture of the desired state or condition of the operation. Then, taking the data obtained in the accounting procedures, the condition that was planned and is desired can be compared with the actual state of affairs or condition as it exists at any time. Then, management knows when and where to make changes in the operating procedures. These relationships are shown in Figure 10-1.

It is obvious that planning is the number one step. It must come before control. It is also obvious that there is need for a budget in developing the planning that is needed. So, the budget provides the needed organized procedure for planning.

Control and People

The budget is not a control in itself, but does provide a way to exert control. It provides a way of controlling what happens through the people who work in the operation. So, if the budget is to have a controlling influence, it has to be known and must be followed by the operating personnel all the way down the line. In this sense it is a measuring device such as a ruler or a yardstick, and not a device for prodding people.

The fact that people are so highly involved produces a problem. All control devices are resisted by people to some extent, and the budget is a control device. So, the budget must be realistic as far as its relationship to people is concerned. If the budget is too restrictive and it is impossible for people to meet its goals, then it will be a negative factor in the operation of the business rather than contributing to efficiency and profitable operation. If, on the other hand, it is too loose, it will not do the control job it can, and efficiency and profit will suffer. The budget must be constructed so that it is fair and so that people are capable of attaining the goals that the budget reflects.

The Coordinating Function

If the budget is constructed in the right way, all employees in all parts of the operation will be able to see where they and what they do fit into the overall picture for the establishment. Such a budget shows a picture of the total foodservice operation, not just the part that may be of special concern to one department.

Thus, the operating budget can be a valuable factor in gaining coordination. It can help to solve the problem where there is little or no integration of

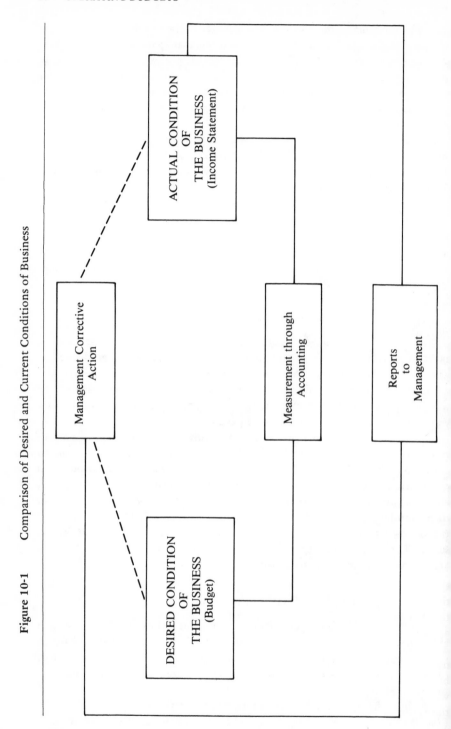

Figure 10-1   Comparison of Desired and Current Conditions of Business

he different departments. This is usually the result of individual employees ot being able to see the total picture, and so continuing from day to day to do heir work with little knowledge or concern for what is happening in other parts of the operation.

With well-prepared operating budgets available to them, workers can see where they are and what they do to fit into the total picture. Then it is easier for managers and supervisors to achieve the coordination that is needed for efficient operations.

So, the operating budget can:

> Help to plan the foodservice operation on the all-important dollars and cents basis.
>
> Provide a basis for control of the operation.
>
> Provide a way of coordinating and integrating the various operations and departments to produce an effective total operation.

Some foodservice people appreciate the importance of operational budgeting, but are reluctant to get involved because of questions for which they do not seem to have good answers. They seem to be concerned about such things as who should make up the budget, when it should be done, and how one actually constructs a budget.

When and Who of Budget-Making

First is the matter of when the budget should be made. Generally, the operating budget should cover a year's duration—the fiscal year for the establishment. So, the operating budget should be made up in advance of the fiscal year.

How far in advance is a logical second question. The answer depends on the kind of foodservice establishment, how much advance planning is needed, and when the operating figures that are to be used in constructing the budget become available.

Remember that the budget is not a one-shot deal that is made once during the year and that is it. It is not a static document, but a dynamic one. So, while the original operating budget may be constructed at a time before the start of the fiscal year, the budget is being worked on continuously during the year and updated as conditions change.

The question of who should make the budget is a major one, because if a number of people are involved, the results will be much more valuable. If the budget is to be used as a control device, it is going to be used by the people who are responsible for maintaining the sales and cost figures that are stated in the budget.

So, operating budgets are usually much more effective when the supervisors who have the responsibility of maintaining the cost and sales figures have a part in constructing the budgets. They certainly should have a part in making that part of the budget that concerns their part of the operation. They often may have valuable input relating to other parts of the operation as well.

To get this participation, the budget-making process must start at the lowest level of supervision at which there is assignment of responsibility for certain operating figures. This may be several steps down the line from top management in a large foodservice firm. Management may have all of the direct responsibility for supervision in a small firm.

Assuming that the foodservice establishment has several levels of management, the budget will start at the lowest level and move up through the line of operations, being reviewed at each step of the way. However, changes that are made at the higher levels should be made only after they have been discussed with the supervisors at lower levels. If this principle is not followed, cooperation from those supervisors may be less than it should be when the final budgetary plan is introduced.

Top management levels have responsibility for the final budget. In some operations this means approval by one person who holds the top position. In others, it could be a group of several people who give final approval.

Types of Operating Budgets

There are a number of types of operational budgets, and management must decide on the type of budget that fits the particular operation best, before anything can be done in constructing the budget that will be used. Budgets are classified into three general types:

Fixed

Flexible

Variable

The fixed budget is one that is geared to a single level of sales, while a flexible budget is geared to two or more levels. The variable budget is constructed in such a way that cost figures are available for any level of sales that the operation might reach.

The simplest operating budget is the fixed budget, in which management budgets at only one level of sales. It is sufficient in foodservice operations where costs and sales vary little from one year to another. Some kinds of industrial feeding operations, smaller restaurants, and school foodservice programs are examples of this kind of operation.

Even though the fixed budget is the simplest form of budgeting, what has to be done to construct a fixed budget is very similar to what has to be done to construct more complex types of budgets.

In constructing a budget that will be of value, the sales forecast is probably the most important item to be considered. This is so because the major costs in a foodservice operation are related directly to sales volume. So, step one in developing the budget is to make a forecast of the sales that are expected during the period of time covered by the budget.

The operator can use two kinds of information in making the forecast of sales. One type is based on facts collected about past experience in the business. Sales records, which show sales in terms of dollars and also in terms of the number of persons served over various periods of time, provide this kind of information. A daily sales analysis record provides a way of having this information readily available. It should show the total number of covers (place settings) and the dollar value of those covers, as well as any additional information relating to why volume of business might have been higher, lower, or at the normal level over any given period.

The other kind of information needed to make a forecast of sales is based on assumptions. It is information on what the owner thinks, assumes, or feels is going to occur in the future. Numerous things influence these assumptions, but they should be factors that enable the owner to make an accurate estimate of future business conditions. Indicators of the economy, both national and local, are valuable. So is information on the general trends of the business for which the forecast of sales is being made. Is the sales trend upward, or is it downward? How was it a year ago? Two years ago?

By combining facts on the past sales history of the business with information on which assumptions can be based, the operator can make a reasonably accurate estimate of the sales potential of the business over some future period. Assuming the forecast is made for a year ahead, it will be necessary to break the forecast down into parts of the year. These shorter periods of time may be quarters or months. Any variations from month to month, including seasonal variations, must be considered when allocating the forecasted sales to the various months of the year.

Constructing a Fixed Budget

An example of a restaurant (which will be called the Superior Restaurant) will be used to show how a sales forecast can be developed. Over three fiscal years, this restaurant has produced the following volumes of sales:

	Year One	Year Two	Year Three
Food	$45,000	$48,000	$51,000
Beverage	15,000	16,000	17,000
Total	$60,000	$64,000	$68,000

In the Superior Restaurant, the number of food covers served has shown little variation, staying at about 25,000 covers per year over the three-year period. The average check, in dollar terms, has gone up from $2.40 in Year One to $2.72 in Year Three.

Totals of Sales

A check of the books of the restaurant provides information on the totals of sales for the individual months of Year Three. The data show that food sales consistently are at approximately a 3 to 1 ratio in relation to beverage sales. (See table 10-1.)

Things That May Affect the Business

The sales information is factual and provides a good picture of what has happened in the three-year period. But it is also necessary to consider any things that may have an influence on the business and could alter the sales totals picture in the year ahead. Has anything especially influenced the business during those three years for which the sales data have been analyzed? Are there changes in prices of items on the menu that might result in additional increases in the average check in the year ahead? Have there been generally normal business conditions over the three-year period; or are there some significant factors that have affected the monthly income as it is broken down?

The operator answers these questions to the best of his ability and concludes that he will continue to serve 25,000 covers in the year ahead, and that his 3 to 1 ratio of food sales to beverage sales will continue. He does, however, foresee about a 5 percent increase in the average check, which would bring it up to $2.87 in Year Four.

Table 10-1   Monthly Sales for Year Three

Month	Food Sales	Percent of Total Food	Beverage Sales
January	$ 2,550	5	$ 850
February	4,590	9	1,530
March	5,100	10	1,700
April	5,610	11	1,870
May	5,100	10	1,700
June	4,080	8	1,360
July	2,550	5	850
August	2,550	5	850
September	4,080	8	1,360
October	4,590	9	1,530
November	5,610	11	1,870
December	4,590	9	1,530
Total	$51,000	100	$17,000

Making Some Assumptions

It is now time to introduce some assumptions to be added to the factual data to predict what is likely to happen. This is a matter of stating what the operator thinks will happen during the budget period that, in this case, is the next year.

What factors indicate that there might be an increase in the number of covers that will be served in Year Four? To answer that question takes a consideration of the national economy, the local economic conditions, and any increase or decrease in the competition. All factors such as these need to be evaluated.

Let us assume that, even though the overall economic situation shows some problems, a change in the amount of competition, some changes in the eating-out habits of the people in the community, and some other local changes offer enough evidence to support the expectation of a 10 percent increase in the number of covers for the next year. This would mean increasing the 25,000 covers of the past year to 27,500 at the predicted check average of $2.87.

With this information at hand, it is predicted that total sales for Year Four, the one for which the budget is being constructed, will amount to $78,925. This figure is obtained by multiplying the expected 27,500 covers by the expected average check of $2.87. Keeping the ratio of food sales to beverage sales at 3 to 1, the estimate of sales becomes:

Food	$59,195	75%
Beverage	19,730	25%
Total	$78,925	100%

That is the prediction for the total year.

Monthly Sales Forecast

It is now possible to forecast the sales by months for the year ahead, on the basis of the *total* sales figures.

With no factors to indicate otherwise, it seems that the seasonal pattern of the firm's business in Year Four will be the same as it has been in the previous year. So, using the monthly percentages of total sales already determined (Table 10-1), a forecast of gross dollar figures by months can be made. This provides a forecast for Year Four that makes a good basis on which to determine the likely cost figures for the period ahead.

The Budgeting of Expenses

Now that the sales forecast has been made, the next step in the preparation of the operational budget for the Superior Restaurant is to estimate the expenses that would be incurred in making those sales. This means

Table 10-2   Monthly Sales for Year Four

Month	Food Sales	Percent	Beverage Sales
January	$ 2,960	5	$ 986
February	5,327	9	1,775
March	5,920	10	1,975
April	6,510	11	2,170
May	5,920	10	1,975
June	4,736	8	1,578
July	2,960	5	986
August	2,960	5	986
September	4,736	8	1,578
October	5,328	9	1,775
November	6,510	11	2,170
December	5,328	9	1,775
Total	$59,195	100	$19,730

bringing together estimates of what costs will be from the department heads for their parts of the operation in a big foodservice establishment. In the case of a relatively small operation such as the Superior Restaurant, the development of these cost estimates would be the responsibility of the manager who, in some cases, may also be the owner.

The restaurant has been in operation for a number of years, and its management should have available the figures on the cost of sales for both food and beverages, and should know what these ought to be in the year ahead. But it is not a difficult task to calculate what the cost of sales should be for any volume of business if the menu prices, the cost of food, the cost of beverages, and the sales mix or ratio of items sold are known.

For some reason, many foodservice people think there is some magical ratio of the cost of food and beverages to sales to which they have to refer for any operation. This is a fallacy, and it is easy to see why. The ratio of the cost of food and beverages to sales depends on menu prices, the prices paid for food that is purchased, and the sales mix. So, it is obvious that the ratio of food and beverage costs to sales will be different for each individual operation. Also involved in this variation is the efficiency with which the particular establishment operates.

In the case of the Superior Restaurant example, the ratio of cost of food to food sales has been running consistently at 38 percent, and the similar ratio for beverages has been 30 percent. Since no change is anticipated in the relationship of costs to prices or in the sales mix in the year ahead, these figures will be used for Year Four budgeting. These ratios can then be applied to the figures for estimated sales; and the part of the budget concerned with cost of sales will be constructed as follows:

SALES

Food sales	$59,195	75%
Beverage sales	19,730	25%
Total sales	$78,925	100%

COST OF SALES

Food	$22,495	38%
Beverage	5,920	30%
Total Cost of Sales	$28,415	36%

The Operating Expenses

Next is a consideration of the expenses of operation. The following accounts are kept in the books of the restaurant. Each needs to be considered in determining the operating budget for the coming year.

1.	Salaries and Wages	7.	Heat, Light, and Power
2.	Employee Meals	8.	Operating Expenses
3.	Payroll Taxes	9.	Advertising
4.	Laundry and Linen	10.	Insurance
5.	China, Glass, Silver, and Utensils	11.	Licenses
		12.	Telephone
6.	Ice and Fuel	13.	Misc. Operating Expenses

Salaries and Wages   The sales forecast predicts that the Superior Restaurant will serve 27,500 covers in the year ahead. Based on past experience, it is not hard to determine the amount of labor needed to serve that many people and maintain the level of service of the establishment. So, taking the wage scale and this information, the figure for wages and salaries can be projected.

Employee Meals   What is done about the cost of employee meals varies among foodservice operations. Some do not try to calculate the actual costs of meals provided to employees. Instead, they make periodic cost checks and set up an average ratio which they then use in calculating costs. In other cases, the actual costs are determined on the basis of the number of employees and what it actually costs to feed them.

Payroll Taxes   Payroll taxes can be calculated on a percentage-to-payroll basis, with provision made for the following:

Social Security payments

State unemployment insurance

> Federal unemployment insurance
>
> Workman's Compensation
>
> Accident and health insurance
>
> Other benefits

When the ratio of the cost of these benefits to the cost of payroll is determined, this ratio can be used for projecting this portion of the labor cost in budgeting for the future.

Other Operating Costs   The historical records of the business provide information for estimating the other operating expenses. These expenses normally show little variation with small increases or decreases in the volume of sales. Past experience usually offers a good indication of how much change can be expected in these expenses at different levels of sales. However, with continuous inflation, the other operating costs assume a more important place in the total cost picture. They move up drastically and can become a major factor. It should be kept in mind that these expenses are controllable, and in high inflationary periods such control assumes much greater importance.

Occupancy Costs   Such items as rent, depreciation, some kinds of insurance, and property taxes are considered occupancy costs. These are not going to vary with different volumes of sales. Since these costs are fixed, they can be forecast almost exactly, if any expected changes that will cause increases in any of the items are taken into consideration.

The Annual Fixed Budget

The annual fixed budget then can be completed. It looks like the example (Figure 10-2). This is a typical lineup of a fixed budget for a small restaurant operation such as the Superior Restaurant. The particular figures have been arbitrarily selected. Figures would vary for each foodservice operation.

For a larger establishment, there would be much more detail than in this example. The food and beverage costs would probably be broken down into categories such as meats, poultry, fish, fresh and frozen fruits and vegetables, groceries, dairy products, etc. Operating expenses would probably also be broken down by departments, especially if there is a division of the responsibility for supervision along departmental lines.

The Monthly Fixed Budget

Again, the annual budget needs to be broken down by months. The data on sales projected by months are available. So, those costs that go up and down in close relationship with sales—the costs that are called variable

Figure 10-2   The Superior Restaurant
Annual Budget

		(Percent)
SALES		
Food	$59,195	75
Beverage	19,730	25
	$78,925	100
COST OF SALES		
Food	22,495	38
Beverage	5,920	30
	$28,415	36
TOTAL GROSS PROFIT	50,510	64
OPERATING EXPENSES		
Salaries & Wages	22,100	28
Employees' Meals	1,580	2
Payroll Taxes	1,180	1.5
Laundry & Linen	1,180	1.5
China, Glass, Silver, and Utensils	1,975	2.5
Ice & Fuel	395	0.5
Heat, Light, & Power	1,975	2.5
Supplies	3,160	4
Advertising	1,580	2
Insurance	790	1
Licenses	395	0.5
Telephone	115	0.2
Misc. Operating Expense	1,580	2
TOTAL OPERATING EXPENSE	$38,045	48.2
PROFIT BEFORE OCCUPANCY COSTS	12,465	15.8
Occupancy Costs	3,940	5
PROFIT BEFORE INCOME TAXES	$ 8,525	10.8

costs—can be estimated by applying the yearly budgeted percentages. Usually, fixed costs are apportioned by dividing the figure for yearly gross costs by the number of accounting periods.

An example will clarify this procedure. The sales forecast for January projects food sales amounting to $2,960 and beverage sales amounting to $986. Consider heat, light, and power; insurance; and occupancy costs as being fixed costs, and all others as variable costs. Then the budget for the month of January would be as in the example for the Superior Restaurant (Figure 10-3).

In this example, note that lower-than-average January sales resulted in a decrease in the profit percentage, because of the effect of fixed costs that cannot be lowered in a period of lower sales.

The annual budget could be broken down into monthly budgets at the time it is constructed; but the recommendation is to do the monthly budgets for no more than three months at a time. It is important to keep the budget dynamic, subject to change, and as current as possible. Projecting budgets for more than two or three months at a time would make the annual budget less reliable, since what will be happening at the end of a year is a lot more uncertain than what will be happening a couple of months from the present time.

Figure 10-3   The Superior Restaurant
Budget—Month of January

SALES			(Percent)
	Food	$2,960	75
	Beverage	986	25
TOTAL SALES		$3,946	100
COST OF SALES			
	Food	1,125	38
	Beverage	296	30
TOTAL COST OF SALES		$1,412	36
TOTAL GROSS PROFIT		2,525	64
OPERATING EXPENSES			
	Salaries & Wages	1,105	28
	Employees' Meals	79	2
	Payroll Taxes	59	1.5
	Laundry & Linen	59	1.5
	China, Glass, Silver, and Utensils	99	2.5
	Ice & Fuel	20	0.5
	Heat, Light & Power	165	4.2
	Supplies	157	4
	Advertising	79	2
	Insurance	66	1.7
	Licenses	20	0.5
	Telephone	88	0.2
	Misc. Operating Expenses	79	2
TOTAL OPERATING EXPENSE		$1,995	50.6
PROFIT BEFORE OCCUPANCY COSTS		530	13.4
	Occupancy Costs	328	8.3
PROFIT BEFORE TAXES		202	5.1

Constructing a Flexible Budget

If it were possible to make accurate predictions for a year in advance, the fixed budget would be sufficient to meet the needs of the food-service establishment for operational budgeting. But even the best procedures for estimating will not provide figures on forecasted levels of sales that will be accurate for that long a period. Many things that are not evident when the budget is being constructed may cause wide discrepancies between what is forecast and what the actual sales volume turns out to be.

A foodservice business operates at varying levels of sales and varying levels of efficiency. So, a budget that is based on a sales volume and does not reflect actual conditions will be only of limited use in controlling day-to-day operations. To meet this problem, a flexible budget can be used to provide a better relationship to actual conditions.

Nature of the Flexible Budget

A flexible budget is a series of budgets, each based on a different level of sales. This makes it possible for the operator to select the level of sales that he forecasts as the most likely and logical level for the period being considered.

Then, the operator can select one or more other sales volume levels, which are different from the one forecast. These can be the next most likely, or the ones that might happen if certain things occur.

Many operators select a level of sales below the one forecast and another level of sales above that forecast. In the case of the Superior Restaurant, if the manager felt that they may do 10 percent more business or they might do 10 percent less business than the volume of $78,925 forecast, he could set up his budget on the basis of three sales levels. (See Figure 10-4.)

Calculating Costs at Each Sales Level

To complete the flexible budget for the Superior Restaurant, costs at each of the three levels of sales must be calculated. Variations will be likely in some of the cost percentages at sales above or below the forecast $78,925 volume. Costs of food and beverage would change at each of the three levels of sales, but the ratio of these costs to sales should stay about the same.

So, calculating food and beverage costs is then a matter of applying the expected 38 percent food cost and the 30 percent beverage cost to the additional volumes of sales. After this is done, the cost of sales part of the flexible budget will look as shown in Figure 10-5.

Calculating Operating Expenses at Each Level

Operating expenses must be calculated at each of the levels of sales in the same way they were calculated for the level of sales in the fixed budget. Some of the operating expenses will stay fairly constant for the various sales levels; other operating expenses such as labor can be expected to show some changes from one level of sales to another. How much depends on the particular establishment.

Figure 10-4   The Superior Restaurant
Sales Forecast

	90%	100%	110%
Food	$53,275	$59,195	$65,115
Beverage	17,755	19,730	21,705
Total	$71,030	$78,925	$86,820

Figure 10-5   The Superior Restaurant
Cost of Sales Budget

		90%	100%	110%	Percent
Food		$20,245	$22,495	$24,745	38%
Beverage		5,325	5,920	6,510	30%
	Total	$25,570	$28,415	$31,265	36%

For example, the manager of the Superior Restaurant might find that even though the volume of sales went down 10 percent, he would still have to maintain the same labor force. This would mean then that his ratio of labor cost to sales cost would go up, while his profit percentage would go down. Of course, he might be in a situation where he could lay off some of his employees, or be able to use part-time people, or in some other way make labor savings. In that case, he might not experience the changes or at least to the same degree. What is highly important is that he be able to predict what will happen if sales go above or fall below what he expects them to be.

After the adjustments for each of the levels of sales are made for labor and other operating costs for the example of the Superior Restaurant, the flexible budget can be completed. An example is shown in Figure 10-6. For purposes of simplification, the operating expenses other than labor have been summarized.

It takes more time and work to construct a flexible budget than to construct a budget for a single level of projected sales. But, the flexible budget is a much more effective management tool. By budgeting at different levels of sales, management is prepared in advance for changes that take the level of sales above or below the expected level of the forecast. So the extra time and effort required is repaid in terms of the increased operating efficiency that results from use of the flexible budget.

Making Use of the Operating Budget

The operating budget has some major uses in the management of a foodservice operation, in both planning and controlling.

As a Planning Tool   The operating budget can be of value in many ways as a planning tool. If the operator knows in advance what the operation will produce, he can increase efficiency in such areas as employee scheduling, purchasing, and planning the financial needs of the business over different periods of time. There can be many dollar savings in the course of a year in all of these areas, when good advance planning is done on the basis of the operational budget.

Figure 10-6   The Superior Restaurant
                   Flexible Budget

		90%	100%	110%
SALES				
	Food	$53,275	$59,195	$65,115
	Beverage	17,775	19,730	21,705
TOTAL		$71,030	$78,925	$86,820
COST OF SALES				
	Food	20,245	22,495	24,745
	Beverage	5,325	5,920	6,510
TOTAL COST OF SALES		$25,570	$28,415	$31,265
TOTAL GROSS PROFIT		45,460	50,510	55,555
OPERATING EXPENSES				
	Salaries & Wages	21,700	22,100	22,800
	Employees' Meals	1,530	1,580	1,650
	Other Operating Expenses	13,500	14,365	15,100
TOTAL OPERATING EXPENSES		$36,730	$38,045	$39,550
PROFIT BEFORE OCCUPANCY COSTS		8,730	12,465	16,005
	Occupancy Costs	3,940	3,940	3,940
PROFIT AS PERCENTAGE OF SALES		6.74%	10.8%	13.9%

As a Control Tool   The operating budget has special values as a control tool, providing a basis for intelligent interpretation of data on the performance of the business. It is in this context that the values are realized. The operator looks at his income statement to find out if his business over the past period has performed as well as expected. Without an operating budget, his expectations are little more than some vague ideas about what he thought should have happened. If, however, he has an operating budget, these expectations are stated clearly in terms of dollars and cents. He can compare this budget with the income statement and he can easily see where the actual operation over the year varied from the expected operation.

Using this comparison, the operator can see readily whether his expected profit goal has been attained. If it has not been reached, or if it has been exceeded, he can determine why this is so by comparing the costs that he had budgeted with the actual costs during the year. Then, he can look for the things that are causing these variations in his operations and make changes that are needed.

While a year is mentioned in this discussion, the comparison could be for a month or a three month, or some other period.

Operations Analysis Sheet

The operations analysis sheet in Figure 10-7 is an example of a form that can be used to facilitate the comparison of the budgeted expenses

Figure 10-7 Operations Analysis Sheet
The Superior Restaurant
Month of January

	(1) Actual $	(1) %	(2) Budget $	(2) %	(3) Dollar Variance	(4) Percent Varia	(5) Actual $	(5) %	(6) TO-DATE Budget $	(6) %	(7) Dollar Variance	(8) Percent Variance
SALES:												
Food	3150	73.9	2960	75.0	+190	−1.1	3150	73.9	2960	75.0	+190	−1.1
Beverage	1110	26.1	986	25.0	+124	+1.1	1110	26.1	986	25.0	+124	+1.1
Total	4260	100.0	3946	100.0	+314		4260	100.0	3946	100.0	+314	
COST OF SALES												
Food	1210	38.4	1125	38.0	+85	+0.4	1210	38.4	1125	38.0	+85	+0.4
Beverage	339	30.5	296	30.0	+43	+0.5	339	30.5	296	30.0	+43	+0.5
Total	1549	36.4	1412	36.0	+128	+0.4	1549	36.4	1412	36.0	+128	+0.4
TOTAL GROSS PROFIT	2711	63.6	2525	64.0	+186	−0.4	2711	63.6	2525	64.0	+186	−0.4
OPERATING EXPENSES												
Salaries & Wages	1150	27.0	1105	28.0	+45	−1.0	1150	27.0	1105	28.0	+45	−1.0
Empoyees' Meals	72	1.7	79	2.0	−7	−0.3	72	1.7	79	2.0	−7	−0.3
Payroll Taxes	60	1.4	59	1.5	+1	−0.1	60	1.4	59	1.5	+1	−0.1
Laundry & Linen	68	1.6	59	1.0	+9	+0.1	68	1.6	59	1.0	+9	−0.1
China, Glass, & Silver	107	2.5	99	2.5	+8		107	2.5	99	2.5	+8	
Ice & Fuel	17	0.4	20	0.5	−3	−0.1	17	0.4	20	0.5	−3	−0.1
Heat, Light, & Power	165	3.9	165	4.2	—	−0.3	165	3.9	165	4.2	—	−0.3
Supplies	175	4.1	157	4.0	+18	+0.1	175	4.1	157	4.0	+18	+0.1
Advertising	94	2.2	79	2.0	+15	+0.2	94	2.2	79	2.0	+15	+0.2
Insurance	66	1.5	66	1.7	—	−0.2	66	1.5	66	1.7	—	−0.2
Licenses	17	.4	20	0.5	−3	−0.1	17	0.5	20	0.5	−3	−0.1
Misc. Operating Expenses	98	2.3	79	2.0	+19	+0.3	98	2.3	79	2.0	+19	+0.3
Telephone	17	.4	8	0.2	+9	+0.2	17	0.2	8	0.2	+9	+0.2
TOTAL OPERATING EXPENSES	2106	49.4	1995	50.6	+111	−1.2	2106	49.4	1995	50.6	+111	−1.2
PROFIT BEFORE OCCUPANCY COSTS	605	14.2	530	13.4	+75	+0.8	605	14.2	530	13.4	+75	+0.8
Occupancy Costs	328	7.7	328	8.3	—	−0.6	328	7.7	328	8.3	—	−0.6
PROFIT BEFORE INCOME TAXES	277	6.5	202	5.1	+75	+1.4	277	6.5	202	5.1	+75	+1.4

with the actual expenses. In this example, the first two columns show sales and expenses for the month. The first column lists the actual dollar figures and the actual percentage figures, while the second column provides the budgeted figures. The third column shows the result of the comparison, listing the variance of the actual figures from the budgeted figures in terms of dollars. The fourth column presents the variances in terms of percentages. The last four columns show the to-date or accumulated amounts, following the format of the first four columns.

Both dollar values and percentages are shown in the operations analysis sheet. The variances in dollars are of interest, of course, to the management of the operation; but far more important are the variances in the percentage figures.

The figures in this form represent the same example of the Superior Restaurant for the month of January. In the case of the Superior Restaurant, it is evident that sales and profit went above the expectations that had been budgeted for January. The comparison also shows that the increase in the profit percentage was the result of good control of operating expenses. However, the comparison also shows that food and beverage costs were a little higher than had been estimated in the budget. A check to see what the reasons are is in order.

Operational Budgets for New Establishments

So far, the consideration of budgets has been related to the Superior Restaurant as an establishment that has been in business a number of years. Therefore, management has historical data on which to base budgeting. A new establishment would not have these figures from the past to use, and management would have to look elsewhere for guidance in constructing the budget.

The time for making an operating budget for a new operation is before any financial commitments have been made. The owner needs to know before he invests his money whether or not the proposed operation will produce enough profit to make it worth his while to make the investment. So, the first item that he will need to budget is his profit figure. If he is not able to get a reasonable return on his investment, there is no point in making the investment. He would do better to put his money elsewhere.

To determine the likely profitability of the venture, there needs to be a forecast of expected sales. Making this forecast is more difficult with a new business than for one already in existence and with a history of sales in past years. A fairly good estimate can be made by multiplying the number of seats in the establishment by the expected seat turnover, and then multiplying that figure by the expected average check.

Once the figure for the expected number of customers is obtained, salary and wage costs can be calculated. Some of the other operating expenses cannot be easily determined, but industry guidelines for foodservice establishments of similar size and type can be used. The occupancy cost determination is much easier. Occupancy costs can usually be determined before the place is opened.

After subtracting the total of the budgeted profit figure, the operating expenses, and the occupancy costs, the dollar figure left represents what is available for the purchase of food and beverage raw materials. If this figure is realistic in terms of the menu price structure and the sales mix that is projected, then the budget is completed.

If, however, the amount of money left for purchasing food and beverage raw materials is not consistent with the proposed price structure and sales mix, more has to be done. The menu price structure and the rest of the budget will have to be considered again, since if at this point the proposed operation as it was planned is not realistic and feasible, drastic changes will have to be made to make it so.

Since there is no backlog of figures from other years of operation, budgeting for a new operation has a lot of uncertainties. So, the budget should be prepared for only a short period into the future. Then, as soon as the first operating figures become available, it should be revised.

Summary

If a foodservice business is to be operated profitably, there must be planning and projection of the way the business is to go as it is operated and developed. Management must set goals, develop plans that make attaining those goals possible, and then coordinate people and procedures to be successful.

The operating budget is a basic tool that can be of much assistance to management in planning, coordinating, controlling, and directing the progress of the business.

Development of operating budgets is not difficult. The amount of time and effort that goes into this activity is repaid many times by the effective guidance that can be realized in comparison of actual figures with the figures representing the expectations of management for periods of time ahead.

The operating budget is a tool that does much to make possible the profitable operation of a foodservice establishment, and should be one of the planning tools for every such operation.

Questions

1. What is the operating budget and for what is it used?

2. List the three major functions of a manager or a management team.

3. How does the budget have a controlling influence in a business?

4. Who in the foodservice operation should participate in the construction of the budget?

5. Name the three general types of operating budgets.

6. Which expenses of operation accounts need to be considered in determining the operating budget?

7. Explain what a flexible budget is and the use it has.

8. How is the operating budget used as a planning tool?

11

Using Break-Even Analysis

No foodservice business will exist for very long unless enough income is realized to pay the expenses and provide some profit. But profits will not come automatically. The operator must plan for them. To do this successfully, he must have a good understanding of the things that affect profits and then must make business decisions on the basis of what that understanding provides.

That means the foodservice operator must plan expenses and establish effective ways to control costs before they are incurred. He must determine what combination of products, what volume of business, and what amounts of labor are needed, in order that the business generate sufficient profit that he can realize an adequate return on the money he has invested. In other words, costs, volume, and profit must be an analyzed objectively.

A number of tools or methods can be used in making this objective and critical analysis. Break-even analysis is one of the most effective. It offers a method of using facts and figures to make business decisions more effective. It also provides a good way to understand the interrelation of volume, costs, and profit.

Analysis Reveals Break-Even Point

The term *break-even analysis* comes from the so-called break-even point, where a business is breaking even—not making a profit, but at the same time not showing a loss. This is the point at which the total expenses exactly equal the total income. Every business has a break-even point.

From the point of view of management, the fact there is a break-even point where expenses and receipts are equal is of great importance when analyzing the relationship of costs, volume, and profit. This analysis is essential if decisions are to be good ones that will keep the business on a profitable basis.

The operator is interested in knowing what his profit or loss would be at any given volume of sales. He also needs to know which volume of sales must be reached in order for the business to produce the amount of profit that was established as one goal. He needs to know the volume of sales that will be added to offset a reduction in selling price. Also, he is concerned about what the profit will be if fixed expenses or variable expenses are increased or decreased.

An analysis using the break-even point can provide answers to these kinds of questions. Break-even analysis provides a tool with which the operator can find out much about the business. It is a tool that gives data on which to base decisions so that the business returns enough profit.

Information Needed for Break-Even Analysis

A certain amount of data is needed to make use of break-even analysis in a foodservice operation. It is information that can be found in statements and reports. Most of the information is operating data, found in the income statement or, as it is more often called, the profit and loss statement. But the data as they come from that statement are not in detailed enough form to use in break-even analysis. So, the data must be modified.

One thing that must be done is to separate the costs into those that change as the volume of business changes and those that do not. These are called variable costs and fixed costs respectively. To make this separation requires that the operator know the different kinds of costs associated with his business and the characteristics of each. Then, he can determine if a particular cost goes into the variable cost category or the fixed cost category.

Fixed and Variable Costs

The following definitions and descriptions of both variable and fixed costs should make this procedure easier.

Fixed Costs   Fixed costs are the costs that are involved in just being in business. These costs are there even if nothing is produced. They do not change with changes in the volume of sales. They remain constant or fixed within a rather limited range of sales volume. The size of the existing plant and the capacity of the equipment hold the volume within that limited range.

Included in fixed costs are rent, insurance, depreciation, property taxes, and interest. There are other costs that management can arbitrarily classify as fixed costs. Advertising expense is a good example. If management decides to budget a specific number of dollars for advertising in the year, regardless of what the volume of sales is, then it is a fixed cost, since it is not going to change with changes in volume of sales.

Variable Costs   Variable costs are costs that change in direct proportion to the volume of sales. Direct materials (food), direct labor and supplies are variable costs. As the volume of sales goes up, there is a proportionate increase in these costs, since more food, more labor, and more supplies are needed. The reverse is true when the volume of sales goes down. Smaller amounts of variable costs are incurred.

Costs should be considered in the light of the definition that fixed costs are those that tend to remain relatively constant regardless of changes in output, while variable costs are those that fluctuate with changes in output.

Analyze the chart of accounts and find those expense accounts that will vary proportionately with volume; these are the variable costs. Also, find those that will stay fixed for the budget period; these are fixed costs.

Semi-Variable Costs   There is one complication. Some costs cannot be classified as either fixed costs or variable costs. They contain a fixed element and also a variable element. So, they are called semi-variable costs.

These semi-variable costs change as the volume of production or sales changes, but they do not change in direct proportion as variable costs do. Examples of these semi-variable costs are expenses for utilities, supervision, and administration. A 10 percent increase in the volume of sales can mean a 4 or 5 percent boost in these costs. However, they also have a fixed characteristic. Some part of these expenses would still be left if sales were to drop to zero.

In break-even analysis, semi-variable costs create a problem, since break-even analysis deals only with fixed and variable costs. The semi-variable costs have to be separated into their fixed and variable parts, so that they can be utilized. There are various statistical methods of doing this. Sometimes it is done by an "educated guess," after analyzing the makeup of the semi-variable costs.

Using the Scatter Graph

One of the simplest ways of making the separation is to use a scatter graph or, as it is sometimes called, a scatter diagram. This method provides a graphic picture of the relationship between the semi-variable expense and a variable activity such as the sales volume, the number of covers served, the direct labor cost, or the direct labor hours. Each semi-variable expense is analyzed in this method to determine the variable rate of increase.

Taking the electricity expense as one of the semi-variable expenses (as an example), the fixed and variable cost of electricity can be determined by the following steps:

1. Collect data for electricity expense from the previous operating statements. Relate these figures to the number of covers served, which is a variable base of activity. These are then put in chart form under the headings of Time Period, Number of Covers Served, and Electricity Expense. A column for Plotted Points is also made part of the chart, as shown below.

Time Period	Number of Covers Served	Electricity Expenses	Plotted Points
1st 10 weeks	1,250	$300	A
2nd 10 weeks	2,750	$375	B
3rd 10 weeks	3,000	$425	C
4th 10 weeks	3,250	$365	D
5th 10 weeks	1,750	$325	E

2. Then, on a sheet of graph paper, construct a horizontal axis to represent the covers served. Construct a vertical axis to represent the electricity expense (Figure 11-1).

3. Next, plot the data from the chart onto the graph paper. The number of covers served should be measured off along the horizontal axis, and the electricity expense along the vertical axis. For each combination of number of covers and electricity expense, there is a point, which should be marked A, B, C, D, and E. These points can be added to the chart.

4. Draw a straight line so that it comes as close as possible to all of the points that are plotted on the graph. The points will not all be on the line. Some will be above the line. Some will be on the line, and some will be below. Draw the line so that about the same number will be above as below. The line will be a sloping line.

How to Use the Graph

The graph shows a number of things of value to the owner or manager of the establishment:

The fixed cost part of the electricity is at Point F where the drawn line intersects the vertical axis (the y-axis) which represents electricity expense. Reading up on this axis, it can be seen that the fixed portion of the electricity expense is about $240 per 10-week period.

The slope of the line that is drawn in represents the variable cost rate of electricity expense per unit of production.

143

Here is how the variable cost rate per cover served can be obtained from the graph (Figure 11-1):

1. Multiply the $240 figure obtained from the graph (the fixed portion of the electricity expense) by 5, which is the number of 10-week

Figure 11-1   Scatter Graph of Fixed and
Variable Expenses
(Per 10-Week Period)

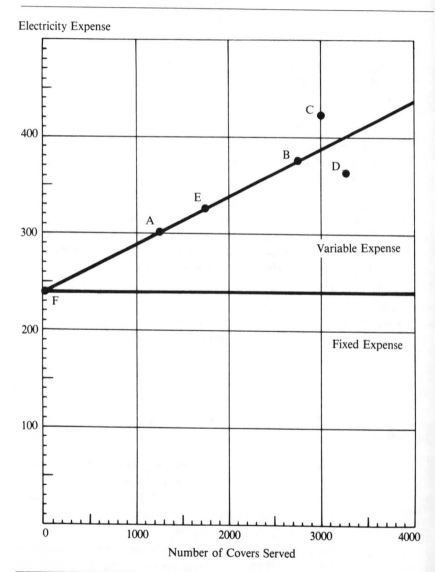

Electricity Expense

periods. The resulting figure is the annual fixed cost, which in this example is 1200, or $120 per month.

2.   Subtract this annual fixed cost of $1,200 from the annual total expense, which is $1,790. The difference is $590, and this is the variable cost.

3.   Divide the variable cost of $590 by the total number of covers, which is 12,000. The 0.049 cents figure obtained is the variable cost rate per cover served.

Estimate at Any Level

This procedure provides the information needed to estimate the amount of an expense at any level of activity of the business. The example of 850 covers served in one month will show how this is done. The calculation is done in this way:

$$\text{Total Expense} = \begin{array}{c}\text{Fixed Cost} \\ \text{For One Month}\end{array} + \begin{array}{c}\text{Variable Cost} \\ \text{Per Cover}\end{array} \times \begin{array}{c}\text{Number} \\ \text{of Covers}\end{array}$$
$$= \$100 + .049 \times 850$$
$$= \$141.65$$

Thus, the total expense figures out to be $141.65.

This technique can be used to find the fixed and variable base of activity or expense such as sales, direct labor hours, direct labor cost, and of course the one used in the example, number of covers served. The procedure separates the fixed and variable cost elements of a semi-variable expense; and thus makes it possible to proceed with the break-even analysis that uses only fixed and variable costs.

Mathematical Determination of the Break-Even Point

There are two methods of determining the break-even point once the semi-variable expenses have been analyzed and all costs have been classified as fixed or variable. One of these is a mathematical method; the other is a graphical method. Either method can be used to obtain a clearer picture of the relationship of cost, volume, and profit in a foodservice establishment.

There are four steps to follow in using the mathematical method of determining the break-even point:

Step 1   Determine the net sales, the fixed expense, and the variable expense incurred by the business for a past accounting period.

Step 2   Calculate the percentage of variable expense to net sales. In the profit and loss statement for the Popular Restaurant that will be used as an example (Figure 11-2), net sales are shown as $100,000, and the variable expense is listed as $68,000. So, to find the percentage of variable ex-

Figure 11-2   The Popular Restaurant
Profit and Loss Statement

	Amount	Per Cent Ratio	Classification of Expenses Fixed	Variable
Net Food Sale	$100,000	100.0%		
Cost of Food Sold	39,000	39.0		$39,000
	$ 61,000	61.0%		
Operating Expenses — Controllable				
Salaries and Wages	$ 30,000	30.0%	$ 6,000	24,000
Laundry, Linen and Uniforms	2,400	2.4	1,700	700
China, Glass and Silver	1,500	1.5	1,000	500
Cleaning and Other Supplies	900	.9	400	500
Utilities	2,400	2.4	800	1,600
Repairs and Maintenance	1,100	1.1		1,100
Advertising and Promotion	1,000	1.0	1,000	
Administration and General	2,400	2.4	1,800	600
Total Operating Expense	$ 41,700	41.7%		
Gross Operating Profit	19,300	19.3		
Fixed Expenses				
Rent	$ 5,000	5.0%	$ 5,000	
Property Taxes and Licenses	1,500	1.5	1,500	
Insurance	400	.4	400	
Interest	900	.9	900	
Depreciation	3,500	3.5	3,500	
Total Fixed Costs	$ 11,300	11.0%	$24,000	$68,000
Net Profit Before Taxes	$ 8.000	8.0%		

pense to net sales, divide the $68,000 (variable expense) by the $100,000 (net sales):

$$\$68,000 \div \$100,000 = 68\%$$

Variable expense, then, is 68 percent of net sales.

Step 3   Subtract this percentage figure, 68 percent from 100 percent. This shows that 32 percent, or in other words 32 cents of every sales dollar, is left to cover the fixed expense and provide profit.

There are several names for this percentage figure. It is known as marginal income ratio, as contribution margin, contribution ratio, and profit-volume ratio (PV). This percentage stays the same for all levels of volume, so long as there is no change in the selling price, variable expense, and fixed expense.

Step 4   Divide the dollar amount of fixed expense, which is $24,000, by the 32 percent obtained from the Step 3 calculation; and this will give the break-even point:

$$\$24,000 \div 32\% = \$75,000$$

Thus, $75,000 is the break-even point with the example's volume of sales, fixed cost, and variable cost.

There is a basic break-even formula that can be used to do this four-step calculation. The figures for fixed cost, variable cost, and sales volume are put into this formula; and the result is the break-even point:

$$\text{Break-Even Point (B.E.P.)} = \frac{\text{Fixed Cost}}{1\,(100\%) - \dfrac{\text{Variable Cost}}{\text{Sales}}}$$

Applying the Formula   An example of how this formula can be applied is provided in the case of the Popular Restaurant, the profit and loss statement for which is given in Figure 11-2. Substitute in the formula the data below from the profit and loss statement.

Fixed Cost   = $ 24,000
Variable Cost = $ 68,000
Sales   = $100,000

This substitution shows the following calculations:

$$\text{B.E.P.} = \frac{\$24,000}{1 - \dfrac{\$68,000}{\$100,000}}$$

$$\text{B.E.P.} = \frac{\$24,000}{1 - 68\%}$$

$$\text{B.E.P.} = \frac{\$24,000}{32\%}$$

$$\text{B.E.P.} = \$75,000$$

On the basis of these data, the $75,000 of sales, which is the break-even point, equals the sum of the fixed costs and the variable costs. There is neither a profit nor a loss. The calculation result can be proved in the following manner:

Sales	$75,000
Less Variable Cost (68% of Sales)	$51,000
Amount available for Fixed Costs and Profit	$24,000
Less Fixed Costs	$24,000
Profit or Loss	0

The break-even point of a foodservice establishment can be calculated in this manner with a fair degree of accuracy.

Effectiveness of the Break-Even Analysis   How effective this break-even analysis is depends upon certain things about costs and profit that are assumed. These basic assumptions include the following:

> The selling price will not change.
>
> The sales mix will stay constant.
>
> The costs can be classified into fixed and variable classifications with a reasonable degree of accuracy.
>
> Fixed costs will remain constant within the limits established.
>
> Variable costs will vary in direct proportion to changes in volume of sales.

If there is a change in any of these assumptions, the break-even analysis will not provide an accurate basis for making decisions. If there are changes everything must be recalculated in terms of the new situation.

Using Break-Even Analysis   With the limitations of break-even analysis in mind, and an understanding of how cost, volume of sales, and profit are related, it is easy to project future profits at different volumes of sales. With that information at hand, budgeting for the operation can be done more easily and more effectively.

Probably the best way of demonstrating the use of break-even analysis in foodservice operations is to answer some of the commonly asked questions to which this procedure can be applied. The data in the profit and loss statement for the Popular Restaurant (Figure 11-2) will be used in these examples.

Examples

Question No. 1   What is the profit before taxes when the sales volume of the business is $120,000 annually?

Using the data for the Popular Restaurant, that firm's profit and loss statement shows:

> Profit Volume Ratio = 32%
> Fixed Costs   = $24,000

The desired sales volume would be:

> Projected Sales   = $120,000

Using these data, the formula will provide the answer to the question.

> Sales × Profit Volume Ratio – Fixed Costs = Profit

The calculation is done as follows:

Projected Sales	$120,000
Profit Volume Ratio	× .32
Contribution	$ 38,400
Less Fixed Costs	$ 24,000
Profit	$ 14,400

So, the answer to the question is: Profit before taxes at a volume of sales of $120,000 would be $14,000.

Question No. 2   What volume of sales is needed to earn a predetermined rate of profit? In this particular case the operator is considering $10,000 a year as a fair profit, and needs to know what sales volume will be necessary to earn that much.

This $10,000 is in effect a fixed cost; and the data from the Popular Restaurant's profit and loss statement is as follows:

Fixed Cost   = $24,000
Profit Volume Ratio = 32%
Desired Profit   = $10,000

This formula is used:

$$\text{Required Sales Volume} = \frac{\text{Fixed Costs} + \text{Profit}}{\text{Profit Volume Ratio}}$$

The calculation is as follows:

$$\text{Required Sales Volume} = \frac{\$24,000 + \$10,000}{32\%}$$

$$\text{Required Sales Volume} = \frac{\$34,000}{.32}$$

$$\text{Required Sales Volume} = \$106,250$$

So, the answer to the question is: It will take a sales volume of $106,250 to provide $10,000 a year profit.

Question No. 3   What volume of sales is needed to offset a 5 percent reduction in selling price without reducing the profit?
From the computations of Question No. 2, the following information is known:

Sales   = $106,250
Profit Volume Ratio = 32%
Fixed Costs   = $24,000

Two calculations must be made to obtain the answer to this question. This formula is used for the first calculation:

$$\text{Sales} \times \text{Profit Volume Ratio} - \text{Fixed Costs} = \text{Profit}$$
$$\$106,250 \times .32 - \$24,000 = \$10,000$$

The calculation is as follows:

Sales	$106,250
Profit Volume Ratio	$\times$ .32
Contribution	$ 34,000
Less Fixed Costs	$ 24,000
Profit	$ 10,000

The second calculation makes the needed adjustment for the 5 percent reduction in the selling price. This formula is used:

$$\text{Required Sales Volume} = \frac{\text{Desired Profit} + \text{Fixed Costs}}{1 - \dfrac{\text{Present Variable Cost Percent}}{\{1 - \text{Proposed Reduction (\%)}\}}}$$

$$\text{Required Sales Volume} = \frac{\$10,000 + \$24,000}{1 - \dfrac{.68}{1 - 5\%}}$$

$$\text{Required Sales Volume} = \frac{\$34,000}{1 - \dfrac{.68}{.95}}$$

The calculation is as follows:

$$\text{Required Sales Volume} = \frac{\$34,000}{1 - .716}$$

$$\text{Required Sales Volume} = \frac{\$34,000}{.284}$$

$$\text{Required Sales Volume} = \$119,718$$

So, the answer to the question is: It will take an increase in sales of approximately 11.27 percent in order to reach the sales volume necessary to offset a 5 percent reduction in selling price.

Whether selling prices should be reduced or not in foodservice operations depends a great deal on whether the establishment can increase the volume of sales enough to offset the effects of the price decrease. This is related to whether the operation has capacity enough to produce the higher number of covers served.

Question No. 4   What will the profit be if fixed and variable costs change?

Assume in this example that the operator has bought new equipment for which he has paid $3,000. As a result of this new equipment, he can reduce his variable costs by one-fifth, but this new equipment increases his fixed costs by

$3,000. If his sales total $100,000, what is his profit?

Three calculations must be made to find the answer to this question. First, it is necessary to determine a new profit volume ratio. Since present variable costs are 68 percent of sales, a 20 percent reduction in variable costs would be 0.68 minus 20 percent of 0.68 or 13.6, which is 54.4 percent.

$$0.68 - 0.20(0.68) = 54.4\%$$

So, the new profit volume ratio is that figure subtracted from 100:

$$1(100\%) - 54.4\% = 44.6\%$$

The second calculation involves use of the break-even formula:

$$\frac{\text{Fixed Costs}}{\text{Profit Volume Ratio}}$$

The calculation is as follows:

$$\frac{\$24,000 \text{ (present fixed costs)} + \$3,000 \text{ (new fixed costs)}}{44.6\%} = \frac{\$27,000}{.446}$$

The new break-even point is $60,540.

The third calculation is then made to determine the profit. Here is the formula to be used:

$$\text{Sales} \times \text{Profit Volume Ratio} - \text{Fixed Costs} = \text{Profit}$$

The calculation is as follows:

$$\$100,000 \times .446 - \$27,000 = \$17,600$$

The answer to the question is: With reduction in variable costs by 20 percent and an increase of 20 percent in fixed costs, and a sales total of $100,000, the operator's profit would be $17,600.

Note that the 44.6 percent profit volume ratio results in a greater profit at the level of $100,000 in sales than the 32 percent profit volume ratio does at the same level of sales. The former is $17,600 profit while the latter is $8,000 profit.

The following can be concluded:

> As sales go above the break-even point, a high profit volume ratio will result in greater profits.

> As sales fall below the break-even point, a high profit volume ratio will result in greater losses.

Determining the Closing Point   There are times in the operation of a foodservice business when it costs more to stay open than it would to close for those hours. So, it is important to the operator to know the "closing point" of the operation—to know the unprofitable hours of operation. The break-even point formula can be used, with a little adjustment, to provide this kind of information, since the significance of the closing point is based on the relation of operating costs to total sales.

In determining the closing point, attention is directed to variable costs. Fixed costs are disregarded, since they go on whether the establishment is open or closed. To find out the closing point for a day, select the minimum operating costs for a day. These costs, which are sometimes referred to as opening costs, are incurred when the foodservice establishment opens its doors for the day. Assume that the following represents the minimum operating costs for the day:

Food Cost	40% of sales
Payroll	30% of sales
Other Variable Costs	10% of sales
Fixed Costs	$40
Total Costs	$40 + 80% of sales

To compute the closing point mathematically requires having one figure expressed in dollars. Fixed costs that are expressed this way were eliminated, so it will be necessary to pick another expense that is in dollars. Payroll is a good one, since it is easy to determine what the minimum operating staff is. Assume that the payroll for a minimum operating staff is $42.50 for the day. Assume, also, that the other variable costs together are about 8 percent, since some of these costs are fixed, being part of semi-variable costs. The minimum operating costs are as follows:

Food Cost	40%
Payroll (minimum)	$42.50
Other Variable Costs	8%
Total (Minimum Operating Costs)	48% + $42.50

Using these figures, the closing point can be determined. The formula to use is:

$$\text{Closing Point} = \frac{\text{Minimum Operating Costs (\$)}}{1 - \text{Minimum Operating Costs (\%)}}$$

The computation is as follows:

$$\text{Closing Point} = \frac{\$42.50}{1 - .48}$$

$$\text{Closing Point} = \frac{\$42.50}{.52}$$

$$\text{Closing Point} = \$81.73$$

So, the closing point is approximately $82.00 in sales per day. If sales are less than this amount, more is lost by opening than if the establishment remained closed for the day.

By the use of this formula, it is also possible to determine if it is profitable to open the foodservice establishment to serve breakfast, and if it is profitable to stay open later in the evening. It is done by analyzing food costs, labor costs, and variable costs for the time period.

Graphical Determination of the Break-Even Point

The other way in which the break-even point can be determined is the graph method. It provides the same information that is obtained by the mathematical method.

There are three steps involved in the construction of a conventional break-even chart. The following data will be used to illustrate how the chart is constructed:

	Month Number 1	Month Number 2	Month Number 3
Monthly Sales	$7,595	$8,400	$9,300
Number of Operating Days	31	30	31
Average Sales Per Day	245	280	300
Monthly Profit	775	1,050	1,250
Average Daily Profit	25	35	40

Here are the three steps:

Step 1   On a sheet of graph paper, construct a horizontal axis and a vertical axis as in the graph shown in Figure 11-3. Then, on the horizontal axis, mark off a scale in terms of dollars for expense. Draw the fixed expense line from Point A to Point A^1, so that it is parallel to the horizontal axis. This line represents the fixed expense at all levels of sales.

Step 2   Plot the total expenses at Point B. This point represents the total fixed costs and the variable costs, which are given as $46,000, on the vertical axis, at a sales volume of $50,000. Draw a line between Point A and Point B, which will be known as Line B. The area between Line B and Line A represents the variable expense at different levels of sales.

Step 3   Plot Point C at the point where total expenses on the vertical axis represent total sales on the horizontal axis. Draw a straight line from 0 through Point C. This is Line C.

The break-even point is at Point D, where the total cost (the TC line), which is Line B, intersects the income line which is Line C. This shows that the amount of sales necessary to break even is $39,474, or roughly $40,000.

To determine the profit, count the squares between C and B. Since each

Figure 11-3   Conventional Break-Even Chart

Expenses
(In Thousands of Dollars)

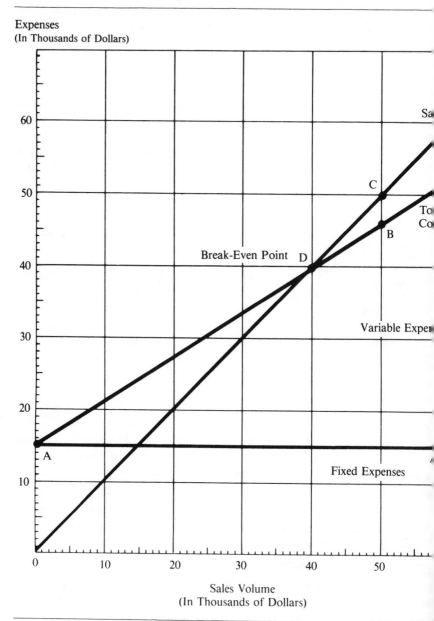

Sales Volume
(In Thousands of Dollars)

square represents $1,000, and there are four squares between C and B, the profit at a volume of sales of $50,000 is $4,000.

Constructing a Daily Break-Even Chart

A simple daily break-even chart can be constructed on graph paper using figures that can be obtained from the profit and loss statement. It is not necessary to separate the fixed and variable costs. Only the average daily sales and the average daily profit need be used. As an example, assume that the following data represent business activity during the past three months:

Sales		$50,000
Less Costs and Expenses		
Food Cost	$20,000	
Variable Expenses	11,000	
Fixed Costs	15,000	
Total Expenses		46,000
Net Profit before Taxes		$ 4,000

Basically the same steps followed in preparing a conventional break-even chart should be followed for the daily break-even chart. Plot the sales line, Point 0 to Point Y (Figure 11-4) in the same way as for the conventional break-even chart. Then, plot the average sales per day, marked as S1, S2, and S3, on the sales line, Point 0 to Point Y. Each square on the chart is equivalent to $5.00.

Plot the average daily profit (P) directly under the respective period, utilizing the squares as a guide. Since each square is equivalent to $5.00, and the average daily profit for S3 was $40.00, plot a point marked P3 eight squares directly under S3 ($300 average sales per day). Plot another point marked P2 located seven squares under S2; and plot a third marked P1 five squares under S1.

Then, draw a line connecting Points P1, P2, and P3. It may not be possible to connect all of the points with a straight line, if the sales and profit figures are used for a period longer than two months. So, draw the "best fit" line, or draw a straight line through the high-profit or the low-profit points.

The break-even point is where the sales line and the profit line cross each other. In this particular example, the break-even point is approximately $150 per day in sales.

From Figure 11-4, it is easy to determine the profit at various levels of sales by counting the squares between the sales line and the profit line. For example, if sales are at $325 per day, the profit would be approximately $47.00, obtained by counting off the squares and finding that they total 9½, and then multiplying that 9½ by $5.00, since each square is equivalent to $5.00. The chart can be used to determine profit under many different assumed conditions.

The graph in Figure 11-4 is easy to make, and it is easy to interpret. It is not as accurate as a detailed analysis of the fixed costs and the variable costs of the foodservice operation. However, even if it is not as accurate as the mathe-

Figure 11-4   Daily Break-Even Chart

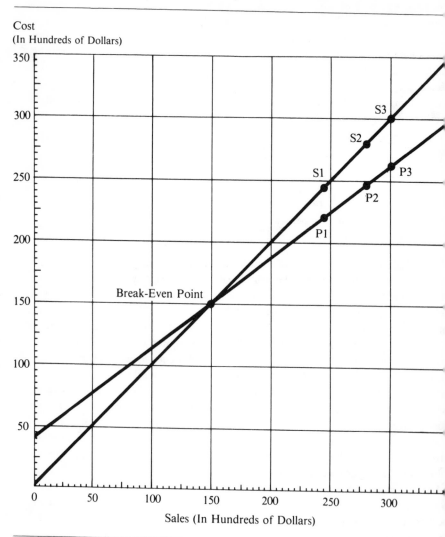

Cost
(In Hundreds of Dollars)

Break-Even Point

Sales (In Hundreds of Dollars)

matical formula method, it does provide to management a good picture of the operations of the establishment.

Summary

Break-even analysis is an effective management tool for projecting income, expense, and profit under assumed conditions. It enables management to use facts and figures that are available in gaining a better understanding of how volume, costs, and profits relate to each other. In so doing, management is in a better position to make better decisions.

There are two ways of determining the break-even point—mathematically and graphically. The former is more precise, but the latter also offers much of value.

The need to separate costs into fixed and variable classifications presents a problem. It is an especially difficult problem since semi-variable expenses must be separated into their fixed and variable components.

The major limitation is the assumption that the basic figures will not change. This means that break-even analysis is more effective in planning for the short range, since forecasts of what future income and expenses are likely to be are not very reliable. But with an understanding of these limitations, much of value can be obtained from break-even analysis in planning and in controlling the things that affect profit in a foodservice establishment.

Questions

1. To what kind of questions can break-even analysis provide answers?

2. Explain the difference between fixed costs and variable costs.

3. What are semi-variable costs?

4. What is the function of the scatter graph?

5. Show the four steps in the mathematical method of determining the break-even point using fixed costs of $24,000, variable costs of $68,000, and sales of $100,000.

6. For what kinds of questions will break-even analysis provide answers? Give two examples.

7. Describe the graphical method of determining the break-even point.

12

Employee Training

Vital to the successful operation of any business are effective employees, because to a great extent the profitability of the operation depends on their performance. This is especially so in the foodservice industry, where a large amount of labor is used, and where, by the nature of the business, productivity is lower than in many other businesses.

Labor costs are taking a continually larger part of the sales dollar, while at the same time the problem of finding well-qualified employees gets more difficult. Seldom does the foodservice operator find personnel who are fully qualified for the job they are employed to do.

Certainly, a good employee training program is essential for a foodservice operation, if the employees are to acquire the knowledge, the job skills, and the right kind of work habits so they can perform efficiently. Training foodservice personnel is one of the best ways to increase the overall efficiency of the establishment, and as a result increase the profits. It is the responsibility of management, not only to see that employee training is done, but also to ensure that it is done correctly and at the right time.

Several kinds of training should be the concern of operators of foodservice establishments. There is training that is part of the orientation program for new employees. There is training for employees who have been on the job, to improve their performance. There is also training for employees for supervisory and other management positions.

Advantages to Both Employees and Management

An effective training program is an advantage to both employees and management. These gains can be measured in more take-home pay for employees and in higher profits for management. Advantages realized by employees include:

more job satisfaction

greater earning power

more chance for advancement

greater sense of security

more motivation

Advantages that management obtains include:

more production

better work methods and habits

lower operating costs

less supervision of workers required

more skilled workers

less labor turnover

Who Does the Training?

The question of who does the training is a major one, and many times the success or failure of the training program depends on the answer.

Too often in the foodservice industry, the training of employees is looked on as something extra that does not get adequate attention. New employees are given a few words that describe their duties and then they are turned over to another employee who may have many years of experience, but experience in doing things incorrectly.

The selection of the instructor is important to the success of the training program. There is really no one good answer to the question of who should train employees. However, it should be kept in mind that a training program in a foodservice operation is not designed to add to the employee's formal education. It is to provide ideas and knowledge of the job and skills, and to improve work habits. A good training program is oriented around the operation itself and its goals and systems.

Also, the person who is to do the training must have an interest in teaching and know something about the principles of learning. A competent instructor should be understanding and patient. The results of the training program depend on how good the instructor is, and how well he is prepared to conduct the training program. The preparation for instructing takes much more time than

159

the actual time of instructing employees. So, whoever is to do the training must have time to get ready. Management has a responsibility to see that this time is provided. The instructor must be familiar with the problems that workers in the establishment face daily. He needs to be able to communicate effectively.

Attributes of a Successful Instructor

There are some characteristics of successful instructors that make a good checklist for rating effectiveness. The successful instructor:

Knows the subject matter well.

Plans the lessons in detail.

Uses tact in dealing with trainees.

Is able to hold the interest of the trainees.

Is flexible and ready to change when better methods of instruction are found.

Is interested in each trainee as an individual, and in each trainee's values and goals.

This kind of person will do the training job in the way it should be done.

Methods of Training

A number of methods of training are used in employee training programs. These include:

Lectures

Conferences

Demonstrations

Visual presentations

On-the-job training

These methods can be used, but not all training programs or training situations are suited to one method for all training. A combination many times proves more effective. It is up to management to select the method or methods that will be most effective in the training situation.

Probably most frequently found in training of foodservice people is the on-the-job training method. This method provides the employee an opportunity to earn money while receiving training. In an on-the-job training program, the instructor can use lectures, discussions, and demonstrations, keeping in mind that he is trying to teach the skill of performing a task more efficiently while the worker is already on the job.

A successful on-the-job training program must be well planned. A number of things should be done if the training program is to be successful. These include:

> planning the objectives of the program in advance
>
> selecting the instructors and the trainees carefully
>
> determining what methods and equipment are necessary
>
> putting what is to be taught into writing
>
> following the rules and principles of learning

Steps in an On-the-Job Training Program

The four major steps in the on-the-job training method are:

Preparation

Presentation

Application

Follow-up

These are based on principles of habit formation which involve motivation, demonstration, and practice.

This step-by-step procedure can be of value to a management person who is not a professional educator, but does have the task of providing needed training to the employees. Use of this procedure provides the element of control to the training process and makes it possible to stay away from the haphazard unplanned efforts that many times are called training in foodservice operations.

Here is a brief description of each of the four steps that the instructor should follow in employee training.

Preparation   The trainees must be prepared for learning. Find out what they already know about the job. Give them a clear understanding of what the training program is all about, what is expected of them, and what value the program can be to them. It is usually necessary to inform and convince employees of the importance of the training.

It is not easy to change someone's work methods that have become a firmly entrenched habit with so much repetition. So, there is a selling job to do on what the results will be of learning new methods or techniques of doing the job. It is essential that the employees realize how the training they are to receive will affect their performance on the job and their opportunities for advancement.

Also, it is important to put the employees at ease. A new learning experience is an emotional experience for employees. They may have fears about whether they will learn or not. In some cases, they may have a resistance to the training program that needs to be minimized or overcome.

Presentation   Before the employees can apply what they learn in the training program, they must have a clear picture of the job to be done. It is at this time that the instructor can "de-skill" the job into simple step-by-step procedures, and can emphasize the key points clearly, completely and patiently. Table 12-1 indicates how this is done.

The instructor should take plenty of time to be sure that the trainees understand each step. Much of the success of the instruction will depend on this understanding. The instructor, by demonstrating, describing, and asking questions (to see if what he is teaching is understood) can ensure a successful learning experience. The trainees will understand thoroughly what they are to do and how to do it.

One point at a time is the rate of progress to be followed. The instructor should not move on to the next until he is sure the trainees know the point he has been discussing. It is pretty much a matter of tell, show, demonstrate, and question, with emphasis on the key points.

Application   This is where the trainees try out what they have been taught. They have a chance to practice what they learned, under the supervision of the instructor. They perform the job on their own, but they have a chance to ask about anything of which they are not sure. The instructor is there to correct anything they have forgotten or not learned.

At this point, if the instruction has been good, the employees should understand the job and the correct way to do it. This part of the training program takes considerable time on the part of the instructor. Close supervision is needed as the trainees try to follow the established pattern for doing the job. This close supervision is essential so mistakes can be pointed out and corrected, to ensure that the pattern finally established will be the correct one. The instructor can reduce the close attention as the trainees get the pattern well in hand, and let them perform the job without assistance.

Follow-up   The trainees are really on their own in this step. Yet, it is a step that is of utmost importance for a successful training experience. Unfortunately, in many foodservice training programs, not enough attention is given to the follow-up stage. The instructor assumes that he has trained the workers by the time the third step has been completed, and forgets the importance of checking.

A good instructor will follow up on the training given in the first three steps, and will check occasionally to see if the employees are doing the job in the correct way. It is essential, too, that the employees know to whom they should go for help if they run into difficulties.

Table 12-1   "De-Skilling the Job"

Use of Mixer—Medium Size Bench Model

Steps	Key Points
1. Place bowl in bowl support.	1. Bowl has three hook holes on outside of rim which are used to hold bowl in position: One in center back, one on each side.
	2. Place bowl into position with center back hook hole in correct contact with hook found in center back of support rim and with two side hook holes over two small posts found on either side of supporting rim.
	3. These three points must be correctly adjusted or paddle (or beater) will not move freely in the bowl.
2. Attach paddle, beater or dough hook.	1. Have lift handle in lowered position.
	2. Place paddle (beater or dough hook) inside the bowl. Bring top of paddle up onto rod, push up and turn to the right to lock into position.
3. Pull lift handle up.	To bring bowl into position.
4. Set speed.	Correct speed for mixing ingredients is important—otherwise splashing or over-mixing may result. SEE INSTRUCTIONS ON RECIPE CARD.
5. Start motor.	Turn switch to "on" position.
6. Stop mixer when through mixing.	Turn switch to "off" position.
7. Lower the lift handle.	This lowers the bowl.
8. Release paddle (beater or dough hook).	Push up, turn to the left, then pull down.
9. Lift bowl from rack support.	
10. SAFETY RULE.	Never put your hand or spatula inside the bowl when paddle is in motion.

Source: Establishing and Operating a Restaurant. U. S. Department of Commerce.

Length of Training Period

The question of how long a training period should be is, again, not one that can be answered easily and with only one answer. It will vary according to the job to be learned, the ability of the employee, and the ability of the instructor to teach effectively. The amount of training employees need varies a great deal. Some may not need any training at a particular time. Some may require more than others. Several employees being trained for the same job may require different periods of time.

Management has responsibility for control of the variables listed above. Attention to what specific job the employee has and what he needs to learn is one area where management needs to function. Certainly, it is management's responsibility to see that good instructors are used. Management also has a measure of control in the selection of new employees by hiring employees with ability and employees who can be more easily trained. The control of these variables has a major influence on the training period. They make it possible to train employees in shorter time and at less cost.

Changing Characteristics of Foodservice Workers

Of significance in connection with training programs are the changing characteristics of workers. Many younger people may have different values and different views on work than older employees who have worked for a period of years. They want jobs to be challenging. They want to have some say in regard to what they are required to do. They may not place as high a value on work, and may place more value on alternatives. Training programs must take into consideration the characteristics of workers, if they are to produce the desired results.

Management Holds Key to Successful Training

The attitude of management is an important factor in how effective a training program can be. First, management must be convinced that there is value in a training program; and management must be willing to do what is necessary to make an effective training program possible.

Most foodservice operations have some kind of training for employees. It may be as simple as a list of written instructions, a breakdown of the duties of the job, and descriptions of what employees are expected to do. It may involve such things as checklists, posters, booklets, demonstrations, and meetings of employees.

Many times these training programs accomplish little. The reason may be that the planning was poor, the instruction was not done well, or management did not provide the necessary support to the efforts. All too often, programs of this kind are failures because management views a training program in the wrong perspective. Management sees training as something designed to solve a specific problem that is causing difficulty for management. Instead, the training should be viewed as an essential, continuing part of the regular job that management has in the conduct of the business. Many times, management considers supervision in this light, but does not apply the same understanding to training.

Also, management must show employees that it has a sincere interest in the training program. If there is not this indication, supervisors and employees will not get involved in training programs with interest and enthusiasm.

One aspect of an active interest in training is a recognition that an effective training program is really a relationship between management and its employees that involves doing certain things and expecting certain things in a kind of two-way relationship. Management must:

> Convince employees that training is to their advantage.
>
> Show an active interest in training, that is made known to employees.
>
> Provide adequate training conditions, including time, space, and supplies and equipment, as well as qualified instructors.
>
> Establish effective communication and instruction.

At the same time, management should expect from the employees:

> evidence of interest
>
> courteous attention
>
> cooperation
>
> a desire to learn

Management has another obligation that many times may not get the consideration it should. Management should provide opportunity for employees who have been trained, are excellent workers, and have the potential for more challenging assignments. Training should not only prepare workers to perform more effectively the job in which they are now engaged, but also should prepare them for further training for more sophisticated work in the operation.

Sometimes the completion of training can be recognized by management in such a way that employees not only have the feeling of being better able to perform their duties, but also that management looks at them in a different light now that they have successfully completed a training program. Anything that relates reward in one form or another with successful completion of training offers a valuable assist in developing interest in and support for a training program.

Summary

Training of employees is one of the major functions of management. Employee training is an essential, continuous responsibility that management must recognize as being as important as the everyday supervision of employees. The effectiveness of employee training will be in direct relationship to the willingness of management to plan, organize, and guide the training effort.

The rewards from a good training program are many. On-the-job training is an excellent method for increasing efficiency and productivity and, as a result, the successful and profitable conduct of the business.

If training is to be effective, management must enlist the active participation of employees; convince employees of the value of the training program; demonstrate management interest in training; and plan the program well in advance, so that all that is required for successful training is available.

Allowing employees to learn a job by trial and error, which is sometimes called experience, can be very costly. The money put into training can be one of the most profitable investments that can be made.

Questions

1.   With what kinds of employee training should operators of foodservice establishments be concerned?

2.   List advantages to management and advantages to employees of an effective training program.

3.   What are the characteristics of a good instructor?

4.   Combinations of methods of training are better than one method. Name five methods of training from which management can select.

5.   What are the four major steps in the on-the-job training method? Describe briefly what happens in each method.

6.   Describe how the attitude of management toward the training program can affect the outcome of training efforts.

7.   What should management expect from employees who are participating in a training program?

13

Purchasing Food

Good food purchasing can probably be best described as having the right product, at the right place, at the right time, and at a price that you wish to pay. It is one of the major activities in the operation of any food-service establishment.

Food purchasing, just like the procurement function in any manufacturing enterprise, has much influence on the success or failure of the firm. The food-service operation, like a manufacturing enterprise, receives food supplies (raw materials), manufactures them into various dishes (products), and then serves (distributes) them to customers. Anyone can pick up a telephone and give an order to a purveyor, but ordering is not purchasing. Purchasing, or buying, is a complex activity with well-defined procedures that must be followed to achieve good results.

Food Buyer Needs Variety of Knowledge

Food purchasing for a foodservice establishment is a major responsibility. It is not a job to be passed along to whomever happens to be available. There must be a person responsible for purchasing activities who can base food-buying decisions on the following:

knowledge of the needs of the establishment

knowledge of the market in which he buys

knowledge of the products he must purchase

knowledge of the procedures he must use

knowledge of the results, including handling, of his purchases

Only with a knowledge of these things can the food buyer make wise buying decisions. Much of the success or failure of the business firm depends on these buying decisions; whether the firm be restaurant, inplant feeding, hotel, or any other type of foodservice operation.

Know Your Needs

Determining the needs of the establishment is the starting point for successful food purchasing. All too often, food buying is done with no clear picture in the mind of the buyer as to just what his needs are. The questions of what, where, when, and how must be answered before the actual purchase is made. If they are not, the results can be over-buying, under-buying, waste, dissatisfied customers, and lost profits.

To determine needs, the food buyer has to consider several things that affect the food requirements of the establishment. These include: the menu, the forecast, inventory, available capital, specifications, personnel, and past purchasing experience.

The Menu   Your menu determines what you buy. Unfortunately, many operators fit the menu to their purchases, rather than fitting their purchases to the menu. There may seem to be some temporary advantage in fitting menus to "good buys," but it is impossible to maintain the desired character of the operation if this becomes the procedure. Your menu is the key to your operation. It sets the tone, or class, of the establishment. In addition, the price-cost ratios of the various items should be set carefully to assure the desired profit. This cannot be done by working backward from purchases made at random. The menu, developed as a result of experience with customer demands and in light of optimum profit, should determine what you buy and in what form you buy it.

The cyclical menu can be of much help to the food buyer. He knows well in advance which items he must work with and is able to concentrate on and become familiar with these products. Also, by lending itself to more accurate forecasting, the cyclical menu aids in pinpointing the quantities needed.

The Forecast   Quantities to be purchased are influenced by what you expect to happen. Accurate forecasting does much to answer the question of how much to buy. Customer counts, records of customer choices among menu items, weather conditions, business ups and downs, special events, and all the other things that affect sales also affect purchasing. These things contribute to effective forecasting, indicate the changes that need to be made in planned menus, and show the increases or decreases in quantities needed.

Good forecasting is essential if there is to be good purchasing. This is especially so for items of which you buy substantial supplies well in advance of use.

Inventory   If knowledge of the inventory (goods on hand) is combined with the forecast, the food buyer can have a clear picture of the quantity he must purchase to meet the expected needs. For this knowledge to be of real value, however, it has to be accurate and current. Good inventory records must be kept up-to-date to be useful. If goods are ordered when sufficient quantities are on hand, or if duplicate orders are made, capital and storage space are tied up unnecessarily. You can avoid this by buying only as the need arises.

Capital on Hand   Closely allied with the size of the inventory is the amount of capital that can profitably be spared for advance purchasing. Many operators carry large inventories in the belief that they have profited by large-quantity buying. Often, however, the quantity saving is less than the return that could be attained if the capital tied up in inventory were put to other uses such as advertising, or improvement in facilities or decor.

There is no universal answer to guide the operator in the amount of capital that should be invested in inventory. It will vary with different types of food-service operations. It will vary, also, with the availability of markets. A summer resort that is far from markets will, of necessity, have to carry a relatively larger inventory than a restaurant located in a large city near sources of supply.

Many operators, however, carry more inventory than they need. The results are higher capital costs and higher food costs due to greater difficulty in controlling large stocks. Often, there is increased spoilage and theft when inventories are too large.

Other Factors   Other factors influence needs. The specifications for your products and the type of personnel that you employ affect what food you have to buy.

Another factor is experience with past purchasing. The good and bad buying experiences of the past can offer much in the way of direction. Many times, foodservice operators make the same food-buying mistakes over and over, in spite of the evidence in purchase records and lowered profit figures. Make the buying records do the job they can for you. Use them to check and analyze your buying methods to see if there is room for improvement.

Know the Market

In filling the food needs of a foodservice establishment, operators have numerous choices among the various sources of supply. Regardless of which one, or which combination, is selected, you should have a good knowledge of the market in order to buy more effectively.

Knowing the market involves finding out what sources of food are available; what foods can be obtained from each purveyor; and what the qualities, brands, and price ranges of the food are. It also means maintaining contact with the market to determine which supplies can best meet the needs of your establishment at a given time.

Select purveyors with a reputation for honesty and integrity, and get to know how they operate and how you can best use their services. Meet the salesmen and get to know them. Get acquainted with the products they have to offer. Make comparisons and choose the firm which can best fill your needs.

Knowledge of the market extends beyond a knowledge of people and firms. It also involves knowing about the flow of supplies through the marketing channels, the seasonality of supply, the fluctuation of prices and the effects of weather, business conditions, and other factors related to the supply of the food items you need.

Sources of Supply

Generally, the choice of a supply source is among wholesalers, institutional suppliers, salesmen of manufacturers of food products, truck jobbers, brokers, and cooperatives. The choice among suppliers, as well as the number of firms in each category, varies according to the location of the foodservice establishment. The choice is widest for locations near large urban centers. Also, some suppliers provide practically a complete line of products, while others specialize in one or a few lines.

Certain types of products may be offered by certain types of suppliers, and which one offers what varies considerably among products. For example, the operator is likely to get supplies of fresh fruits and vegetables from a terminal market wholesaler, jobber, or a vendor who specializes in the produce line. On the other hand, canned foods are usually purchased from a food manufacturer's house or a grocery wholesaler. Also, meat is available from salesmen of the large packers or from local vendors.

The Purveyor   Selecting the right purveyor is necessary for successful purchasing. It is obvious that you should select a purveyor who has a reputation for honesty and integrity. Less obvious is the need to pick one who understands the type of business you operate and who is interested and able to service you. If the quantity or quality of product you buy is not that usually handled by a particular vendor, you may create a situation that will result in higher prices or less satisfactory service than you can get elsewhere.

It is your responsibility to inform your vendors exactly what you expect from them. They cannot do their job properly unless you do this. Chances are that your purveyors want to help you in every possible way because the financial condition of their customers is important to them.

Your food salesman can be of considerable value to your operation. He can advise you as to the best use of products and he will keep you up-to-date on new products as they come onto the market. Your food salesman also should have a knowledge of the price situation in the market—both current and for the immediate future. This knowledge can help you to plan your buying to take advantage of the best market values.

Seasonality of Foods

The seasons for foods (all foods have a seasonal supply characteristic) are of much concern to the food purchaser. The choices between fresh, canned, and frozen items vary depending on the season. Certain fresh items, which are inexpensive and plentiful when in season, are prohibitive in cost when that season is over, and they should be purchased in canned or frozen form until the next peak season arrives. Certain foods, such as fresh fruits and vegetables, have relatively short, large-supply seasons, although some supplies are available over the year as shipments reach the markets from more distant producing areas. There are times in the year when the arrival of the new pack of canned or frozen products may result in attractive buys among what is left of the previous year's packs.

Seasonality in meat supplies involves a relatively long-time cycle. For poultry and dairy products, the cycle is somewhat shorter. Effects of severe weather conditions on the movement of food supplies through marketing channels are also of some concern to the food purchaser. Weather-caused delays in shipments and deliveries may require menu changes. The impact of adverse weather on certain crops may also result in short supply and/or price increases.

Sources of Market Information

There are several sources of market information. Among these are state and federal market reports, trade association reports, and the purveyor or his representative. State and federal departments of agriculture issue market reports which provide information about wholesale supplies, prices, and market conditions for such agricultural products as fruits and vegetables, poultry, eggs, and meats. Local or national trade associations usually base their information on the U.S. Department of Agriculture reports, tailored for local conditions. Some suppliers provide their customers with market information through weekly or monthly publications, and the food salesman is often an excellent source of current market knowledge.

An occasional visit to the market for fresh fruits and vegetables can be of

Figure 13-1   Supply Chart Showing Seasonality of
Fruits and Vegetables
Nearby Supplies—Boston

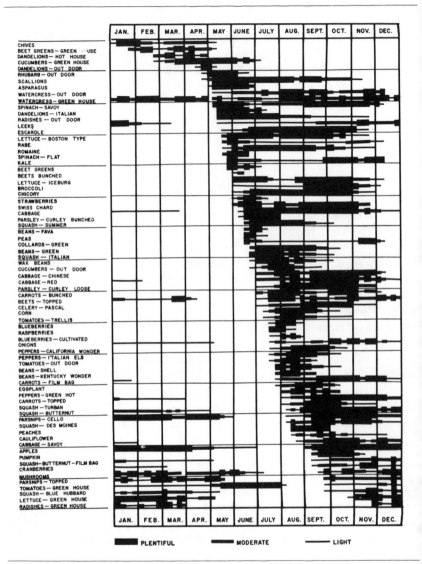

considerable value. It provides an opportunity to find out what is available, what the price ranges are, and what range of quality there is from which a choice can be made. Purchasing fruits and vegetables "sight seen" is preferable to telephone ordering. All of this information and knowledge about the markets nables the food buyer to have the widest choice of action. Only in this manner an he buy competitively, and this is the basis of good purchasing.

A craftsman would never attempt to create a product without a thorough nowledge of its raw materials. The same principle holds for the foodservice perator. You must understand the raw materials you use in your establishment. nderstanding means the ability to recognize the parts that quality, weight, rades, standards, and performance play in choosing the proper foods.

It is not enough that the operator know what he wants. He must also be ble to transmit his knowledge to the purveyor and other members of his own rganization. He does this through a set of specifications, clearly written, to void any misunderstanding concerning the standards that the materials he urchases must meet.

What You Should Know about Foods

Know Quality There are certain signs or indicators of uality that can be of value in recognizing qualities of items purchased. Color, ize, shape, odor, and degree of firmness indicate condition, maturity, or ripe- ess that affect the flavor, texture, and the "cookability" of foods.

The presence of defects, such as cuts, bruises, insect or disease damage, eformities, and mechanical injury, are indications of a loss of quality. Some dditional aspects of quality are not visible unless the product is cut. Dark center r hollow heart of some vegetables are examples of internal conditions that ou cannot see unless the vegetables are cut and inspected. Marbling and fineness f texture in meat products is another example.

Four major checks on the quality of food purchased are appearance, exture, size, and color. Whoever is responsible for purchasing food should be cquainted with the characteristics of products to the extent that he can check n these factors and have an adequate guide to product quality.

Know Weight Factors Weight of product offers much of alue to the purchaser who needs to check the quality and value of food pro- ured. Fruits that are heavy for their size are likely to have more juice than those hat are light for their size. Large turkeys are likely to produce more meat in roportion to bone than lighter-weight birds. Eggs of certain weights per case are arger in size than those of lesser case weight. Cans of certain sizes or weights rovide more product for the money than smaller sized cans. Beef from heavier nimals has quality characteristics different from those of meat from lighter- veight animals. These are all examples of the significance of weight in the urchasing of food supplies for the foodservice establishment.

Know Grades and Standards There are certain standard uides for foods that can do much to indicate what can be expected of a roduct, although not all products are graded. Standards are measurements of quality, weight, extent, value, or quantity. The quality standards for food products establish certain levels or degrees for the characteristics that make up the quality of the product. Grades are market classifications of quality. They reflect the relationship of the quality of the product to the standard established for the product, and they indicate the degree of variation from that standard. For example, a particular grade of beef indicates the quality of that meat. This, in turn, involves such things as the amount and distribution of fat, color and texture, amount of meat in relation to bone, and the age and sex of the animal. A particular grade of canned foods reflects the count, the syrup density, the size of the product, color, and other characteristics of the food in the can.

Grades are shown by the use of certain stamps or markings indicating the quality of the products which have been graded. One set of such grade symbol represents the official U.S. Department of Agriculture standards of quality, Figure 13-5. Although the U.S.D.A. grades are widely used, federal grading is on a voluntary basis, and many products are not graded. Private grades are more flexible than the U.S.D.A. grades and may show variation from season to season, but they are also good indicators of quality. There are also private grades or brands which represent certain qualities offered by manufacturers and distributors. Knowledge of grades and standards, and use of these grades in purchasing, are useful tools.

Performance The food buyer should know what the performance factors of different foods are under operating conditions. Certain classes of products that are satisfactory for one operator may be less than satisfactory for another. The buyer should purchase according to the use to which the product is to be put. It may be a complete waste of money, for example, to use a choice grade of beef from which to grind hamburger. The key is in buying for a particular use.

Writing Specifications

The use of specifications is one of the most important phases of good food purchasing. To be effective, these specifications should be in writing in order that there be no misunderstanding concerning them. Also, unless specifications are down in black and white, deviations from them are more likely to occur.

When writing specifications, keep in mind that they are simply a set of standards that clearly define the product as you wish to purchase it. A specification can be as brief or as elaborate as is necessary to meet the needs of your operation. All specifications should, however, contain certain basic information such as:

> name of the product
> federal grade, brand, or other quality designation

size of container or unit on which prices will be quoted

the quantity required in a container or per pound

In addition, any other information that helps describe the condition of the product, as you wish it to be delivered to your establishment, should be included in the specification. This information might include:

For canned goods   Type or style, pack, syrup density, count or portion size, specific gravity

For meat products   Age, cutting style, weight, sex condition, condition on receipt, amount of pre-preparation

For fresh fruits and vegetables   Variety, fill of container, place of origin

For frozen products   Condition on receipt (temperature)

For dairy products   Butterfat content

This is only a partial list, intended to show examples of the type of information that should go into a good food specification. What will finally go into a specification depends on the needs of the particular establishment. Figure 13-4 shows some sample specifications.

Tests Play Vital Role   To develop specifications for an establishment, it may be necessary to run a series of tests on the various products. These include:

cutting tests for canned goods

yield tests

cooking tests

shrink tests

taste tests

There is no easy road to developing specifications. Testing products and writing specifications is a laborious process. But, once the job has been completed, the investment in time and labor will pay off by taking the guesswork out of your food purchasing.

Know the Procedure   Knowing what is good buying procedure, and then doing the food buying in line with the requirements of good procedure, are essential for effective procurement. A good purchasing procedure includes the use of specifications, proper ordering procedures, and proper record keeping. Lack of proper buying procedure will often nullify knowledge of needs, market, and product. Also, a properly organized purchasing routine will save you time, eliminate chances of error, and assure that you have foods at the right place, at the right time.

It does no good to invest time and effort writing a clear, concise set of food specifications if they are not properly used in the purchasing procedure. Copies of the specifications must be put into the hands of the suppliers. This enables the seller to know exactly what the buyer wants when he orders a specific product. It also provides a means of resolving differences with the supplier when unsatisfactory products are delivered. Some establishments send out a list of foods needed, with the specifications stated for each item, to two or three suppliers. Each supplier inserts the price at which he will supply each item and returns the list. The buyer then telephones the supplier who gets the order.

One method of simplifying the use of specifications is to organize them into a book and assign a code designation to each specification. This provides positive identification of each item, without lengthy explanations on the order form. For example, the notation B-22 might be used to indicate to the supplier that he is to refer to your specification number B-22 for sirloin of beef when filling your order.

Developing the Order

There are various ways in which the needs for food are translated from the production plans to the order received by the vendor. Those responsible for production often use an order sheet (such as shown in Figure 13-6) that shows the quantities required for the meals planned during the period covered by the order. These are reviewed by the buyer, who uses his knowledge of market conditions to make some changes and then proceeds to obtain bids before placing the order. One method of recording bids on such products as meats and produce, which usually are ordered more often than other products, is to use a daily order sheet.

Another system involves use of a purchase order book. The listings of products are arranged in commodity classes. All the items to be ordered are indicated, and there are columns for entering the bid received from each supplier asked to make a bid. When the bids are in, the lowest bid for each item is circled usually with a different colored pen or pencil. Then, the items to be ordered from each vendor are transferred to a multiple copy purchase order form Figure 13-7. One copy usually goes to the vendor, one to the receiving clerk, one to the accounting office or manager, and one remains in the purchasing office.

If purchase orders are not written for all products purchased, it is important that some notation be sent to the receiving clerk and accounting department. If necessary, a copy of the daily order sheet may serve this purpose. Lack of coordination with other departments can cause a great deal of confusion in receiving and accounting for food purchases. When purchase orders are used they should provide the following information:

the amount of each item being purchased

the specification of the item being purchased

the price for the item, as provided by the supplier

expected date of delivery

any other information necessary to a particular purchase

Ordering Staple Items

Ordering goods that are regularly kept on hand in your establishment can be simplified by the use of either a par stock or a simple mini-max principle (Figures 13-2 and 13-3).

Par Stock   If ordering is done at regularly stated intervals, a par stock can be established and used as an ordering guide. This involves establishing a stated amount of stock that you have determined must be kept on hand to fill the needs of your operation. Once this has been done, it is necessary only to replenish your supply to this par at order time. For example, if ten cases of peaches were determined to be an adequate stock to carry you (with some margin of safety) from one delivery to the next, at each order time you would order whatever number of cases were needed to bring the count up to ten.

Mini-Max   When ordering and delivery times are flexible, a minimum as well as a maximum (par) stock can be set; and goods are ordered only when the minimum is reached. The minimum should be large enough to guarantee a supply between the time of ordering and the time of delivery. Applying this principle to the example using peaches, and establishing a minimum safety stock of, for example, three cases, you would order only when your stock of peaches fell to that level. Of course, by using this system, the size of your order for any one product would always be the same.

Standing Orders   Standing orders with purveyors are quite commonly used for certain products. If the supply of goods on hand is closely watched and any buildup or depletion of inventory corrected immediately, such orders can be used successfully. The danger in using standing orders is in the failure of the purchaser to supervise proper receipt of the products and the current inventory, with resulting discrepancies.

Bids in Competitive Purchasing

Obtaining bids from purveyors is the key to competitive purchasing. Without a survey of the market, and the range of prices available at a given time, it is impossible for the food buyer to purchase effectively.

Figure 13-2   Principles of Ordering

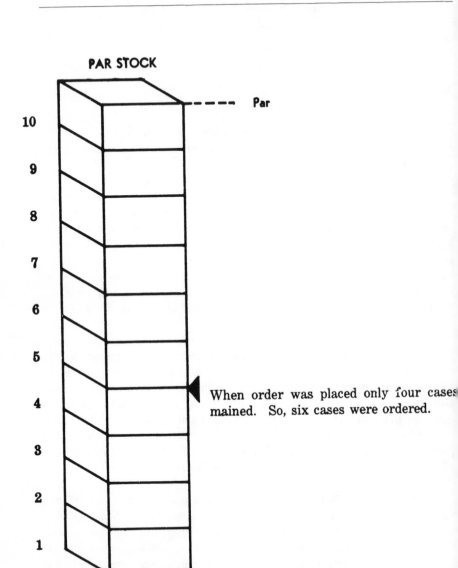

PAR STOCK

---- Par

When order was placed only four cases mained.   So, six cases were ordered.

Order enough so that total number of cases goes back to par each time.

*The figures 1 to 10 used above are for purposes of example only Numbers of units that represent par, maximum, and minimum will vary depending on the requirements of the individual food service establishment.

Figure 13-3   Principles of Reordering

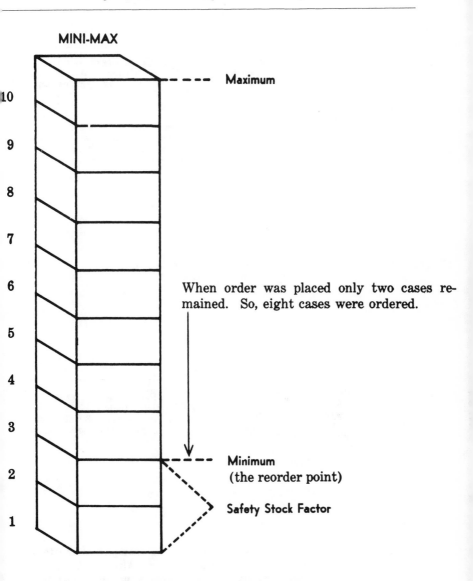

MINI-MAX

- - - - Maximum

When order was placed only two cases remained. So, eight cases were ordered.

Minimum
(the reorder point)

Safety Stock Factor

Order is not placed until stock falls to minimum point. Then, enough is ordered to return stock to maximum point.

Figure 13-4   Sample Specifications

Beef Rib, Oven Prepared
Upper Half U. S. Choice
Grade 30-35 lbs. Cut 4 inches
and 3 inches from eye muscle
at 12th and 6th ribs, respectively. Chine bone, blade
bone, and all cartilage removed. One inch average fat
cover. Deliver at 32-40° F.

Eggs, Fresh Whole
U. S. Grade AA. Jumbo,
minimum weight 30 oz./doz.,
or 56 lbs. per case. Not more
than 4 days should elapse between grading and delivery.
Not over 10% of the eggs
below minimum weight. 2%
allowance for breakage.

Butter, Chip
U. S. Grade AA. Case of
6/5# packages, 72 count. Deliver 32-45° F.

Chicken, Fryers
U. S. Grade A, 24 case, New
York dressed, 2-2¼ lbs.,
fresh killed. Under refrigeration not more than three
days. Deliver at 30-40° F.

Pear Halves, Canned
Bartlett, peeled, U. S. Grade
B, No. 10 cans, 30/35 count,
18-22 Brix. 62-63 oz. drained
weight.

The above specifications are intended only as examples of the form
and type of information that might be included. Although U. S. D. A.
grades are used here, brands or private grades may be substituted.
Note that these specifications have been kept as simple as possible
while still providing ample information to identify the product. If
necessary, however, they can be expanded to provide more exacting
standards.

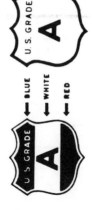

Bids may be open or sealed. The open bid may be in the form of a weekly price list from the purveyor, or it may be obtained daily by telephone, and recorded on the daily order sheet illustrated in Figure 13-6. Sealed bids, used most extensively by public institutions, provide maximum protection against misunderstanding and collusion. Sealed bids are based on product specifications submitted to the vendor. It is extremely important that these specifications be complete in every detail. They should include the degree of service expected from the vendor so that acceptance of the low bid, where required by law, will not leave a lack of proper delivery time or some similar limiting factor. Once the

Figure 13-6   Typical Order Sheet

DAILY ORDER SHEET						
Need	On Hand	Item	Amt. Ord.	Purveyor		

Figure 13-7 Typical Purchase Order Form

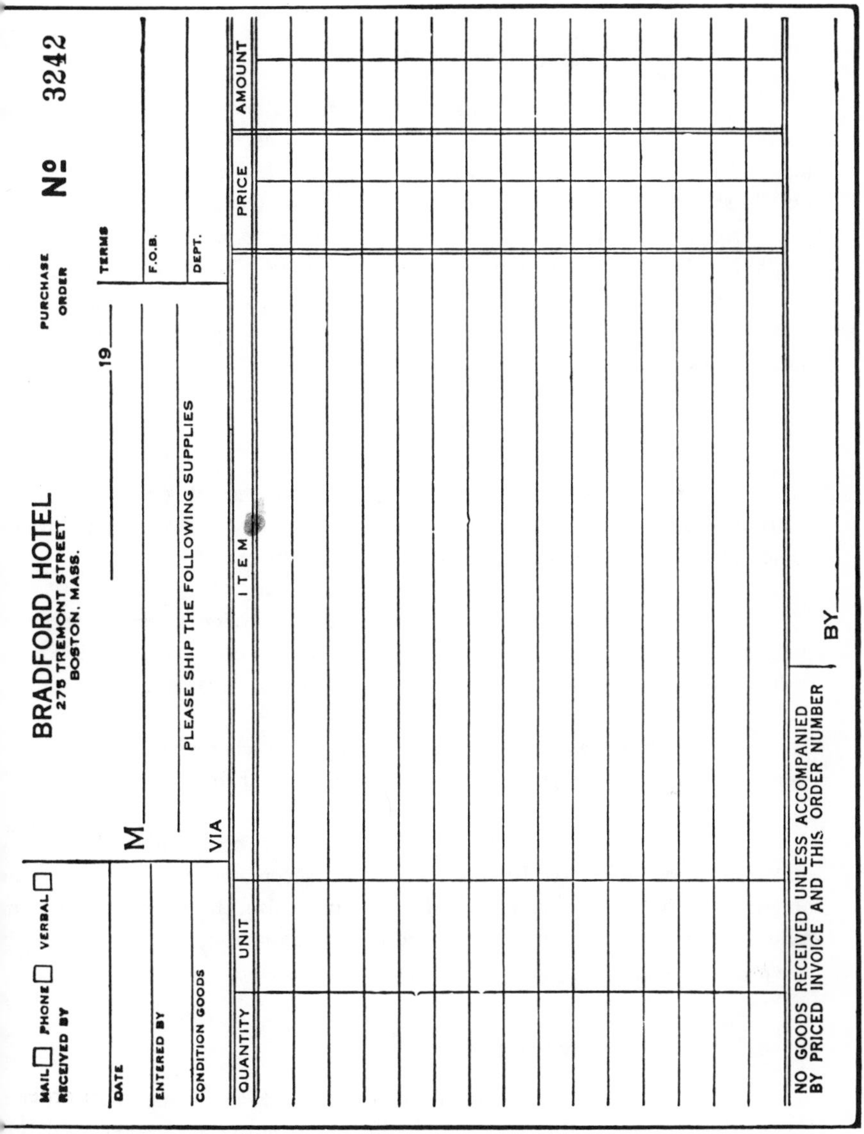

MAIL ☐ PHONE ☐ VERBAL ☐
RECEIVED BY

DATE

ENTERED BY

CONDITION GOODS

BRADFORD HOTEL
275 TREMONT STREET
BOSTON, MASS.

PURCHASE ORDER No 3242

_____ 19___ TERMS

M_____ F.O.B.

PLEASE SHIP THE FOLLOWING SUPPLIES DEPT.

VIA

QUANTITY	UNIT	ITEM	PRICE	AMOUNT

NO GOODS RECEIVED UNLESS ACCOMPANIED BY PRICED INVOICE AND THIS ORDER NUMBER

BY_____

bid has been accepted, it may be too late to correct a misunderstanding arisin from incomplete specifications.

Contract Buying

In some circumstances, when it is necessary for a foodservi operation to assure the supply to stabilize the price of a product, purchasin may be done on a contract basis. The contract between buyer and vende usually stipulates that a minimum quantity of goods will be purchased at a give price, over a stated time. The price may be fixed or it may have some degree flexibility. Because of the unpredictability of market fluctuations, it must I recognized that there is a certain amount of risk involved in contract purchasin Contract purchasing is usually done only by larger enterprises with experience purchasing staffs.

Relationships with Salesmen

A good food buyer will have an established policy in h relationships with food salesmen. Although this policy will vary with circur stances, there are certain basic features that should be included.

Who Can Order   Have a clear understanding in regard your ordering procedure. The vendor should know who is authorized to pla orders, and he should accept orders only from those so designated.

When to Call   Designate a time when you would like sale men to call, and make sure that you are available at that time.

Acceptance of Gifts   To buy competitively, the foo buyer must be objective. By prohibiting the acceptance of gifts, you avo obligations to vendors or to individual salespeople. Also, the prices you pay mu reflect the cost of these gifts to the vendor. In the long run, you gain nothing b accepting such gifts and you lose independence of action.

Know the Results

Good purchasing does not end with the giving of an order t the vendor. To ensure that good purchasing practices are not wasted, you mu determine that the goods received at the establishment are exactly the goo ordered. In addition, the handling of the goods after they are received is mo important in the preservation of quality and quantity. This means the maint nance of good receiving and storage practices. Another factor that must be tie in with good purchasing is a periodic review of the acceptability of the produc Is the product fulfilling the requirements of management and the custome

Although these areas may not be the responsibility of the purchasing agent, they must be coordinated with purchasing by management as a means of control. If the product does not meet management and customer requirements, information must be passed along to the food purchaser so that he can change the purchasing practice concerned.

Receiving   If no check is made on purchases as they are received at the establishment, there is no assurance that the food purchased meets the specifications. It is vital that the person responsible for receiving food be trained to recognize deviations from the specifications. It is at this point that these deviations are most easily rectified. Of course, not all operations can afford a full-time receiving clerk. The important thing is that the responsibility for this function be clearly assigned. It can be assigned to an employee on a part-time basis in combination with other duties. However, he should be responsible only to the manager or auditor for the receiving function.

Storage   All foods are perishable. Improper handling, between the time of delivery and the time foods are used in production, can greatly alter their character. In addition, loss through theft is always a possibility. Good storage control will minimize these problems and assure that food, as it is finally used in production, will conform to the desired standards.

Product Review   Management is constantly faced with this question: Does the food we purchase do the job we want it to do? Answering this question means keeping a close check on customer reaction to discover if the product is acceptable in your operation. Tastes change, fads come and go, and the alert operator adjusts purchasing to fit the desires of customers. This means that sales records must be kept and analyzed. Can the loss of an item's popularity be traced to some deficiency in purchasing, or is it a production or a service problem? The operator who maintains a close contact with the desires of his customers is able to adjust to change before the operation is adversely affected.

Summary

The right product, place, time, and price are the essentials of good food purchasing for a foodservice establishment. The person responsible for purchasing must know the needs of the operation, the market, products to be purchased, procedures to use, and the results of the purchases. Determination of needs requires information on the menu, a forecast, a report on inventory, knowledge of the extent money can be spent, as well as experience.

There is a choice of suppliers that varies according to location, a seasonality to food supplies, and a variety of sources of market information all of concern to foodservice buyers. Specifications and the use of grades assist in making good selections. Cutting, yield, and cooking tests are used in developing specifications.

Using the par stock or mini-max principles can simplify ordering items that are regularly kept on hand. Sometimes standing orders are used. Obtaining bids is a key to competitive purchasing, and use of order forms assists in determining the best selections.

Checking the results of purchases, the handling of the purchased food, and how well it meets the need is an essential part of good food buying.

Questions

1.   The food purchaser for a foodservice establishment should have knowledge of many things, if the food purchasing decisions are to be good ones. List things about which the food buyer should be well informed.

2.   What should be considered by the food buyer in determining the needs of the foodservice establishment?

3.   Explain how seasonality of foods affects the form in which various products should be purchased.

4.   Describe the signs or indicators of quality that can be of value to the food buyer in determining the quality of food items.

5.   Explain the difference between standards and grades.

6.   Prepare a sample specification for: (a) canned peas; (b) fresh apples; and (c) meat.

7.   In developing specifications for a foodservice operation, several tests are conducted. Name five of these tests.

8.   Explain what par stock and mini-max are, and their value in the ordering of staple food items.

14

Purchasing Beef

The purchase of beef represents major expenditures for many foodservice establishments, since it is a high-cost item and such relatively large amounts are purchased. Poor purchasing practices, mistakes, and bad judgment in this important purchasing task can have serious repercussions on the establishment's total food cost and on profits. So, good beef purchasing is an area of concern for most foodservice people.

To do good purchasing of beef, the buyer needs knowledge, information, judgment, and experience. From this base, he then develops the skills that ensure good buying. An effective buyer must know what the foodservice establishment needs are. The buyer must also know about the market, especially the market for beef. He, of course, needs a knowledge of beef and beef products; and he must know about the procedures involved in doing the best job of buying beef and then in handling and storing it after purchase. Some of this information can be acquired easily and remembered; other information should be referred to when needed, but it is important to know where it can be obtained.

Know the Needs of the Establishment

The foodservice buyer must keep in mind the needs of the operation for which he is buying and then find the products available on the market that will meet those needs. He must be aware of alternate choices that will meet the needs when the primary selection is not available. Every food service operation is different and the combination of needs for one particular place differs from that for another. So, determining the needs, first of all, is a major responsibility of the buyer. Then, he must have those needs translated into the specifics of the market, to perform his job most effectively.

In any planning of beef purchasing, the start must be made with the menu. This is the basis of the food production aspects of the establishment, and the purchasing operation must meet the needs of production. The menu indicates the items to be purchased, and it also shows the timing of the purchases.

Advance Menu Knowledge

To do an effective job, the buyer must know in advance what the menu requires. How much advance notice varies from one operation to another. All too often this important need is forgotten, and the buyer is forced to get items from any place he can with no opportunity to obtain the best price. Sometimes, even, a compromise must be made on quality.

So that the buyer has enough time to do an effective purchasing job, the menus should be made out well in advance of the time of purchase. If a cyclical menu is used, the buyer has much of the information on what is to be purchased and when it is needed, well in advance of the time of need. Also, the fact that the cycle menu can provide more accurate forecasting, helps provide the information needed on what quantities should be purchased.

Good forecasting is essential to good planning of purchases. That and the menu provide the information or knowledge that the buyer must have. The menu indicates what he should buy and when the items will be needed. The forecast indicates the number of covers that will be served, and this tells the buyer how much of each item will be needed. What, when, and how much are the questions for which answers must be available, if purchasing is to be planned efficiently.

Determining Quality Needs

The quality of beef that the foodservice operation needs has a big effect on the job of the purchaser. What quality should be bought? This varies among establishments, since there is no one quality that is going to fit the needs of all kinds of operations. Also, there is no one grade or quality that will meet all of the needs to which beef is put. For some uses, a particular quality is needed; for other uses, lesser quality is needed.

To determine the needs of a particular operation, it is necessary to consider the kind or class of foodservice and the type of customers or clientele that are served. Generally, the customers of an establishment that has a high menu price structure will want better quality meat than the clientele of a place with lower prices. Often, institutions will want a lower grade than many other kinds of foodservice operations.

It is important that the beef be purchased for the use intended, and this usually means the use in a particular establishment. Buying according to use is a way in which lower purchase costs and higher consumer satisfaction can be realized. This means making the use of the important factor in what is purchased, rather than the type of establishment, or the operator's desire that nothing but U.S.D.A. choice beef be used. Many times, the results would be better in terms of cost and customer satisfaction, if prime or choice beef steaks and ribs are purchased, and lower grades are selected for use as pot roasts, hamburger, swiss steak, and similar menu items.

A testing program to determine what quality grade is needed for the various items on the menu can be conducted. In this way, the foodservice operator can decide the quality grade that best suits the product that he sells. The program of testing should include tests of yield, cooking tests, and taste tests. The data obtained will answer the questions of cost, cooking results, and customer satisfaction with the menu item.

What Size and Weight Cuts to Buy

Involved in good purchase planning is a decision on what size and weight of the various cuts of beef are needed. The yield for particular cuts and the size of portions desired are things that must be considered in reaching this kind of decision. Different weights of particular cuts of meat yield appreciably different amounts of edible meat; and this is a significant factor in selecting from among the available weight ranges. The yield tests provide information that enables the operator to determine which weight ranges will give him the best value for his particular operation.

Publications such as the *Institutional Meat Purchase Specifications* of the U.S. Department of Agriculture, and the *Meat Buyers Guide* of the National Association of Meat Purveyors provide information of value to foodservice operators who buy beef in quarters or larger units and are interested in estimating the weights of the primal fabricated cuts from these units.

Other things may affect what weights and sizes of beef cuts are to be purchased. The personnel employed by the operation and their capabilities is a major factor. Also, the equipment that is available in the establishment affects what weights and sizes can be used effectively. These would seem to be obvious limiting factors, but in many instances, these considerations are overlooked or not given adequate attention.

Importance of Portion Size

Much beef is purchased in portion-ready form, including such items as prefabricated steaks and chops. In these cases, the portion size can be related to the purchase price easily. But oven-ready or cuts that have not been prefabricated present more of a problem. For example, an oven-ready rib weighing 20 lbs. will yield an 8-oz. portion of sliced beef that has a greater thickness but a smaller diameter than the same portion from a rib weighing 25 pounds, all other factors being equal. In that case, what weight rib to buy may depend on how the operator wants the sliced rib to appear on the plate.

Whether to Make or Buy

How much pre-preparation should beef have when it is purchased? This is a question that gets more attention now than in earlier times. It is a question of considerable importance from a cost point of view. The food service operator needs to decide whether to buy beef carcasses, sides, quarters or primal cuts and do a large part of the butchering on the premises; or to have the supplier provide portion-ready or oven-ready cuts all prepared to go into the oven or broiler.

In recent years, there has been a disappearance of the butcher from most foodservice operations, and a greater dependence on portion-ready and oven ready meat. There are, however, still foodservice operations that do butchering that involves breaking down larger cuts into smaller cuts.

In order to decide whether to make or buy, the operator needs to determine the exact cost to put a portion of beef on the table in front of the customer. Involved in this cost figure are:

all cost of material

cost of labor to prepare the portion

cost of handling the meat from the time it arrives at the foodservice operation

Some other factors must also be considered in addition to exact portion cost. What control of quality is there in the establishment? How skilled are the meat preparation personnel? Also, can the local purveyors meet the exact specifications of the establishment for preportioned and prefabricated cuts? As the trend toward eliminating the large bones and the heavy fat from beef and breaking down the carcass into primal and smaller cuts has accelerated, it is much easier to get the specifications met locally than it was in the past.

Methodology of Comparison

An example will illustrate how the make-or-buy decision can be made. The foodservice operator in this case has a choice between purchasing a primal rib (U.S.D.A. Institutional Meat Purchase Specification Number 103) at $1.40 per pound; or a roast-ready rib (U.S.D.A. Institutional Meat Purchase

Specification Number 109) at $1.85 per pound. The operator needs to determine which to select.

First to be determined is the comparative price of the two ribs ready to be put into the oven. On the butcher's test card (Figure 14-1) is shown the breakdown of primal rib. The rib, which has a purchase price of $1.40 per pound, has, by the time it is ready to cook, a value of $1.956 per pound. That is a difference of 55.6 cents from the as-purchased price of $1.40; and that figure of $1.956 per pound is about 11 cents per pound more than the cost of the roast-ready rib ($1.85).

So, the decision on whether or not to get the rib and break it down in the foodservice establishment depends on the cost comparison, and also the cost of breaking down that rib on the premises. If the labor and handling costs are appreciable, the decision should be to buy the roast-ready rib, as would be the case also when the cost of the roast-ready rib is lower, as in the example. In making this comparison, it is important to know whether it will be possible to eliminate labor cost if the roast-ready product is purchased. Or, will the labor be there anyway and perhaps be better engaged in breaking down the larger cut?

The changes in the meat industry that have seen more and more beef broken down into cuts near the production areas and shipped, some in frozen form, to the distribution areas, have produced a large increase in the use of ready cuts, and a disappearance of butchers except from the large foodservice establishments. The two test cards have considerable use for the food purchaser in making purchase comparisons.

The Butcher's Test Card The butcher's test card (Figure 14-1) shows exactly what happens to the primal rib from the time the butcher at the foodservice establishment receives it as purchased until it is ready to go into the oven after he finishes breaking it down. It shows the byproducts obtained in this process that can be used in the operation, with market prices assigned to them. Subtract the value of these byproducts from the original purchase price of the rib, and the result is the value of the now ready-to-cook rib. In this example, the value has gone up from $1.40 per pound to $1.956 per pound.

There is a ready-to-cook multiplier at the bottom of the test card. This figure is obtained by dividing the ready-to-cook cost per pound by the as-purchased price per pound. Thus, $1.956 divided by $1.40 equals 1.40. This is the cost multiplier, which can be used to determine the ready-to-cook value per pound of a similar size primal rib when price changes occur, without the need to make another yield test. It means that the ready-to-cook price is 1.40 times the as-purchased price.

The Cooking Loss Test Card The other test card (Figure 14-2) shows what happens to the rib between the time that it goes into the oven

Figure 14-1 Butcher Test Card

ITEM Roast Rib #103 **GRADE** Choice **DATE**
PIECES 1 **WEIGHING** 30 **LBS.** **OZ.** **AVERAGE WEIGHT**
TOTAL COST $ 42.00 **AT $** 1.40 **PER** lb. **SUPPLIER**

Breakdown	*No.*	*Weight Lb.*	*Weight Oz.*	*Ratio to Total Weight*	*Value Per Pound $*	*Total Value $*	*Cost of Each Lb.*	*Cost of Each Oz.*	*Portion Wt. in Oz.*	*Portion Cost*
Short ribs		2	4	.08	1.00	2.25				
Boneless meat		4	0	.13	1.20	4.80				
Bones		3	0	.10	.06	.18				
Fat		3	0	.10	.06	.18				
Cutting loss			4	.008	1.40	.35				
Rib, 3x4, oven-ready		17	8	.583	1.956	34.24	1.956	.122		
TOTAL		30	0	1.00						

Remarks:

Ready to Cook Cost Multiplier
1.40

Figure 14-2 Cooking Loss

COOKED 5 HOURS 45 MINUTES AT 325 DEGREES
REMOVED FROM OVEN AT 140 DEGREES INTERNAL TEMPERATURE.

Breakdown	*No.*	*Weight Lb.*	*Weight Oz.*	*Ratio to Total Weight*	*Value Per Pound $*	*Total Value $*	*Cost of Each Lb.*	*Cost of Each Oz.*	*Portion Wt. in Oz.*	*Portion Cost*
Ready-to-cook weight		17	8	.583	1.956	34.24				
Cooked weight		14	0	.47						
Loss in cooking		3	8	.12						
Usable trim		1	0	.03	1.20	1.20				
Bones and waste		1	8	.05						
Carving shrink			8	.02						
Salable meat		11	0	.368	3.22	35.44	3.22	.201	8	1.61
TOTAL										

Remarks:

No. of Portions 22
Portion Cost Multiplier 2.30

and the time it is on the plate of the customer. It measures the loss that occurs in cooking.

In the example, there are 11 pounds of salable meat remaining after the shrinkage during the cooking process and the trim loss in the carving process. The ready-to-serve portion cost is $3.22 per pound; and that figure compares with the $1.40 cents per pound paid to the supplier when the meat was purchased. The test card also shows that an 8-ounce serving would cost $1.61. So, the ready-to-eat cost multiplier indicates that every pound of this meat that is put into the portions of meat served to the customers costs 2.30 times the price that was paid for the meat to the meat supplier. This means that if there is a 10-cent increase in the as-purchased price of primal rib, the ready-to-serve cost per pound will increase by 23 cents.

Variety in Cuts of Beef

There is a great variety in the forms and cuts of beef that are available. They range from whole carcasses to the small individual retail cuts and consumer-size portions. Which cuts to buy for a foodservice operation will depend on a number of factors. What is the size of the establishment? Where is it located in relation to the suppliers? What kind of menu is being used? How capable are the personnel and how many are there? What are the facilities? Even though the amount of beef foodservice people buy in fabricated form is increasing relatively rapidly, there are still operators who purchase beef in the larger wholesale cuts.

In fabricating beef, the side is divided into forequarters and hindquarters. Then the hindquarter is broken down by taking the flank from the loin and round sections. The rump is taken from the round, and then the round is cut up into the top round, the bottom round, and the knuckle. The forequarter is broken down by dividing the brisket, chuck, and shank from the plate and rib. This separates the forequarter into two parts. Then, the carcass is broken down to a greater extent into the smaller cuts. The Beef Cuts Chart (Figure 14-3) shows the various wholesale and retail cuts and shows from what part of the carcass each cut comes. Also, there is additional information on the chart regarding cooking method. Figure 14-3 was prepared by the National Live Stock and Meat Board and shows the cuts most commonly found throughout the United States. In some sections, especially in New England, the method of cutting and the names of cuts traditionally have differed from those usually found in the rest of the country.

The Disappearing Butcher

Cuts of beef purchased by foodservice operators range all the way from a side of beef to an individual serving. Some big foodservice operations that use a great deal of beef buy the larger cuts and a butcher breaks down the

Figure 14-3   Beef Cuts

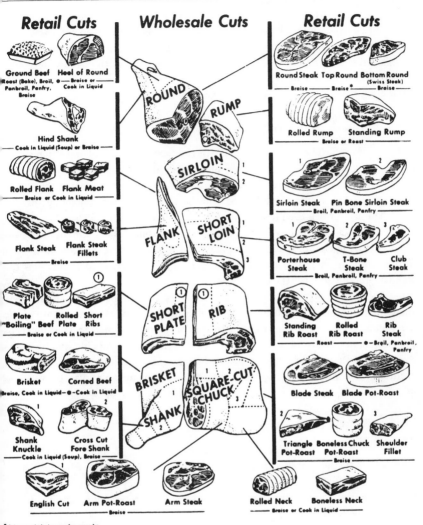

Source: National Live Stock and Meat Board

side into smaller cuts on the foodservice premises. Multi-unit foodservice companies often have butchers at the central commissary where beef is broken down into the smaller cuts from the wholesale cuts and the smaller cuts sent out to the various units.

But, the trend is very evident. Butchers are disappearing and are found much less frequently in foodservice operations than in the past. More and more beef is now being purchased in portion sizes all ready to cook, such as individual steaks and chops, and in the oven-ready sizes, such as pretrimmed rib roasts.

The old way of buying large wholesale cuts and fabricating the beef on the premises requires much more in the way of facilities than the storage necessary for holding a supply of the smaller size cuts until they are used. Also, higher labor costs have made the cost of fabricating on the premises much higher.

Standardization of Names of Meat Cuts

There are differences in the names of cuts of meat depending on where in the country the meat is purchased; and this has provided difficulty for food buyers. But there is a change under way, most evident at the retail food store level, where there had been more than 1,000 retail meat-cut names.

The uniform meat identity program developed by the National Live Stock and Meat Board has reduced the many names to about 300 standard names for fresh cuts of beef, pork, lamb, and veal. The uniform meat identity labels have information on the type of meat, the primal or wholesale cut, and then the standard retail name for the cut.

Table 14-1 lists the popular names for many retail beef cuts, and the new standard names under the uniform meat identity program. More and more of the meat industry is moving into line with this program, designed to take much of the confusion out of the names used for cuts of meat. It is possible that, in states that have laws regarding names of food items including meat cuts, there will eventually be provisions requiring that standard names for cuts be used on menus.

Meat Specifications

Using specifications in the purchase of beef is one way of ensuring that the product purchased is what is needed and what has been ordered. Specifications should be in writing, so that they are clearly understood by the supplier and so that there will not be misunderstandings regarding them, and resulting deviations from them.

Certain basic information should be in the specifications so that the specifications are really a set of standards that clearly define the product as the foodservice operator wants to purchase it. A specification can be elaborate or it can be simple; it can be long or brief. What form it takes depends on what is needed to meet the requirements of the particular foodservice operation. However, all specifications should contain:

> name of the cut that is desired
>
> federal grade, brand, or other designation of the quality wanted

federal designation of yield wanted

size or unit on which the supplier will be quoting prices

quantity required in a container, or the quantity per pound of the product if count is also a measure that is used

The specification should also include any information that helps to describe the condition of the product as the foodservice operator wants it delivered to his place of business. In the case of a beef specification, this information might include the age of the animal; the cutting style; weight; sex condition; condition at the time the product will be received, including the state of refrigeration, the amount of pre-preparation that should be done, the style of trim, and the packaging.

An example of a specification for beef will serve to illustrate what should be included. Figure 14-4 is typical of what a foodservice operator might work out, based on his own yield test, as being the product needed for his establishment. This particular specification happens to be very similar to U.S.D.A. Institutional Meat Purchase Specification Number 176.

The U.S.D.A. Institutional Meat Specifications

The foodservice operator may not want to develop his own specifications to meet the unique needs of his business. Having a specification that is so different from the needs of other customers might mean that suppliers will charge extra or will not be interested in providing products that meet this specification.

Specifications that have been prepared to meet foodservice needs can be used. Most popular of these are the U.S. Department of Agriculture Institutional Meat Purchase Specifications. They are often referred to as "IMPS." The Institutional Meat Purchase Specifications for Fresh Beef are Series 100. They may be purchased from the U.S. Government Printing Office, Washington, D.C. 20250.

The U.S.D.A. Acceptance Service

Another service of the United States Department of Agriculture that is of much value to meat purchasers is the U.S.D.A. Acceptance Service. This service is designed to ensure that the meats purchased comply with the detailed specifications that have been approved by U.S.D.A.

The specifications are provided to an approved supplier. Then, after bids have been made by that vendor and accepted by the foodservice purchaser, a grader inspects the beef order to see if what is being provided complies with the specifications. If the products meet the specifications, the meat grader will accept them and certify that they meet the specifications. There is a charge for this service which sometimes is paid by the supplier and other times is paid by the purchaser, depending on the arrangements between them. The additional

Table 14-1   Standard Names for Cuts of Beef

Traditional Names	Standard Names
Shoulder Roast	Beef, Chuck, Shoulder Pot Roast, Boneless
London Broil	Beef, Chuck, Shoulder Steak, Boneless
Stewing Beef	Beef, Chuck, for Stew
Short Ribs	Beef, Chuck, Short Ribs
Short Ribs Barbecue	Beef, Chuck, Flanken Style Rib
Soup Bones	Beef, Marrow, Bone
Soup Neck Bones	Beef, Chuck, Neck Bones
Chuck Roast, Blade Cut	Beef, Chuck, 7-Bone Pot Roast
Chuck Steak, Blade Cut	Beef, Chuck, 7-Bone Steak
Chuck Roast, First Cut	Beef, Chuck, Blade Roast
Chuck Steak, First Cut	Beef, Chuck, Blade Steak
Blade Steak, Bone In	Beef, Chuck, Top Blade Steak
California Chuck Roast	Beef, Chuck, Under Blade, Pot Roast
California Chuck Steak	Beef, Chuck, Under Blade Steak
Chuck Eye Pot Roast	Beef, Chuck, Mock Tender
Blade Steak Roast	Beef, Chuck, Top Blade Roast, Boneless
Blade Steak	Beef, Chuck, Top Blade Steak, Boneless
Boneless Chuck and Undercut Roasts	Beef, Chuck, Eye Roast, Boneless
Boneless Chuck and Undercut Steaks	Beef, Chuck, Eyesteak, Boneless
Brisket, Double Cut	Beef Brisket, Point Cut, Boneless
Brisket, Single Cut	Beef Brisket, Flat Cut, Boneless
Skirt Steak	Beef Plate, Skirt Steak, Boneless
Flank Steak	Beef, Flank Steak
Shin Center Cut	Beef, Hind Shank, Center Cut
Shin End Cut	Beef, Hind Shank, Cross Cuts
Rib Roast 7-inch cut	Beef, Rib Roast, Large End Ribs 6–7
Club Rib Roast (Rib Roast 1st 3 Ribs)	Beef, Rib Roast, Small End Ribs 11–12
Rib Steak	Beef, Rib Steak, Large End, 7th Rib
Delmonico Steak, Bone In	Beef, Rib Steak, Small End, Ribs 11–12
Boneless Sirloin Steak	Beef, Rib Steak, Small End, Boneless Ribs 11–12
Delmonico Steak	Beef, Rib, Eye Steak
Delmonico Steak Roast	Beef, Rib, Rib Eye Roast, Ribs 6–12
Beef Riblets	Beef, Rib, Back Ribs
Top Rib Roll	Beef, Rib, Rolled Cap Pot Roast

cost that is involved will be more than offset by the advantages obtained by large-scale foodservice meat purchasers.

Information on the Acceptance Service and how it can be related to the foodservice meat purchasing program can be obtained from Livestock Division of the Consumer and Marketing Service, U.S. Department of Agriculture, Washington, D.C. 20250.

The Sources and Supply of Beef

There are two major sources of the nation's beef supply. One is from dairy animals that are sold for meat after they have outlived their useful-

Table 14-1   Continued

Traditional Names	Standard Names
Club Sirloin Steak	Beef, Loin, Top Loin Steak,
Club Sirloin Steak, Boneless	Beef, Loin, Top Loin Steak, Boneless
T-Bone Steak	Beef, Loin, T-Bone Steak
Porterhouse Steak	Beef, Loin, Porterhouse Steak
New York Sirloin Steak	Beef, Loin, Shell Sirloin Steak
Rump Steak (Short Cut Rump Steak)	Beef, Loin, Top Sirloin Steak, Boneless
Tenderloin Roast	Beef, Loin, Tenderloin Roast
Tenderloin Tips	Beef, Loin, Tenderloin Tips
Tenderloin Steak	Beef, Loin, Tenderloin Steak
Top Round Steak (first cuts)	Beef, Round, Top Round Steak, First Cut
Top Round Steak	Beef, Round, Top Round Steak
Braciole (thin cut top)	Beef, Round, Top Round Steak, Butterfly
Top Round Roast (Top Round Steak Roast)	Beef, Round, Top Round Roast
Tenderettes	Beef, Round, Cubed Steak
Round Tip Roast	Beef, Round, Bottom Round, Rump Roast
Bottom Round Roast	Beef, Round, Bottom Round Roast
Swiss Roast	Beef, Round, Bottom Round Roast, Center Cut
Swiss Steak (Sandwich Steak)	Beef, Round, Bottom Round Steak
Eye Round Roast	Beef, Round, Eye Round Roast
Eye Round Steak	Beef, Round, Eye Round Steak
Top Sirloin Roast (Face Rump Roast)	Beef, Round, Tip Roast
Face Rump Steak	Beef, Round, Tip Steak
Top Sirloin Steak	Beef, Round, Tip Steak, Cap Off
Beef Kabobs	Beef, Round, Cubes for Kabobs
Cube Steak	Beef, Chuck, Cubed Steak
Beef Cutlets	Beef, Chuck, for Cutlets
Bottom Round Stew Beef	Beef, Round, for Stew

Note: The standard names for beef cuts state: (1) the kind of meat (Beef); (2) the primal or wholesale cut (Chuck, Hip, Loin, or Round); and the retail cut (such as Blade Roast). Thus, stated is the kind of meat, where the meat comes from on the animal, and from what part of the primal cut the meat came. Labels that reflect this information are in use in retail stores.

ness as milk producers in dairy herds. The other is from animals that have been bred for beef production and have been raised for that purpose.

Most of the meat from dairy animals is in the lower grades and is used for processing into meat products. Very little ever gets to the institutional and retail outlets.

Most of the beef in the better grades comes from animals specifically bred to produce high quality beef. Most of these animals are fattened in feedlots for the last 3 to 6 months before going to slaughter. Under those conditions, their physical activity is restricted, and they are fed a high energy diet to obtain the most economical gains in weight and to cause fat to be deposited in desirable areas, and so produce the marbling that is desirable in meat. These animals

Figure 14-4   Sample Specification

ITEM Boneless Strip Loin
1. GRADE U.S.D.A. Top Choice
2. WEIGHT 14-17 pounds
3. AVERAGE THICKNESS OF SURFACE FAT ¾ inch (1 inch maximum at any point except for seam fat).
4. CONDITION ON RECEIPT Chilled
5. ADDITIONAL REQUIREMENTS
   a. All bones to be removed by scalping, producing a smooth inner surface.
   b. Flank edge to be removed by a straight cut, perpendicular to the outer skin surface, starting at a point on the rib and not more than 6 inches from the extreme outer tip of the loin eye-muscle, and continuing on a straight line to a point on the butt end not more than 4 inches from the extreme outer tip of the loin eye-muscle.

---

produce high quality beef. Animals that are allowed to feed on grass pasture do not produce as high a quality.

About three-quarters of all the beef produced in the United States is sold as fresh meat; and this includes about all of the beef that comes into the U.S.D.A. grades of prime, choice, good, and commercial, as well as about half of the beef in utility grade. The other 25 percent of the beef produced is lower grade and goes into processing for meat products.

Small Percentage Grades Prime

Much is heard about U.S. prime in foodservice operations, but prime grade carcasses make up only a very small percentage of the total amount of meat that is graded. It is very expensive to produce such high quality beef. Meat of this grade has a great deal of fat, which means heavy trimming of the carcass, with substantial reduction in the amount of edible meat that is obtained.

Most of the beef that meets the prime grade requirements goes into hotel and restaurant outlets, and is used in foodservice operations where the check average is high, and the demand is for the best quality without too much concern for price.

Much Transportation Is Involved

There was a time many years ago when the meat supply was grown in the eastern part of the United States; but as the country developed, the location of large-scale meat production moved west. The places where beef is produced are now far away from the places where most of the beef is used. There is about a thousand miles from the open range to the storage box of a restaurant for the average pound of meat.

Animals are slaughtered and the dressed beef is chilled and ready to move to the distant markets within two days. Normally, four or five days are needed to transport beef from midwestern packing plants to the wholesale branches of the meat packing firm. Then, the meat usually is sold to foodservice operators and retailers within a few days after it reaches those wholesale outlets. This adds up to about ten to twelve days between the time the beef animal is slaughtered and the time the meat arrives at the foodservice establishment.

There is a value in this lapse of time, as far as beef is concerned, since it provides an aging period. From about the time the animal is slaughtered until fourteen days of holding time go by, the beef gradually increases in tenderness. But after that two weeks in storage, there is very little change in the degree of tenderness. Beef is held longer in storage in some cases, but this is to obtain more aged flavor rather than to increase tenderness.

Market Sources of Beef

There are many kinds of firms operating in the market, some supplying one kind of beef and others supplying other kinds. Foodservice operators usually buy their supplies of meat from a branch of one of the packing companies that has purchased the cattle, slaughtered the animals, and then put onto the market cuts of various types and sizes.

Beef supplies can also come from a service wholesaler. He does not buy cattle and is not in the slaughtering business. Instead, he purchases meat from the packers and distributes it to customers. Some packers sell their production of meat through these independent service wholesalers, through brokers and through agents, as well as selling it at their own central plant and its branches. Packers also sell directly to customers who purchase in trucklots or carlots.

Branches of the packing companies were usually located in cities with population of 50,000 up. In recent years, many branches have been closed in smaller cities. The packer's branch offers a full line of meat, provisions, and poultry. Sales are made to local retailers, wholesalers, and institutional buyers. Some of these buyers go to the branch location and pick out their supplies of meat. Others place their orders by telephone. Some give their orders to the salesmen of the packer who call at the business locations.

There are several kinds of independent service wholesalers. Full-service wholesalers buy carcasses from the packers and break down the carcasses into wholesale cuts which they distribute to their customers. Other wholesalers are institutional suppliers who specialize in distributing meat to the foodservice industry. Some of these firms also provide a line of other foods needed by foodservice people. There are wholesalers who bone-out the lower-grade beef carcasses and sell the meat to retailers and to processing plants. There are also wholesale firms that specialize in distributing frozen cuts of meat and frozen meat products. Another group is called truck wholesalers or peddlers. They operate refrigerated trucks, buy meat from a packer or a wholesaler, and resell it. Then there are the meat processing firms which manufacture and sell a wide variety of meat products to foodservice operators and other users.

The kinds of firms that are available in a particular location and the range of products that they offer differ from the situation in other locations. But generally, foodservice operators can find suppliers who can meet their needs although in some areas the number of suppliers may be limited and the range of choice may be restricted.

Changes in Volume of Slaughter

The changes that occur from week to week in the number of livestock being sold for slaughter is one of the reasons for price changes. When there is a week in which less livestock is slaughtered, the packers have less meat available for sale a week to two weeks later. Since there is less beef available to buy, the meat dealers compete with each other to get what is available, and they are more likely to pay higher prices to get it. The result is an increase in the prices of beef.

Then with prices up, the volume of slaughter increases, and larger supplies of meat become available. With larger supplies, there is less competition among dealers. They are reluctant to pay higher prices, and are inclined to offer less. So, the level of prices goes down.

It is difficult to forecast what numbers of livestock are going to be slaughtered week after week and month after month, since there are so many things that affect the decisions of the people who own those animals to send them to market. The supplies of feed, the cost of feed, the weather, and the time of the year are all factors that play a part in the decision to market livestock. Many times, it is how the market seems to be to the producer that affects the decision. He may have a hunch that it is going up or that it is going lower, and he acts accordingly.

Cost of feed has an effect on whether animals will be taken off grass feeding and put in feed lots to be fattened up for higher grades. If feed is too costly or scarce, animals that were to have been fed in feedlots will be sent to market. This beef will be of lower quality, and will bring down prices.

Price Changes

Of much concern to the meat buyer are the changes in prices, and an understanding of what changes occur as well as the reasons they occur. Since meat accounts for such a large part of the food expenditures in many foodservice operations, small changes in prices can be of much importance. There are various reasons for the fluctuation of prices on the wholesale markets for livestock. These fluctuations are reflected in the prices of the meat produced from those animals.

Seasonal Variation

There are seasonal variations in the supply of animals that move to market. Usually, the slaughter of cattle reaches its lowest point of the year in late June and early July. Then, in late July or in August, slaughter increases and continues upward until it reaches the high level of the year in October and November. The increase from low-volume point to peak point generally is about 25 percent, but this varies a great deal from year to year.

There is, as well, a difference in the kinds of animals that go to market. The fall slaughter is usually made up of a relatively large proportion of lower grades of cattle, since it has large numbers of grass-fed animals. On the other hand, the spring slaughter has a high percentage of cattle that have had special feeding in feedlots and which produce the higher grades of meat.

The Cattle Cycle

In addition to the seasonal variations in the year, there is another variation in supply that is of longer term nature, but that also results in beef prices moving upward and downward. This variation is the cattle cycle. It reflects the buildup in animal numbers to a peak and then the decline of those numbers to a low point before another buildup occurs. This cattle cycle may take several years from the time the low point in cattle numbers is reached until the buildup in numbers reaches its peak. Or, the time interval may run as long as six or seven years.

As might be expected, prices are higher when the number of cattle is lowest. As a result of these higher prices, producers of livestock increase the number of animals. This increase goes on until enough meat moves to market to force prices down. More and more of the larger number of animals move to market, and the level of prices continues downwards. These lower prices discourage livestock producers from keeping large numbers of animals. So, they cut production until prices start to move up again. Then, the cattle cycle starts over again.

These things affecting prices are going on at the same time, and they have an effect on the prices of meat to foodservice operators. The person who does the beef buying for a foodservice establishment must know what is happening in the meat markets, if he is to do the purchasing job most effectively. Only in this way can he intelligently evaluate the prices asked. However, these prices may not always be based on market conditions. Sometimes they are related more to what competitors are able to get, or what the supplier thinks the purchaser is likely to pay. In some cases, the supplier just wants to obtain a specific price.

A buyer who knows what the market situation is has information that often enables him to obtain a better price. Also, if he is knowledgeable, there is less likelihood that he will be paying prices that are not based on market conditions. Since wholesale meat prices fluctuate daily, it is necessary for the buyer to keep informed of market changes, trends on the market, developments that affect supply and demand and price, and anything else that affects the market, so that he can take advantage of price declines.

Market Information Sources

Information on the market can be obtained from a number of sources. Many daily newspapers have reports on what happens on the livestock markets and on the wholesale meat markets. Trade magazines offer weekly summaries of the receipts and sales of livestock and meat at different markets throughout the country.

The United States Department of Agriculture issues market reports that can be obtained on request without charge. Many times, a reliable supplier's price list provides information on market changes by the changes in the listed prices. The interpretation of the market reports should be done carefully. It is necessary to understand the words used and the grading systems used. The size of lots sold is important. Carlot prices are not available to those who buy only one or two ribs. Also, in purchasing wholesale cuts, the amount of trim must be considered in making comparisons.

More valuable than the daily prices in making comparisons is the indication of trends which the buyer can obtain from the market reports over a period of time. Even when it is not possible to make meaningful comparisons of prices on the wholesale market with prices being asked locally, the reports on the wholesale market provide an indication of when the local prices should be moving down or should be moving up.

Beef Grades

Of great importance to the foodservice buyer are grades as indicators of the quality of the product being purchased. Cattle that the packers buy to slaughter for beef, show considerable variation in quality and yield of meat. The animals may be dairy cows, no longer efficient in producing milk, which are being sent to the slaughterhouse. They may be animals that have been bred for meat production and raised for that purpose. The range in age can be anywhere from one year to fifteen years or more. The animals can vary in weight from a few hundred pounds to many hundreds. The animals may be marketed in one of the five so-called sex conditions.

All of these factors affect the quality and palatability of the meat that is produced from the carcasses. They also affect what yield of meat is obtained, especially how much meat comes from the more desirable parts of the carcass.

Government intervened in a rather confusing marketing situation in 1927 when the U.S. Department of Agriculture set up a voluntary grading and stamping system in order to obtain more order in the marketing of meat. One of the goals was to establish a system of quality identification so that people far away from where the animals and meat were would be able to communicate with others, with all knowing exactly what quality and conditions were being discussed.

Grading systems are designed to sort out things. In this case it was a matter of a grading system that would sort out animals or carcasses, using normal characteristics as a basis, and group them so that they were in relatively uniform groups. By setting up specifications for each group and by standardizing the terminology used, the grading system makes it possible for people who are familiar with the system to communicate with each other in a meaningful way, no matter where they may be located. The federal grades or standards for grades of carcass beef are a result of this effort. They are designed to sort cattle into eight quality grades and into five yield grades.

Quality and Yield

The grade of a beef carcass is based on separate evaluations of two general factors—quality and yield. In reaching these evaluations, the graders consider two sets of characteristics. One group indicates how palatable the lean will be. The other is the indication of the percentage of trimmed, boneless, major retail cuts that can be obtained from the carcass. The first of these two factors has to do with the quality of the carcass. The second has to do with the yield of the carcass.

Quality can be defined as those characteristics associated with the palatability of lean meat, including tenderness, flavor, and juiciness. Yield can be defined as the amount of usable or salable meat obtained from a carcass after cutting and trimming.

There are eight quality grades and five yield grades of beef. The quality grades are designated by words, with prime the top grade term. The yield grades are designated by numbers 1 to 5, with number 1 the highest yield. When a federal meat inspector grades a beef carcass, the evaluation consists of an evaluation for quality and an evaluation for yield. The designations appear on the carcass.

To understand what is involved in grading, it is necessary to know what a federal meat grader does when he is determining the grade of a particular carcass.

Market Class Determination

First, in examining the carcass, the grader determines its market class. This decision depends on the sex condition in which the animal was marketed. The five sex conditions are:

Steer   A male animal that had its male hormones removed at a very young age. (As a result, the animal has muscular development that is more like that of a female than a male, such as less heaviness through the forequarters.)

Heifer   A female that has never produced a calf and is not in the late stages of pregnancy.

Cow   A mature female animal that has had one or more calves.

Bull   A mature male.

Bullock   A male animal, usually slightly fatter than a bull, and approximately 15 to 16 months in age.

It is important that the grader determine the market class for several reasons. For one thing, cow carcasses are not eligible to be graded prime. Also, bull and bullock classes do not go into the usual retail meat channels, and they are graded on the basis of a separate and different set of standards. However, the carcasses of cows, steers, and heifers that are graded for marketing through the normal retail channels do not have any identification of market class. They carry only the quality and yield designations. The bull and bullock carcasses have the word "Bull" or "Bullock" included with the designation of grade to make sure that these carcasses are recognized as bull or bullock.

Steer carcasses usually bring a slight premium over heifer carcasses because they have a slightly higher yield of meat. So, there is some point to the meat purchaser's being able to identify the various market classes. Cow carcasses are likely to be more angular, with more of their weight in the less desirable areas of the carcass, such as the plate, chuck, and shank. As a result, they are less desirable than steers or heifers. When it comes to palatability, if everything else is equal, there is no difference between heifers, cows, and steers.

Age Determination

The grader next determines the age of the animal. As animals grow older, they become less and less tender; so it is important that the grader determine the approximate chronological age of the animal when it was slaughtered. Since age and toughness are related, there are definite age limitations regarding animals that can be put into certain of the grades. This is especially important when it comes to the higher grades. The relationship of age to quality grade, cutability or yield, and market classes is shown in Table 14-2.

How mature the carcass is can be determined by the skeleton characteristics. Characteristics associated with youth are porous red bone, and white, soft cartilages especially on the end of the chine or backbones where they are called buttons. Advanced age is characterized by hard, white, flinty bones, and by cartilages that have completely ossified or turned to bone.

Characteristics of Palatability

There are a number of palatability characteristics, including:

Marbling   This is identified by the flecks of white within the lean. Marbling affects flavor, juiciness, and to some extent tenderness. An abundance of marbling is desirable.

Color, firmness, and texture   Lean meat that is bright colored, firm, and has a fine texture shows the signs of high quality.

Maturity   Though evaluated previously, the grader looks at it again, since youthfulness of the carcass can make up for some small amount of lack of quality.

At one time, conformation was considered as a quality factor. Conformation had to do with the way the carcass is formed; and if there is a thick back with full loins and ribs, and deep, plump rounds, thick chucks, and short necks and shanks, the conformation would be considered superior. These characteristics were considered in determining into which quality grade a carcass was placed. But as a result of research work showing that conformation does not affect the palatability of meat, the United States Department of Agriculture dropped conformation from its list of quality grading factors.

Other Changes

The United States Department of Agriculture also made some other revisions, including a reduction in the marbling requirements for the various grades. Another was the redesigning of the good grade to make it more restrictive and more consistent in eating quality. More meat is now eligible for choice grade and prime grade, and the good grade has been narrowed. The result is that somewhat leaner beef now qualifies for the two top grades than was the case in the past.

U.S.D.A. Meat Grades for Quality

The buyer for a foodservice operation should know what the various U.S.D.A. quality grades represent, and also what the private grades represent. The latter is often more difficult as there is more flexibility in the private grades from year to year.

The U.S.D.A. grades are prime, choice, good, standard, commercial, utility, cutter, and canner, in order from the highest quality grade to the lowest. The three lowest grades generally are used for meat that goes directly into processing. Following are brief descriptions of the grades, indicating the principal differences between them.

USDA Prime   Beef of this grade rates highest in tenderness, flavor, and juiciness. It has abundant marbling—the flecks of fat within the lean—that enhances flavor and juiciness. Roasts and steaks of this grade are cooked with dry-heat methods.

Table 14-2   Carcass Beef From Steers, Heifers, and Cows

Approximate Age Limitations	Quality Grade	Cutability Grade	Market Classes
Max. of 36 months	Prime	1 through 5	Steers and Heifers Only
Max. of 42 months	Choice	1 through 5	Steers, Heifers, and Cows
Max. of 48 months	Good	1 through 5	Steers, Heifers, and Cows
Max. of 48 months	Standard	1 through 5	Steers, Heifers, and Cows
Min. of 48 months*	Commercial	1 through 5	Steers, Heifers, and Cows
No Limits	Utility	1 through 5	Steers, Heifers, and Cows
No Limits	Cutter	1 through 5	Steers, Heifers, and Cows
No Limits	Canner	1 through 5	Steers, Heifers, and Cows

*This grade reserved for carcasses showing evidence of more advanced maturity than those in preceding grades. These carcasses tend to be slightly thick due to a moderately heavy fat covering, but are rather rough and irregular in contour.

USDA Choice   Beef of this grade has a little less marbling than prime grade, but it is high quality beef. Roasts and steaks from the loin and rib are tender, juicy, and with much flavor. Dry-heat cooking is the cooking method for roasts and steaks of this grade. Also, many of the less tender cuts, such as those from the rump, round, and blade chuck can be cooked with dry heat methods, if they are USDA choice grade.

USDA Good   This grade of beef has somewhat more lean than the higher grades. It is fairly tender, but since it does not have as much marbling as the higher grades, it lacks some of the juiciness and flavor.

USDA Standard   In this grade of beef there is a high proportion of lean meat and very little fat. Beef of this grade is generally fairly tender since it comes from young animals. But it does not have marbling and so has less flavor. Moist heat cooking is best since otherwise it would be somewhat dry.

USDA Commercial   This grade comes only from mature animals. It is not naturally tender, even though it may be well marbled. As far as marbling is concerned, it looks similar to the prime grade, and could be confused with it. But, meat from these older animals cannot be in the higher grades. This grade of beef requires long slow moist-heat cooking.

The Yield Grades

There are four characteristics that should be considered in determining the yield grade:

amount of external fat on the carcass as measured over the rib eye of the quartered side

amount of kidney, pelvic, and heart fat

the area of the rib eye muscle at the twelfth rib, in square inches

the weight in the carcass

The yield of meat obtained from the carcass decreases as the amount of external fats, pelvic fats, and carcass weight increase. The yield increases as the rib eye area increases. A carcass in yield group 1, for example, usually has only a thin layer of external fat over the ribs, loins, rumps, and clods. In many parts of the carcass, muscles are usually visible through the fat. A 500-lb. carcass in this yield group—which is near the borderline between group 1 and group 2—might have 0.3 in. of fat over the rib eye, 11½-sq. in. of rib eye, and 2½ percent of its weight in kidney, pelvic, and heart fat.

209

The U.S. Department of Agriculture yield grades are 1 through 5, with yield grade 1 indicating the highest yield and yield grade 5 indicating the lowest yield. Carcasses within any particular grade may vary a great deal in value because of these differences in yield. In choosing between two U.S.D.A. choice grade carcasses, one of which is in yield grade 1 and the other in yield grade 4, there is more value to the yield grade 1 carcass, because it yields a greater percentage of usable or salable meat.

Approximate Yields

For a beef carcass, the cutting loss in the form of fat trim, shrink, and bone varies from 20 to 30 percent and occasionally even higher. If there is a cutting loss of 25 percent, a 300-lb. side of beef would yield 225 lbs. of meat cuts that can be sold and used.

A rule of thumb might be stated as 25 percent waste, 25 percent ground beef and stew meat, 25 percent steaks, and 25 percent roasts for carcass beef. Not all of the steaks and roasts would be from the most tender loin and rib parts of the carcass.

The U.S. Department of Agriculture has made studies of yields and has developed charts which show the yield from wholesale cuts of beef. Tables 14-3 and 14-4 are examples. One shows the yields from the wholesale cuts for a 300-lb. side of beef of yield grade 3. The other shows the yields of cuts from beef quarters, again from a 300-lb. side, yield grade 3. These yields are approximate, but they give a good indication of what can be obtained when the larger cuts are broken down.

Characteristics of Quality Beef

Foodservice buyers need to be able to recognize the signs of quality in beef. In general, quality beef should have a smooth, thin layer of creamy-white fat. The muscles should be thick and bulging. The lean should have a bright red color, a fine texture, and a firm dry appearance. There should be an abundance of fine flecks of fat—marbling—evenly distributed throughout the lean. The bones should have a porous appearance with tinges of red. Cartilage should be white and soft.

Not all graded meat is federally graded. Many of the large packers have their own graders and they stamp the carcasses with their own grade names. These carcasses are referred to as packer graded or packer branded meats. Generally, the packer brands tend to parallel the U.S. Department grades for beef, but the packer has much more flexibility in applying his own grades to carcasses. Some of the production of meat will not be graded at all. There are some purchasers of beef who prefer to buy meat without any grade marking on it.

Table 14-3   Approximate Yields from Wholesale Cuts of Beef (300-Lb. Side, Yield Grade 3)

	% of Wholesale Cut	Pounds
Round (68 lb.)		
Round Steak	39.7	27.0
Rump Roast (Boneless)	14.6	9.9
Lean Trim	17.9	12.2
Waste (fat, bone, and shrinkage)	27.8	18.9
Total Round	100.0	68.0
Trimmed Loin (50 lb.)*		
Porterhouse, T-Bone, Club Steaks	30.6	15.3
Sirloin Steak	49.8	24.9
Lean Trim	6.4	3.2
Waste (fat, bone, and shrinkage)	13.2	6.6
Total Loin	100.0	50.0
Rib (27 lb.)		
Rib Roast (7 in. cut)	67.8	18.3
Lean Trim	12.6	3.4
Waste (fat, bone, and shrinkage)	19.6	5.3
Total Rib	100.0	27.0
Square-Cut Chuck (81 lb.)		
Blade Chuck Roast	33.0	26.7
Arm Chuck Roast (Boneless)	21.5	17.4
Lean Trim	25.9	21.0
Waste (fat, bone, and shrinkage)	19.6	15.9
Total Chuck	100.0	81.0

*Does not include kidney knob and flank.
Source: U.S. Department of Agriculture.

Inspection for Wholesomeness

Another program of the government is concerned with the inspection of meat for wholesomeness. Meat that passes this inspection is stamped with a special marking indicating that it has been inspected by a government inspector and judged to be wholesome. The marking is applied to the carcass and appears on the major cuts.

Table 14-4   Approximate Yields of Cuts from Beef
Quarters (300-Lb. Side, Yield Grade 3)

	% of Quarter	Pounds
Hindquarter (144 lb.)		
Round Steak	18.8	27.0
Rump Roast (Boneless	6.9	9.9
Porterhouse, T-Bone, Club Steaks	10.6	15.3
Sirloin Steak	17.3	24.9
Flank Steak	1.0	1.5
Lean Trim	14.6	21.0
Kidney	.6	.9
Waste (fat, bone, and shrinkage)	30.2	43.5
Total hindquarter	100.0	144.0
Forequarter (156 lb.)		
Rib Roast (7 in. cut)	11.7	18.3
Blade Chuck Roast	17.1	26.7
Arm Chuck Roast (Boneless)	11.2	17.4
Brisket (Boneless)	4.0	6.3
Lean Trim	31.6	49.2
Waste (fat, bone, and shrinkage)	24.4	38.1
Total forequarter	100.0	156.0

Source: U.S. Department of Agriculture.

Under the law, all meat that is processed in plants that sell their products across state lines must be inspected by U.S. Department of Agriculture inspectors, in order to determine its wholesomeness. This inspection has nothing to do with the quality of the meat. Its purpose is to determine whether the meat is suitable for use as human food. The grade markings indicate the quality. Inspection is compulsory; grading is voluntary.

Also under the law, the cleanliness and the operating procedures of the meat-packing plants selling products across state lines are supervised by U.S. Department of Agriculture inspectors, to assure that the meat is not adulterated and that the meat does not become contaminated.

The Purchasing Procedure

A good purchasing procedure that is followed consistently has much effect on how well the job of buying meat for a foodservice operation will be done. A good procedure. means that specifications should be used. Correct ordering practices should be followed; record keeping should be accurate.

Knowledge of the needs of the establishment, of the market, and of the meat itself will be of little value unless the buying procedure is effective. Also included in the advantages of a good buying procedure are savings in time, elimination of errors, and a means of assuring that the needed supplies of beef are at the right place at the right time.

Using Specifications

Copies of the specifications should be provided to the suppliers, so they know exactly what the buyer wants when he places an order for a specific item. The specifications also are a means of settling differences with a supplier, when unsatisfactory products are delivered, instead of what was specified.

Some foodservice establishments send a list of needed items to several suppliers. Each vendor then lists the price at which he will supply each item and sends the list back to the foodservice operator. Then the buyer telephones the supplier to whom he decides to give the order.

Some places organize the specifications into a book and give a number to each specification. This offers a simple way of identifying the particular specification without having to provide a lengthy list of characteristics on the order sheet. For example, the number A-31 might mean to the supplier that he should refer to specification A-31 for sirloin of beef for that particular customer when he fills the order.

From Plans to Order

The needs of the establishment for beef must be taken from the production plans and translated into the order that goes to the vendor. Often production people use an order sheet that indicates the amounts needed for the meals that are planned for the period for which meat is being ordered. The food buyer reviews these lists. He may make some changes on the basis of what he knows about market conditions; and he then gets bids before placing the order.

Often a daily order sheet is used for recording bids on products such as beef. A sample daily order sheet is shown in Figure 14-5. It has space in which to record the daily price quotations of each purveyor who bids. After examining these quotations, the buyer is ready to place the order.

Obtaining Bids

The daily order sheet is actually a way in which suppliers offer their bids, if it is used correctly. It is a form of verbal bidding. Some foodservice operations, especially institutions and other larger operations, use a system of written bids. In many places, public institutions are required by law to issue requests for bids and to get sealed bids from purveyors. Also, in some cases, the order must be placed with the supplier who makes the lowest bid.

Regardless of how formal or informal the bidding system is, it does indicate to suppliers that the purchaser is looking for the best value and is going to compare bids. There may be situations where purchase is made from only one supplier. Foodservice operations in areas where there just are not many sources of supply find this necessary. But, in general, dealing with more than one supplier keeps the suppliers competitive and can mean better value for the purchaser.

Buying on Contract

Larger institutions and other large foodservice firms sometimes make contracts with the purveyor, in order to ensure getting certain beef items over the course of the year, or to stabilize the price on these items. Contracting in this way should be done with care. The contracts should include specifications for the items covered. The question of who is to store the items, the time delivery will take place, and where the deliveries will be made need to be spelled out clearly. The buyer must be well informed about the beef market, the way it operates, and the factors that influence it, or he could find that he has a contract over a long period of time when, though prices are moving downward, he still must pay the price agreed upon at the time the contract was made. Some contracts have provisions for changes in price, for situations in which an item is not obtainable, and for termination of the contract under certain conditions.

Figure 14-5 Daily Order Sheet

DAILY ORDER SHEET

Need	On Hand	Item	Amt. Ord.	Purveyor		

Thus, it is vital that what is involved in contract purchasing be understood, so that the contract method can be of value to the purchaser who wants to be sure of getting what is needed to meet the requirements of the foodservice operation; and also so that the supplier knows well in advance the volume on which he must base his operations.

Relationships with Salespeople

A good foodservice purchaser should have a policy regarding relationships with salespeople who try to sell him products. The foodservice industry has had many problems in the past with bribes, payoffs, and similar arrangements between the people who purchase and the people who sell.

The particular policy that should be followed will vary depending on the circumstances. But there are some basic features that should be included in such a policy, including:

Who can order There should be a clear understanding regarding the ordering procedure for the foodservice establishment. Salespeople should know who in the place is authorized to place the orders, and they should accept orders only from those who have this authority.

When the salesman should call Designate a time when the buyer would like to have salespeople call. It is important that the buyer be there at that designated time.

Acceptance of gifts If the foodservice establishment's buyer is to purchase on a competitive basis, he must be objective. By refusing to consider gifts, he avoids being obligated to any of the supplier firms and to salespeople. There is nothing to be gained by buyers accepting gifts, since the cost of gifts to customers is reflected in the prices that must be paid, and since, by accepting gifts, the buyer loses his independence of action.

Receiving, Storing, and Checking Results

Good buying procedure does not end when the buyer places the order with the supplier. This is especially so when beef is the product being purchased. Beef, as all perishable products, is constantly changing from the time the animal is slaughtered until the meat is eaten by the customer. There are changes taking place in the beef after it arrives at the foodservice establishment and before it is prepared that can eliminate the advantages resulting from a good purchasing program by the buyer. Beef needs to be received, stored, and handled carefully to ensure that the full value of what was ordered is received and reaches the customer.

The person who receives the beef when it is delivered by the purveyor has a major part to play in the complete buying operation. It is his responsibility to do several important things, including:

> certifying that the correct amount and quality of beef has been received
>
> recording the purchase that has been received
>
> making sure that the beef is moved quickly to the correct storage

The receiving clerk should be familiar with the specifications being used by the establishment. He really should be able to recognize the quality of the beef by looking at it, to the extent that he can determine if the beef being delivered meets the specifications. He should also check the temperature when it is an important factor, as in the case of frozen beef.

Beef is an expensive food item, and small differences in the weight of what was ordered and is being paid for and what was actually delivered can make a difference in the food cost budget. Over a period of time, these small discrepancies between the weight stated on the invoice and the weight delivered can mean substantial dollar losses. So, the person who receives the deliveries needs to give high priority to being certain the quantity of beef delivered is the same quantity for which the operation is being billed. His efforts in preventing this kind of loss should be in the form of weighing each item and comparing that weight with the weight listed on the invoice.

The responsibility of the receiving clerk for recording items as they are received should also have high priority, since this is the first step in the control of the accounts payable.

The rapid movement of the deliveries into storage protects the beef against quality loss due to high temperatures. In some operations, the receiving clerk may also date each item with the date of receipt. This ensures the most recently received items are not used before those that had been in storage.

Refrigerating Beef

Beef loses its quality rapidly when held at higher temperatures. The closer the temperatures of the cooler can be maintained to the freezing point, the longer will be the storage life of the beef and beef products. Beef freezes at $29.5°F.$, so an ideal cooler temperature would be $30°F.$ It would be difficult to maintain that temperature all the time; and the recommendation is that the temperature of the beef cooler be between $32°$ and $36°F.$, with a humidity of 85 to 90 percent.

In addition to temperature, other factors affect how long beef can be kept under refrigeration. These include:

the amount of time that has gone by since the animal was slaughtered

the condition of the animal and the treatment received before and during the dressing operation

the size of the cut of meat itself

the amount of meat surface that is exposed to the air

If the receiving, moving to storage, correct labeling and dating of each package placed in the freezer are given the proper attention, then selection of items from storage should be done correctly, and there should be rapid enough turnover of the beef in storage. Time limits that are suggested for meat in frozen storage are in Table 14-5.

Aging Beef

Most beef moves through the market channels relatively quickly between the time the animal is killed and the time the beef is used. However, some foodservice operations are interested in aged beef, as their customers prefer the aged beef flavor and are willing to pay more for it.

Aging is a way of increasing the tenderness of the beef by allowing the enzymes, which are in the muscle tissue of the beef, to break down the connective tissue. This aging process occurs more rapidly at high temperatures than at low temperatures. About the same degree of tenderness can be reached in two days at 65°F. as would occur in ten to fourteen days if the temperature is about 34°F. At higher temperatures, the process would operate more rapidly. How-

Table 14-5	Freezer Storage Time Limits for Frozen Meats at Temperatures at 0°F. or Lower

Meat in Freezer Wrap	Storage Limit for Maximum Quality
Beef (Steaks and Roasts)	6 to 8 Months
Lamb	6 to 8 Months
Veal	3 to 4 Months
Pork (Fresh)	3 to 4 Months
Poultry	6 to 8 Months
Ground Beef	3 to 4 Months
Cooked Meats	3 to 4 Months
Smoked Ham*	2 Months
Sausages*	DO NOT FREEZE
Sliced Bacon*	DO NOT FREEZE

*Flavor of cured and smoked or salted meats deteriorates rapidly when these meats are frozen. Freeze these items only for very short periods of time as an emergency measure.

ever, aging beef at high temperatures enables bacteria carried by the air to go into action, and there will be an effect on flavor. So, the recommended temperature for aging beef is $34°$F. with a humidity of 75 percent.

As meat is aged, the surfaces tend to dry out, and the meat must be trimmed before use. How much trimming loss there will be depends on how long the meat has been aged, the humidity level in the cooler, and the speed at which air currents move in the cooler. Trimming loss, in addition to moisture loss, will vary from 1 to 2 percent at the end of one week to as high as 6 to 9 percent at the end of a four-week period.

Aging beef is expensive when this loss of trim and moisture is considered. So, the minimum time to get the desired conditions should be the rule. Some foodservice establishments age beef for as much as six weeks, but most of the tenderization occurs in the first two weeks. Beyond that time, there will be a small tenderizing effect, but most of the change will be in flavor; and all the time there is a loss of moisture and a loss in trimming.

Summary

The person in a foodservice establishment who is responsible for buying beef must know the needs of the operation, the market, beef and beef products, and the best buying and storage procedures.

Planning the beef purchases involves knowing what to buy, when to buy it, and how much to buy. The answers to these questions are found in the menu and the forecast. Buying for use indicates the quality to be selected. Yield tests, cooking tests, and taste tests are a big help in deciding on the quality needed. The buyer must have knowledge of portion size and the yield obtained from the various cuts that are available.

The amount of pre-preparation that should be purchased can be determined from a comparison of cost figures. Included should be costs of the food, labor for preparation, and handling. The butcher's test card and the test card that shows the cooking loss give the data for the comparisons.

Specifications need to be developed and used if beef purchasing is to be effective. The Institutional Meat Purchase Specifications of the U.S. Department of Agriculture provide a valuable guide.

Foodservice operations usually get their supplies of beef from branches of the packing companies and from service wholesalers. Some foodservice buyers go to the location and pick out their supplies of meat. Other place their orders by telephone or give them to salesmen who call.

There are frequent price fluctuations on the markets as a result of changes in the volume of animals slaughtered, seasonal variations in volume going to market, and the longer-term cattle cycle. Trends in prices reported are usually of more significance than the actual prices that are paid on the wholesale markets.

There are many sources of market information of value to buyers. Newspapers, trade magazines, state and federal departments of agriculture, market reports from private and public agencies, and price lists from suppliers are among these sources. But it takes a good understanding of market terminology and the grading systems in use to make accurate interpretations of this information.

Cattle that move to slaughter vary greatly in weight, age, and sex condition. These are among the factors that affect the quality and yield of the meat. The U.S.D.A. meat grading system sorts out these animals into eight groups or grades, five market classes, and five age categories.

A good purchasing procedure for a foodservice establishment includes using specifications, correct ordering procedures, and accurate record keeping. Objective relationships, which rule out receiving gifts, with vendors and salesmen are an important factor. Asking for bids and comparing prices are an important part of good beef buying.

Receiving and storing of the beef after it is delivered also affects how well the beef purchasing operation is conducted. Checking, recording, and moving the beef quickly to storage are essential. Beef needs correct storage temperatures. The correct moisture in the storage is another important factor. Storing beef for aging can be of value in some foodservice operations.

Many of the suggestions and recommendations in this chapter can be applied to purchase of other items, but the emphasis is on beef since that is the major meat item for many operators.

Questions

1.　　Explain the relationship of the menu and purchasing.

2.　　Why is determination of needs vital in deciding the quality of meat to be purchased?

3.　　Explain how the foodservice operator can determine whether to make or buy as far as beef for his foodservice establishment is concerned.

4.　　What are the following and how are they used: (a) butcher's test card; and (b) cooking loss test card?

5.　　Using specifications in purchasing beef is a way of ensuring that what is purchased is what is needed, and what is delivered is what was ordered. What information should be included in all specifications?

6.　　What are the U.S.D.A. Institutional Meat Specifications?

7.　　Describe the cattle cycle and how it affects supplies and prices for beef to the foodservice operator.

8.　　List palatability characteristics of beef.

9.　　What are the names of the U.S.D.A. grades for beef?

10.　　What is meant by yield grade?

11.   Describe the difference between U.S.D.A. grading and U.S.D.A. inspection of meat.

12.   What things should be considered in determining how long beef should be kept under refrigeration?

15

Purchasing Canned
Fruits and Vegetables

Very few if any foodservice establishments do not purchase food in cans. For most operations these items are a standard part of the regular purchasing. Actually, canned foods were probably the first "convenience foods" used on a large scale by the foodservice industry. In spite of the increasing volume of frozen foods and other forms of products resulting from the advances of technology, canned foods continue to be a substantial and necessary part of the foods purchased by foodservice buyers.

Products among the canned foods that seem to get less attention than they should from buyers are fruits and vegetables. Far too often, canned fruits and vegetables are ordered with insufficient concern for what really is needed, what is requested, and what value is obtained.

Efficient food purchasing for a foodservice establishment requires that information be obtained, evaluated, and applied to the specific purchasing that is to be done. The procedures and practices that result in efficiency in food purchasing are just as important in buying canned fruits and vegetables as they are in buying meat, even though the dollar values involved are much higher with meat. To do an effective job, the person who does the food purchasing must know:

what the foodservice operation needs

the local market and how it operates

products which are available

best use of each product and the type of product

which specific product is needed to meet the need of the foodservice operation

Only with this knowledge and by using it in doing the purchasing can tł right product of the right type and quality, at the right price, be obtained at tł right time. The need to have and use this knowledge applies to food buying ɪ all foodservice operations, regardless of the type.

Knowing the Establishment's Needs

Knowing specifically what the needs of the foodservice oper tion are constitutes the first step in deciding which products to buy. Knowiɪ what the menu is and thus knowing what use is intended for the product to ł purchased provides the buying goal for the food purchaser.

Canned foods of high quality are essential when the menu is designed fɑ high average checks in a for-profit restaurant or hotel dining room. Howeve when the operation is a nonprofit institution with a very limited budget, tł high level of quality may not be the choice.

At both of those extremes, the menu and the intended use would refle the situation and provide to the buyer what he must know in order to make tł best purchasing choice.

Knowing the Market

The buyer's task is to match what is needed with what offered. To do this, the buyer needs to know where the products can be o̶ tained, how the market operates, and what can be obtained from the marke The market in this sense includes the sources of supply and the things th̶ happen affecting the prices that the buyer must pay, as well as the process ɑ getting products to users.

To do this matching, the buyer may need to know whether it is possib to bypass some of the steps in the marketing process to his advantage. The buyɑ certainly needs to have a great deal of information on the availability of particɯ lar grades, styles, types, varieties, counts, syrup densities, specific gravities, aɪ geographic sources of canned fruits and vegetables.

Knowing the Best Use of the Product

An understanding of what type of product is best used fɑ what purpose means knowing much about the cooking and serving of the fooɑ purchased. Baked, stuffed tomatoes offer a good example. To meet the needs when that item is on the menu, the choice would be whole, hand-picked tomatoes. This would be the type of product that would best meet that need. But if the menu calls for au gratin tomatoes, the less expensive, broken tomatoes would be the wise choice. That selection would best meet that need. Selecting between the alternatives is of much importance, since there is a considerable difference in price between the can of whole tomatoes and the can of broken tomatoes.

Purchasing fruit for salads and desserts provides another good example. If the appearance of the salad or dessert is important, the food buyer would purchase the fruit in whole form or half form. But if appearance is not important, the less perfect or broken fruits would be a more economical choice. The nutritional value and the wholesomeness of both forms would not be different, but the cost would. The whole and half units of fruits and vegetables usually cost significantly more than the less perfect fruits and vegetables. Of course, one of the food buyer's responsibilities is to control costs.

The buyer must know enough about the product so that clearly stated specifications can be prepared, and his discussions with suppliers and their salesmen can be effective. If the buyer is to be able to do those things, he must have a good knowledge of each canned food item that is used in the operation.

Buying or Simply Placing Orders

The comparison between the food buyer who just calls a supplier and asks, "What is your price for canned beans today?" and the buyer who requests a price for a particular kind of bean, packed in a certain way, and with other specifications stated as well, really presents the case as far as good buying of canned fruits and vegetables for a foodservice establishment is concerned.

Anyone can do it the first way, but it takes an informed buyer to do it the second way. Asking a supplier for a price on beans means just about nothing to the supplier. What kind of bean? What style of bean? What size? What grade? Those are the questions that need to be answered before the supplier can intelligently state a price. There are many kinds, styles, sizes, and grades.

Obviously that means the buyer must provide information along with a request for a price. In the example of beans, there are grades—fancy (Grade A), extra standard (Grade B), and standard (Grade C). There are types—green or wax, to mention two. There is the style of pack—whole, whole vertical, whole asparagus, french, cut or cuts, short cuts, and mixed.

There is variety—round or flat. There is geographical source—Western Blue Lake or Eastern Blue Lake. There is weight in pounds or ounces, and also whether it is drained weight or not. There is size of bean, which ranges from small to extra large.

There are differences between what each of these terms represents. This

223

example relates to beans, but the same need for more precise information applies to all canned fruits and vegetables.

Sources of Information

There are many places where the person buying food for a foodservice establishment can get the needed information about canned fruits and vegetables. The federal grades and standards offer much product information regarding quality. There also are industry association grades and standards. There are many publications with all types of information. The suppliers of the products that are purchased are also good sources of information.

The United States Department of Agriculture has developed grades and standards for many canned fruits and vegetables. The national, regional, and state trade associations have developed grades and standards similar to the government grades but usually with more flexibility.

The Almanac of the Canning, Freezing, Preserving Industries published by Edward E. Judge and Sons, Inc., 79 Bond St., Westminster, Maryland 21157, is an industry publication that includes data on prices and packs, lists of associations, food laws and regulations, labeling and packaging, the U.S.D.A. quality grades, and a variety of other information about canned foods and frozen foods. Several trade magazines and papers, designed primarily for packers and distributors, contain much information on trends in the industry, the volume of marketing, and current prices and price trends. Foodservice industry publications often have material on effective purchasing of canned foods. Also, there are numerous books on purchasing food for foodservice operations.

All of this information can be available to the buyer and can prove valuable in the buying operation, since a well-informed food buyer can do the most effective food buying job.

Purchasing Canned Fruits and Vegetables

If the buyer keeps in mind the needs of the operation for which food is being purchased, knows the market and its product offerings, and knows the products and the uses for which they are best suited, he is in a position to put a buying program into operation. At this point there are several things the buyer needs to do that will greatly affect how well he performs the buying function and how well he controls costs, while at the same time satisfying needs of the establishment. The buyer should:

Decide the particular type and quality grade of the canned fruits and vegetables that best suit the use for which the items purchased are intended.

Determine by cutting tests which of the products provides the best value for the price paid.

Prepare in writing the information on the type, and the quality grade or brands of the canned fruits and vegetables wanted.

Place the order with a reputable supplier after getting the comparable prices and similar information.

Check the delivered product and see that it gets into storage.

Doing these things will go a long way in ensuring that the best product, most suited for the intended use, is purchased; and also ensures getting value for the money expended and maintaining that value until the product is used.

What Type, Grade, or Brand to Purchase

In deciding on what particular type and quality of canned products to buy the guide, again, is the intended use. Which type of fruit, for example, is best suited for the use stated in the menu? What type of vegetable is best suited for the use stated in the menu?

Take pears, for example. What use is indicated on the menu? Are the pears to be used in salads or in desserts? What type of pear is wanted—whole, halves, quarters, slices, or mixed? What count is wanted—16 to 22 halves in a number 10 can, or 31 to 40 halves in the can? Which density of syrup—light, heavy, or extra heavy? Which kind of pear—Kiefer or Bartlett? Which quality grade— Fancy, Choice, or Standard?

Depending on the answers to those questions is the purchase of the right canned pears at the right price that will meet the needs for use. There is no point in using pears that are packed in heavy syrup, if the use of the pears is in a salad. Neither would fancy quality peaches be a good choice for a peach cobbler.

So, check the menu. Find out how the product is to be used. Then, purchase to meet the need—for style, count, kind, syrup density, quality grade, variety, and the other things that make one offering on the market different from another.

Grades and Standards of Identity

The federal Food, Drug, and Cosmetic Act established minimum quality standards for canned foods. These standards are measurements of quality and weight or quantity. The provisions of the act prohibit movement of misbranded or adulterated foods in interstate commerce. There are penalties for foods that come under the provisions of the act and do not conform to the general requirements of the act. The provisions prescribe that the products meet:

a definition and standard of identity

a standard of quality

a standard of fill

225

Standards of identity have been established for many canned fruits and vegetables, and also for a number of related products such as jellies, jams and preserves, fruit butters, and such items as peanut butter and salad dressings. The grades are market classifications of quality and put products into groups according to established standards of quality. They are promulgated by the United States Department of Agriculture. The canned products must meet the standards of identity, quality (wholesomeness), and fill, of the Food and Drug Administration. The use of the federal grades of the U.S. Department of Agriculture is voluntary.

Definitions and Standards of Identity   This defines what a food is. When applied to canned foods, it states the composition of the product in the can. Included are the name or names of the product, the specific mixture and the ingredients that were used in canning the product. However, the canner does not have to list the ingredients unless he has added other ingredients, such as artificial flavoring, chemical preservatives, herbs, or spices.

Definitions and standards of identity have been established for canned applesauce, apricots, berries, figs, fruit cocktail, cherries, grapefruit, grapes, peaches, pears, pineapples, plums, prunes, juices, jellies, jams, frozen cherry pie, and preserves. They have also been established for canned green beans, wax beans, corn, mushrooms, peas, tomatoes, and tomato products, such as catsup, juice, paste, puree, and pulp, and also miscellaneous vegetables.

Standard of Quality   This defines the minimum level of quality for canned foods. Fruit cocktail, for example, is defined as the food prepared from the mixture of fruit ingredients, in certain forms and proportions, and in a medium such as water, syrup, and juice of different kinds. The standard of quality relates to the amounts of the different kinds of fruit, amount of peel, size of pieces of fruit, condition of the fruit, and similar things. For canned tomatoes, the minimum level of quality is based on drained weight, color, amount of peel, and blemishes per pound.

If the products do not meet the minimum requirement that has been established, they must be labeled as below standard in quality or with the statement: "Good food—not high grade." The reason may be listed, such as poor color, excessively trimmed, or not well peeled. Shown in Figure 15-1 is an example of these markings.

Standard of Fill   This defines how well the can must be filled. Standards of fill vary for different products. For some items, the standard is based on the maximum head space allowed. For example, cans of peas must be filled within 3/16 in. below the top of the double seam. For products such as corn, tomatoes, and potatoes, the standard of fill is based on the minimum percent of water capacity, and the cans must be filled to not less than 90 percent of their total capacity.

Figure 15-1   Canned Vegetable Label

TENDER YOUNG

Sweet
Peas

BELOW STANDARD IN QUALITY
ARTIFICIALLY COLORED

ABOVE LEGEND MANDATORY—PEAS ACTUALLY HIGH QUALITY
Especially selected for Institutional use

NET WT. 6 LBS. 10 OZ.

Other canned products such as apricots, cherries, peaches, and pears must be filled with the "maximum quantity of . . . which can be sealed in the container and processed by heat to prevent spoilage, without crushing or breaking such ingredient." They must be filled as "full as commercially practicable without impairment of the quality of the food products."

If the canned foods do not meet these requirements, the packer can label them "Below Standard of Fill," or "Slack Fill."

Labeling Requirements

The Food, Drug, and Cosmetic Act includes provisions that prescribe certain minimum requirements for labels that must be complied with by all packers and distributors. The labeling requirements are mandatory for all food products shipped in interstate commerce. The Fair Packaging and Labeling Act also contains some mandatory requirements. The law requires that the label contain the following information:

227

the legal name of the product

name and place of business of the manufacturer, packer, or distributor

net contents in weight, measure, or numerical count

variety, style, and packing medium when relevant

the dietary properties, if important

any artificial flavor, color, or preservative

that product falls below the quality of standard of fill required by the law, if such is so

information in English unless an imported product that has a foreign language label and is distributed in an area with a predominant language other than English

a statement of ingredients unless a standard of identity has been established by the government

Syrup Must Be Stated

The law requires that the label state the type of packing medium in which the product is packed. Fruits are packed in syrups consisting of water or juice, and ranging from plain syrup to extra-heavy syrup.

Syrup density is not a factor in grading. But as a general rule, the syrup with the largest amount of sugar is used for the best grades. However, syrup density for the same grades will differ depending on the fruit canned due to the individual differences of the fruit. Table 15-1 illustrates these differences.

The reason for the difference in the syrup density for the 3 products compared in the table is that sweet cherries and grapes would break down if they were packed in a heavier syrup than $35°$ because of the delicate structure of the fruit.

Table 15-1   Difference in Syrup Densities for Fruits

Syrup	Apricots	Brix* Measurement Cherries	Grapes
Extra Heavy	$25°-40°$	$24°-35°$	$22°-35°$
Heavy	$21°-25°$	$19°-24°$	$18°-22°$
Light	$16°-21°$	$14°-19°$	$14°-18°$
Slightly Sweetened	Less than 16	Less than 14	Less than 14

*Syrup density is referred to as the Brix. The Brix is a measurement of sugar content as determined by a reading in degrees on a Brix hydrometer or refractometer, 15 days or more after the fruit is packed. Each degree of Brix can be estimated as one degree of sugar content.

Descriptive Labeling

Many canners and distributors include on their labels more information than that required by law. This information may include the brand name, the grade, words that indicate the size of the product such as jumbo, extra large, small, and words that indicate the maturity of the product such as mature and very young.

Also included may be information about the quantity, directions for use of the product, and information on the best methods of handling and storing the product. Many times the number of cups or the number of servings in the can can be found on the label.

Open Code Dating

In some states, the trend is toward requiring processors to open code date their products so that consumers can know readily by what date a product should be eaten or sold. Massachusetts adopted such open code dating in 1978 and granted a temporary exemption to foods in cans and jars while food processors implement a voluntary plan of open dating.

Nutritional Labeling

Even though manufacturers and processors usually provide information on the nutritional values of their products to foodservice purchasers in a printed form, the advent of nutritional labeling on many of the food packages sold to consumers makes this development of more than passing concern.

In 1973, the United States Department of Public Health's Food and Drug Administration issued regulations for nutritional labeling. This was part of an effort to encourage manufacturers of food products to provide nutritional information in a standardized way on their food packages. The action was the result of increased concern about the nutrition of people in the United States, and the increased pressures of consumer activists.

Any canned, frozen, processed, and packaged food for which a nutritional claim is made by the producer must show the nutritional content. All foods to which nutrients have been added must be nutritionally labeled. Many food items in consumer-size containers have the nutritional information in standard format on the packages.

Since the introduction of nutritional labeling requirements, some individuals and groups have demanded that foodservice operators be required to post or to have stated on their menus nutritional information about the items on the menus. It is possible that the demands for nutritional labeling may extend regulatory action toward this area in the future, although there seems to be recognition of the immensity of the problems that would be involved for foodservice operators.

Grades and Grading

Grades are market classifications of quality. Grading is a process of classifying units of a commodity into groups, according to some established and generally accepted standards.

The United States Department of Agriculture has developed grades for numerous canned fruits and vegetables. These U.S.D.A. grades are:

U.S. Fancy, or U.S. Grade A

U.S. Choice for Fruits, or U.S. Grade B

U.S. Extra Standard for Vegetables, or U.S. Grade B

U.S. Standard, or U.S. Grade C

All canned foods that do not meet the minimum quality standards for Grade C are graded as Substandard; and there must be a prominent statement to that effect on the label.

There is some confusion in the grade listings, since for some products there are Grades A and C, but no Grade B. For other products, Grade C is omitted and there are Grades A and B. Some examples are: fruit cocktail which is graded as A, B, and Substandard; tomato puree which is graded A, C, and Substandard; clingstone peaches which are graded A, B, C, D, Substandard, Grade C Solid Pack, and Substandard Solid Pack. Table 15-2 shows the differences in the grade classifications for a selected number of canned fruits and vegetables.

Which Grade to Purchase

Each grade has a use for which the product is best suited, but no one grade is best for all purposes in a foodservice operation. Even the top grade or the most expensive food item is not best for some uses.

Canned foods sold with the lower grade markings are perfectly wholesome, and they have essentially the same nutritional values. Where they differ from the higher grade and more expensive products is mostly in their appearance and to a lesser degree in their flavor and taste.

In general, Grade A or Fancy is the classification for fruits and vegetables of the highest quality. They have been selected carefully for size, color, maturity, and tenderness. They are practically free from blemishes and defects. So, where appearance and flavor are important, the choice should be Grade A or Fancy.

Grade B (Choice for Fruits and Extra Standard for Vegetables) is of fine quality; but it scores somewhat lower than the higher grade in one or more of the factors. Products that are Grade B do not have so much uniformity in color, size, or maturity, and generally can have more blemishes and defects.

Grade C or Standard is a good quality product, but it does not meet the higher standards of Grade B. Grade C products are just as wholesome and nutritious as the higher grades. The products are less uniform in size and color, less tender, or have more blemishes and defects. If appearance or tenderness are not important, Grade C products are a good choice. For example, Grade C items are good for cooked fruit desserts. They are good in dishes where there is to be additional cooking, and they are good choices when the product is one of several ingredients in a recipe.

Substandard does not mean that the product is not wholesome. All canned foods must be wholesome under the Food, Drug, and Cosmetic Act quality requirements. Substandard means that the food has some quality defect greater than allowed for the Grade C or Standard grade. The fruit, for example, may be considerably broken up. It may be off color, or it may have more than the allowed amount of defects. If form and appearance are not important, substandard foods can readily be used. The substandard canned foods usually are sold as "seconds."

Grades provide information for the buyer on which he can base a choice, so that he gets the quality that is best for the use intended on the menu. This provides a large assist in controlling food costs, since the lower grades can be used to meet many menu needs where appearance is not of great importance. This means resulting savings in food costs.

Grade Scoring Factors

The grades for canned foods are based on scoring factors. These factors include color, uniformity of size, absence of defects, character, flavor, consistency, finish, size and symmetry, liquor or clearness of liquor, maturity, texture, and cut.

There can be variation in any of these factors. Many times the variation results in the product being down-graded, but that does not necessarily mean that it is low in nutritional quality or in eatability. It simply means that the product contains more than the allowed amount of such things as defects, or broken pieces, or off color to be put in the higher grade.

There are some general requirements, in addition to these factors, that canned foods must meet. The fill of the container, the drained weight, and the syrup density are three requirements.

The grading factors vary with the individual canned fruit or vegetable, but the scoring range is the same. Where there is no Grade B for a canned fruit, and there are only Grades A and C, the scoring range is greater. A summary of the total score required to meet the requirements of each grade is in table 15-3.

See Table 15-2 for a listing of products for which there is no Grade B in the canned foods standards. Tomatoes provide an example of the difference in scoring required when there is no Grade B. Canned tomatoes must score 90 points or higher to be in Grade A, since there is a Grade B in the standards for canned tomatoes. But, tomato juice needs to score only 85 points or higher to

Table 15-2 Grade Classification for Selected Canned Fruits and Vegetables

	Grades			
	A	B	C	D or Sub-standard[1]
Apples	x		x	x
Apple Juice	x	x		x
Apple Sauce	x	x		x
Apricots[2]	x	x	x	x
Asparagus	x		x	x
Green or Wax Beans	x	x	x	x
Lima Beans	x	x	x	x
Beets	x		x	x
Blackberries or similar berries	x	x	x	x
Carrots	x		x	x
Cherries, Red Sour Pitted	x	x	x	x
Cherries, Sweet	x	x	x	x
Chili Sauce	x		x	x
Corn (Cream-style Whole Kernel)	x	x	x	x
Fruit Cocktail	x	x		x
Fruit Preserves or Jams	x	x		x
Fruit for Salad	x	x		x
Fruit Jelly	x	x		x
Grapefruit[3]	x	x		x
Grapefruit Juice	x	x		x
Grapefruit and Orange Juice (Blended)	x	x		x
Mushrooms	x	x		x
Orange Juice	x		x	x
Peaches[2]	x	x	x	x
Peanut Butter	x	x		x
Pears	x	x	x	x
Peas	x	x	x	x
Pickles	x	x		x
Pimientos	x		x	x
Pumpkins and Squash	x		x	x
Potatoes – White	x		x	x
Red Raspberries	x	x	x	x
Sauerkraut	x	x	x	x
Spinach and other Greens (Turnip, Mustard, Beet, Kale)	x	x		x
Sweet Potatoes	x		x	x
Tangerine Juice	x	x		x
Tomatoes	x	x	x	x
Tomato Catsup[4]	x	x	x	x
Tomato Juice	x		x	x
Tomato Paste	x		x	x
Tomato Sauce	x		x	x

[1] Anything below Grade C is considered Substandard. Some products are listed Grade D and others are Substandard. Where there is no Grade C, anything under Grade B is considered Substandard.

[2] Apricots and peaches are also graded Grade C Solid Pack, Substandard Solid Pack, Grade D, and Substandard. Grade D may closely resemble the same quality of fruit as Grade C except that Grade D may contain more than one variety of the same fruit. It may or may not meet the minimum Food and Drug standard of quality.

Table 15-3   Scoring Ranges for the Grades of
                 Canned Foods

Grades	When There Is A Grade B	When There Is No Grade B
A (Fancy)	90–100	85–100
B (Choice, Extra Standard)	75–89	–
C (Standard)	60–74	70–84
Substandard	0–59	0–69

be Grade A, since there is no Grade B in the standards for tomato juice.

Occasionally, a canned product will not qualify for a high grade, even though its total score is above the minimum score established for that grade. This is the result of what is called a limiting rule. Each grade factor is given a score range. Under the limiting rule, if a product does not score above a certain scoring range on an important quality factor, it cannot be graded higher regardless of the total score.

Here is an example. In the Score Chart for Canned Peas (Table 15-4), peas that receive a score of 5 or 6 for color cannot be graded higher than U.S. Grade B or U.S. Extra Standard regardless of their total score. That much deficiency in color keeps them out of the higher grade.

Again, knowing the score for canned fruits and vegetables can be of value to the buyer for the foodservice establishment. If the peas are being purchased for a menu use in which color is not important, then he could buy the peas that had been put in Grade B because of the partial limiting rule that keeps peas with the color deficiency from being graded higher. Of course, the Grade B peas will be lower in price than the higher grade.

Drained Weight of Tomatoes

Tomatoes again provide an example. Grading of tomatoes is done on the basis of the drained weight in the can, the wholesomeness of the tomatoes and their color, and also the absence of defects.

Whole tomatoes must have a net drained weight of 54.7 to 67.9 oz., according to the standard for this grade of tomatoes. Grade A whole tomatoes must have a net drained weight of 72.2 to 76.6 oz. Grade B tomatoes must have a net drained weight of 63.5 oz. to 67.9 oz.; and Grade C tomatoes must have a net drained weight of 54.7 to 59.1 oz.

---

[3] There is a "U.S. Broken" Grade for grapefruit.

[4] Grades A and B are distinguished by solid content. Grade A Catsup must have a solid content of not less than 33 per cent by weight and score not less than 85 points. Grade B Catsup must have a solid content of not less than 29 per cent by weight and score not less than 85 points.

233

Table 15-4   Score Chart for Canned Peas

Factor	Points Maximum	Grade A Fancy	Grade B Ex. Std.	Grade C Std.	Sub-Std.
Color	10	9–10	7–8	5–6**	0–4*
Liquor	10	9–10	8	7	0–6*
Defects	30	27–30	24–30	24–26*	0–20*
Maturity and Tenderness	50	45–50	41–44*	37–40*	0–36*
Minimum Score		90	80	70	

*Limiting Rule: Peas receiving this score cannot be graded higher regardless of total score.
**Partial Limiting Rule: Peas receiving this score cannot be graded above U. S. Grade B, regardless of total score.

There is a difference in the Grade A drained weight of 4.4 oz.—from 72.2 to 76.6 oz. That could mean a difference of one or two extra tomatoes. If the same price is quoted for tomatoes with a drained weight of 72.2 oz. and for tomatoes with a drained weight of 76.6 oz., there would be approximately 6 percent more tomatoes for the money in the can with drained weight of 76.6 oz.

This example emphasizes why a simple question such as: "What is your price on tomatoes today?" addressed to a supplier or suppliers, will not produce a good answer. How could they provide comparable quotations with so many variations available in the product? It is necessary to include grade and weight in that question.

Buyers need to know the point spreads that determine the various grades. Canned peas, for example, can score 88 or 89 points and be Grade B. Yet, this lot of canned peas may differ little in quality from another lot that just scored 90 points and as a result is Grade A. That only major difference between these two lots of canned peas will be prices. The Grade A peas will have a higher price than the Grade B.

If the factor of color were the one that was graded low and all the other factors were high, and color is not an important factor in the use to be made of the peas, then the lot scoring 88 or 89 points would be a better buy because of its lower price.

How to determine the point spread so that the comparison can be made is a problem. The time and equipment would not be available to make the necessary tests. But buyers can get the scores for the product being offered by asking for a copy of the grader's certificate.

Use of Brand Names

The brand names offer another way of determining the relative qualities of the canned foods being purchased. Many foodservice buyers depend

Table 15-5   Drained Weights* for Canned Tomatoes,
No. 10 Can

U.S. Grade Classification	Score Points	Drained Tomatoes	Ounces
Grade A Whole	20	65%	67.9
Grade A Whole	19	60%	65.7
Grade A Whole	18	58%	63.5
Grade A Whole	17	54%	59.1
Grade A Whole	16	50%	54.7
Grade A	20	70%	76.6
Grade A	19	68%	74.4
Grade A	18	66%	72.2
Grade B	17	62%	67.9
Grade B	16	58%	63.5
Grade C**	15	54%	59.1
Grade C	14	50%	54.7

*Drained weight is a grading factor for tomatoes only. However, minimum drained weights are required for canned foods by the Food, Drug and Cosmetic Act.
**Limiting rule.

on brand names to indicate quality and to ensure getting the same quality each time the item is bought.

Canners, packers, and distributors grade their canned products. Their grades follow closely the U.S. Department of Agriculture grades. If a canner, packer, or distributor uses the terms Grade A, Grade B, Grade C, or the terms Fancy, Choice, or Standard, the products graded that way must meet the U.S.D.A. standards. If the letters "U.S." are used before the grade letter A or the word Fancy, the product must be under continuous government inspection.

Many packers and distributors use brand labels to indicate grades. One brand or label will mean the highest quality, while another will indicate a lower quality. Usually, the labels are a different color. There is more flexibility in the grades represented by the private brands than there is in the U.S.D.A. grades. One private brand label may represent the minimum requirements of the U.S.D.A. grade, while another label may represent the maximum.

Usually, the canners, packers, and distributors put their best label on the highest quality product. In times of poor crops, however, it is possible that the product carrying the best quality label may be lower than the comparable government grade, because there is so little of the high quality product available. Sometimes when, due to extremely poor crops, the quality of the product is very low, special labels are used, and the usual labels are not used.

Cutting and Cooking Tests

Since not all canned fruits and vegetables are graded, and since there can be variations from time to time in the grades represented by particular labels, the food buyer should make cutting tests and compare the different brands. This is done once a year in many foodservice operations, usually near the end of the canning season. With the results of these tests at hand, the buyer can then select the brands that best meet his needs.

A cutting test is the only way in which firsthand information can be obtained regarding the drained weight, appearance, texture, flavor, and any of the other scoring factors of the product that is in the can. Making a cutting test is not a complicated matter. All that is needed is a shallow pan, a sieve*, a scale, two sample cans of each canned food, and a comparison chart.

The first step is to read the label. Then, check what it states. Open one can and spread the contents evenly over the sieve. Let it stand for about two minutes, and then weigh the product. The net drained weight is the total weight of the product and the sieve, minus the weight of the sieve. Drained weights have much importance in connection with costs. The idea is to see how many portions can be obtained per can. So, the cost per portion becomes the measuring device and can be used in making comparisons.

Next, the product should be inspected for its appearance, texture, and flavor. Look it over carefully from the point of view of the customer of the

Figure 15-2   Score Sheet for Fruit Cocktail

Sample			
Drained Weight			
Clearness of the Syrup			
Color			
Uniformity of Size			
Defects			
Proportion of Fruit			
Character			
Flavor			
Label or Grade			
Vendor			
Cost per Case			
Can or Unit Price			
Price per Serving			

*For commercial cutting, sieves used are specified by the U.S. Department of Commerce, National Bureau of Standards, as to width of screen and the number of wire meshes per inch. For cutting number 10 cans, two screens, 12 in. wide are used. One screen which has 2 meshes to the inch is used for canned tomatoes; the other which has 8 meshes to the inch is used for all other canned foods.

oodservice establishment. Taste the product, again from the point of view of he customer to whom it will be served and who will eat it. Then, form a udgment.

It is then time to give the product a cooking test. Heat it to a serving emperature of 140° to 150°F. Place the product on the heated steam table and et it stand on the line for a period of time. This can be the amount of time that quals a serving period. Then check the product again for appearance, texture, nd flavor. Check how well it held up on the serving line. If the product performs satisfactorily and the price is right, determine how many cases are needed nd place the order. Store the second can unopened so that it will be available or testing in the future.

A score sheet can be used to record the information as these tests are conducted. Figure 15-4 is a sample score sheet that has been used effectively. This particular one is for fruit cocktail and includes the items of special importance n checking that product.

Buy the Correct Unit Size

The size of the unit is another factor that needs consideration n buying canned fruits and vegetables. The unit size may increase the overall ost, if the size of the unit is not correlated with the standard menus which are repared in the foodservice establishment.

In general, the larger the unit size, the less the per serving cost. Also, less abor and less time will be needed in the kitchen for preparing the food. However, this advantage in purchasing large unit sizes can be lost if the unit bought s too large and some of the food is left over and thrown away.

So, foodservice food buyers should purchase canned foods in the unit size which takes care of the need for the number of people to be served and the tandardized recipes of the establishment.

Common Container Sizes

A knowledge of the common can sizes, their contents, and vhat they yield in terms of cups is necessary for most effective buying of canned oods. Labels of cans or jars that may be exactly the same size may state net veights that differ between the two cans or jars. The reason is the difference in he density of the food. An example would be pork and beans on which the abel states one pound, and blueberries with a label marking of 14 ounces—both acked in the same size can.

The chart in Table 15-6 shows the container sizes. Also, Table 15-7 gives nformation for substituting one can for another size, based on what equals one Number 10 can.

Developing Specifications

The only way the food buyer can make known to the supplier exactly what is needed and wanted is to write out definitions of the standards of the products he wants to buy. This means the development of specifications. Specifications should be written in commercial terms, as these are the words that the supplier needs on which to base his prices. If commercial terminology is used, the prices quoted can be on a comparable basis.

The specification can be brief or elaborate, depending on the needs of the establishment. However, all specifications should contain the following basic information:

> name of the product
>
> federal grade, brand, or trade designation
>
> size of the container and the number of units per case on which the supplier will quote a price.

Table 15-6   Common Container Sizes

Industry Term	Container Consumer Description Approx. Net Weight	Approx. Cups	Products
8 ounce	8 oz.	1	Fruits, vegetables, *specialities
Picnic	10½ to 12 oz.	1¼	Condensed soups, small quantities of fruits, vegetables, meat and fish products, *specialties
12 oz. (vacuum)		12 oz.	Used largely for vacuum-packed corn
No. 300	14 to 16 oz.	1¾	Pork and beans, baked beans, meat products, cranberry sauce, blueberries, *specialties
No. 303	16 to 17 oz.	2	Fruits, vegetables, meat products, ready-to-serve soups, *specialties
No. 2	1 lb. 40 oz. or 1 pt. 2 fl. oz.	2¼	Juices, ready-to-serve soups, *specialties, and a few fruits and vegetables
No. 2¼	1 lb. 13 oz.	3¼	Fruits, some vegetables (pumpkin, sauerkraut, spinach and other greens, tomatoes)
No. 3 Cyl.	3 lb. 3 oz. or 1 qt. 15 fl. oz.	5¾	Fruit and vegetable juices, pork and beans, condensed soup and some vegetables for institutional use
No. 10	6½ lb. to 7 lb. 5 oz.	12–13	Fruits, vegetables for restaurant and institutional use

*Specialties—Food combinations prepared by special manufacturer's recipe.

The following items should be included in the specification to help in describing the product wanted, so that the price quoted will be on the item.

> type, style, and variety
>
> packing medium and syrup density
>
> concentration or specific gravity
>
> count or portion size
>
> drained weight
>
> federal certification

A specification that includes all of that information can be readily understood by the supplier, and he can provide meaningful quotations. Here are two examples of what might be included in the specifications.

> *Apricots*   halves, unpeeled, U.S. Grade B (choice), Heavy Syrup, Count-85/96 (Medium size), Minimum drained weight—64 ounces. Quantity required—5 dozen 9/10.
>
> *Tomato Puree*   eastern packs, heavy concentration, U.S. Grade A, Federal certification of grade required. Quantity required—5 dozen 6/10.

Developing specifications takes much time. It is necessary to make cutting tests, cooking tests, and taste tests. But two or three specifications can be developed each month and, by the time the year ends, a substantial number of specifications for canned fruits and vegetables will be available. The goal, of course, is eventually to develop specifications for all food items that are purchased.

In the development of specifications, considerable help can be obtained from the information on the grades and standards established by the government and by industry trade groups. Also, suppliers and their salesmen can provide information of much value.

Table 15-7   Substituting One Can for Another Size

For Institutional Use

One No. 10 can equals . . . . .Seven No. 303	(1 lb.)	cans
One No. 10 can equals . . . . .Five No. 2	(1 lb. 4 oz.)	cans
One No. 10 can equals . . . . .Four No. 2½	(1 lb. 13 oz.)	cans
One No. 10 can equals . . . . .Two No. 3 Cylinder	(46 to 50 oz.)	cans

Source: National Canners Association, Washington, D.C.

Checking at Receiving Time

When the canned fruits and vegetables are delivered, a check should be made to see if the correct quantity and the correct quality are received. It is well to make another cutting test. Make a cutting test of the product that has been received, and also a cutting test of the can that had been left unopened when the earlier cutting test of the sample can was made. Check again for drained weight, the appearance of the product, its texture, and its flavor. Also, do another cooking test to see how the product holds up under actual conditions.

There will be a comparison between the tests for the sample that was provided before the order was placed, and the product that has been received. If the product received is not satisfactory, call the supplier. Usually purveyors are ready to straighten out such situations. Also, if the product is satisfactory, the supplier would appreciate knowing it.

Additional Information about Canned Foods

Canned foods are not indestructible, and they should be handled with care. Cans should not be thrown or dropped. Treatment of that kind can cause considerable damage to the product inside.

Store canned foods in a cool, dry place. Most canned foods will keep indefinitely without spoiling. But a gradual chemical change occurs in canned foods during storage; and if the canned foods are left in storage for a long period of time this can affect flavor and texture. If the canned foods are held in storage where the temperature is high, the chemical change occurs more rapidly, and the effect on flavor and texture will occur sooner. Cool temperatures keep these chemical changes to a minimum.

Excessive moisture in the storage place can cause cans to rust. Rust on the outside of the can does not spoil what is inside. However, badly rusted cans may provide problems.

Cans that swell up can very likely be bad. It is recommended that swells not be used, as it is not worth taking a chance that the products inside are still good.

Once the cans have been opened, the canned foods can be stored in the original can if it is covered and put under refrigeration. Do not let opened canned foods stand in the hot kitchen. Freezing will not harm canned foods, but freezing is not recommended. If canned foods are left over, refrigerate them and use them as soon as possible.

For best results, heat canned foods in cooking utensils rather than in the can itself. Do not overcook canned foods. They have already been cooked and have been lightly seasoned. It is recommended that the liquid be boiled to half of its original volume and then be added back to the product. This conserves a maximum of flavor and nutrients. Heat to a serving temperature of 140° to 150°F.

240

There is no need to boil canned foods. They have been subjected to high heat treatment during the canning process that destroys bacteria and other organisms that can cause food to spoil.

Use the juices and syrups in cooking. When it is possible, use the liquid with the product. Fruit syrups can be used in dessert sauces, baking, gelatin salads, punch, and other drinks. Vegetable juices can be used in sauces, gelatin salads, soups, and salad dressings.

Summary

There are several points that should be remembered if the purchasing of canned fruits and vegetables is to be done effectively. These include:

Determine the needs before ordering.

Check to see if the best quality for the money is being obtained, by the use of cutting tests and cooking tests.

Specify the grade, brand, or other quality wanted and use commercial terms in the specifications.

When the product is received, check to be sure that what was ordered has been received.

A good purchasing program provides the right product at the right place, at the right time, and at the right price. That is the goal of the person who buys the food for a foodservice establishment.

Questions

1. Explain how the use to be made of a canned fruit, such as peaches, should determine what type of product should be purchased.

2. Describe the differences between a food buyer who functions as an order placer and one who does an informed buying job.

3. Under the law that established minimum quality standards for canned foods, the FDA has prescribed that the products meet three standards. What are these three standards?

4. What information is required on labels under the requirements of the Food, Drug and Cosmetic Act and the Packaging and Labeling Act?

5. What is meant by the word Brix?

6. What are the names of the U.S.D.A. grades for canned fruits and vegetables?

7. The grades for canned foods are based on scoring factors. List ten of these factors.

8. What changes occur in canned foods while in storage?

16

Purchasing Eggs

Eggs perform a variety of functions in the foodservice estab-lishment, and are probably the most versatile of foods. Their many and varied uses range from being served in the shell to being major ingredients in cooking and baking and an integral part of desserts. They are a perishable food, but have a shelf life longer than might be expected when they are held under the correct conditions.

The foodservice person who buys food must know a number of things about eggs in order to do an effective buying job. Included are a good knowledge of quality, size, and value; and the uses of each of these qualities and sizes for particular needs of the foodservice operation. Also, attention needs to be given to the value obtained for the money spent in buying eggs.

In addition, the egg buyer should have a good understanding of the mar-keting practices for eggs and should know about grades and other indicators of quality. The buyer must know about egg products as well as shell eggs, since the foodservice industry makes wide use of frozen, dry, liquid, and processed egg products.

Eggs and egg products used in foodservice establishments have their origin as shell eggs, so it is important that foodservice people have a good understand-ing of the egg, how the condition of the various parts that make up a shell egg relate to the quality of that egg. This understanding is of much value in purcha ing; and it helps greatly in ensuring that eggs are given proper care from the time they are delivered until they are used.

Parts of the Egg

The interior of a shell egg has several major parts. These include the shell, the shell membranes, the air cell, the egg white, the chalaza, and the yolk. How they are arranged in the shell and the condition they are in are related very closely to quality. Figure 16-1 illustrates the interior arrangement of the parts of the egg and identifies each part.

Egg Shell   The shell accounts for about 11 percent of the egg. Its principal component is calcium carbonate, and it is porous.

The egg shell ranges in color from a dark brown to a chalky white, depending on the breed of bird that produces the egg. The reason that certain colors predominate in certain areas or regions of the country results from the kind of birds being used to produce eggs in those areas. It is from this situation—less pronounced now than in the past—that consumers have a shell color preference. These preferences go back to when the poultry industry was very different and transportation and refrigeration were not as efficient as they now are. The preferences still exist, however, and foodservice operators still encounter customers who insist on having a white-shell egg or a brown-shell egg.

Actually, the color of the shell has no effect on the quality of the egg. Shell color is not an indicator of quality. The characteristics of the shell that do

Figure 16-1   Interior Arrangement of the Hen's Egg

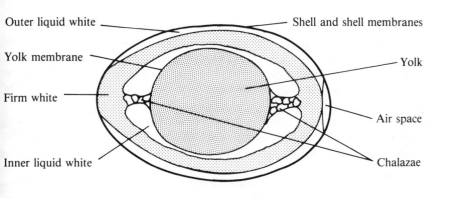

have a relation to quality are a shell that is unbroken, clean, and regular in shape. Those are the things to check on when purchasing eggs.

Shell Membranes   These membranes are very thin, measuring only about 24 ten-thousandths of an inch in thickness. They are inside the shell to protect the egg from outside contamination. The shell membranes are made up mostly of protein.

Air Cell   This part of the egg is an indicator of egg quality. The air cell is normally located at the large end of the egg between the shell membranes. It is not there when the hen lays the egg, but it appears as the egg cools and the contents contract in size and volume. In eggs of high quality, the air cell is small and it stays in a fixed position. Eggs are packed with the large ends up, so that the air cell remains in its normal position.

Egg White   The egg white is also a major indicator of quality. It is composed of both thick albumin and thin albumin, and it makes up about 58 percent of the total egg. Eggs of high quality contain a high proportion of thick albumin to thin albumin. As the quality of the egg goes down, so does this proportion. When the egg is taken out of its shell, the thick albumin helps retain the general shape of the egg.

The white has a high content of essential minerals. The condition of the white gives a good indication of quality; a thin, runny white is a sign of decreased quality.

Chalaza   This albuminous substance fastens the yolk to the center of the egg. It is actually the twisted end of a high-protein membrane that is around the egg to protect it. The appearance of a prominent chalaza in an uncooked or soft-cooked egg may be objectionable to some people, but the fact that it is there shows that the yolk has been well protected. This helps to maintain quality.

Egg Yolk   The yolk makes up about 31 percent of the total egg, is high in fat, and contains valuable proteins. The yolk ranges in color from pale yellow to orange. Some people are concerned that the color of one egg is different from that of another. The exact shade of color depends on the pigments contained in what the hen eats. With different feeds, different shades of egg yolk color can be found.

The yolk is also a major indicator of egg quality. If the yolk is round and upstanding, it is a sign that the egg is of high quality. As quality goes down, the yolk flattens out and loses its round shape.

Changes in Arrangement   There is a definite arrangement of the parts of the egg, and as quality decreases, this arrangement changes. When

he egg is fresh, the yolk is suspended in the center of the white and is kept there
›y the chalaza. At the time the egg is laid, the quality of the egg is at its highest
›oint. As time goes by, the amount of firm white in relation to thin white
lecreases. The air cell increases in size. The chalaza weakens and can no longer
ıold the yolk in the center of the egg.

Understanding Egg Quality

It is essential that those people concerned with the purchase,
torage, and use of eggs in a foodservice establishment understand what egg
juality is, how it can be determined, and how it can be maintained all the way
rom the time the eggs are purchased until they appear on the customer's plate
ıs a menu item. Only through this understanding can the things be done that
vill mean satisfaction for the customer, economical operation, and successful
ooking operations in the kitchen. It is the responsibility of the person who buys
·ggs for the operation to know what good egg quality is and to get the quality
›f eggs needed.

The premise that an egg is never better than when it is first laid is the basis
›n which standards of quality have been developed. The characteristics of
ıormal, freshly produced eggs become the standard that is used in grading eggs.
Γime, temperature, and poor handling practices change these properties or
:haracteristics of freshly laid eggs, and the quality of the eggs goes down.

Candling is used to determine the quality of the shell egg. When the eggs
ıre held before strong light, it is possible to determine the position of the yolk,
he size of the air cell, whether there is blood in the white or blood spots on the
·olk, and other defects such as cracks in the shell. Candlers formerly looked at
:ach individual egg as they held it in front of the light. Now, eggs are examined
ıs they are mechanically moved over banks of specially designed lights.

The Egg Grades

There are quality grades for eggs, with the letters AA, A, B,
ınd C being used to indicate the different grades. In some places, other terms are
ısed to designate the grades. For example, in Massachusetts, the term "Strictly
Fresh" may be used to designate Grade A; the U.S. Department of Agriculture
ıses the term "Fancy Fresh" to indicate Grade AA in one of its quality programs. Terminology such as that usually applies only to eggs sold in cartons
n retail stores and is not of concern to foodservice people, who buy eggs in
juantity. Each state and the United States Department of Agriculture have
·egulations on the quality grades; generally the various specifications are quite
similar.

Table 16-1 summarizes the U.S. Consumer Grades for Shell Eggs. Table
16-2 shows the tolerance for the individual carton or case within a lot.

Table 16-1		Summary of U.S. Consumer Grades for Shell Eggs

U.S. Consumer Grades	At least 80% (lot average)* must be:	Tolerance Permitted From the 80% Requirement**
Grade AA or Fresh Fancy Quality	AA Quality	15 to 20% of the eggs may be of A Quality. Not over 5%*** may be of B, C, or Check quality.
Grade A	A Quality or better	15 to 20% of the eggs may be of B Quality. Not over 5%*** may be of C or Check quality.
Grade B	B Quality or better	10 to 20% of the eggs may be of C Quality. Not over 10%*** may be Dirty or Check in quality.

*In lots of two or more cases or cartons, see Table of Tolerance For Individual Case or Carton Within a Lot for tolerance allowed.
**Within the tolerance permitted, an allowance is made at receiving points or shipping destination for ½ percent leakers in Grades AA, A, and B.
***Substitution of higher qualities for the lower qualities specified is permitted.
Source: Based on United States Department of Agriculture material.

Size and Weight Are Factors

The size of the eggs is not related to their quality, but it is an important factor in purchasing eggs because size and price are closely related. The larger the size, usually the higher the price. This makes size one of the determining factors for value of eggs received for the money spent. So, in purchasing eggs both the grade quality and the size need to be specified.

Table 16-2		Tolerance for Individual Case or Carton Within a Lot

U.S. Consumer Grades	Minimum Quality, By Percent* Required Per Case	Minimum Quality, By Number of Eggs* Required Per Carton
Grade AA or Fresh Fancy Quality	70% AA 20% A 10% B, C, or Check	8 eggs AA 2 eggs A 2 eggs, B, C, or Check
Grade A	70% A 20% B 10% C, or Check	8 eggs A 2 eggs B 2 eggs C, or Check
Grade B	70% B 10% C 20% Check, or Dirty	8 eggs B 2 eggs C 2 eggs, Check, or Dirty

*Substitution of higher qualities for the lower qualities specified is permitted.
Source: Based on United States Department of Agriculture material.

The egg size is expressed in terms of ounces in the definition of what is a Large egg and what is a Small egg, for example. The Large egg must have a minimum net weight per dozen of 24 oz.; the figure for the Small egg is 18 oz. There are similar minimum weights in ounces for each of the other sizes—Jumbo, Extra Large, Medium, and Pewee.

Table 16-5 shows the U.S. Weight Classes for Consumer Grades of Eggs. These are the size classifications established by the United States Department of Agriculture. Just as in the case of the Quality Specifications, the states have size specifications that are very close to these. Also shown are the minimum weights per 30 dozen, expressed in pounds; and the minimum net weight at the rate per dozen for individual eggs.

The ratio of edible portion to the shell, and the ratio of yolk to white do not differ much in eggs of different sizes. So, if shell eggs are to be used for cooking or for promoting a special egg dish, the size that is the "best buy" at the particular time of purchase would be a good choice. However, if the food-service establishment has a reputation for uniformity in the egg dishes on the menu, probably the same size would be purchased on a regular basis.

Generally, Large or Medium eggs are standard choices for breakfast. Customers usually want their breakfast eggs to be larger than the Small or Pewee sizes. When the eggs are to be served as part of another dish and do not retain their identity, then substitution of one size for another, depending on price, can be done with good results.

For example, four Large eggs are equivalent to three Extra Large eggs, or five Medium eggs, or six Small eggs. Each of those numbers of different size eggs will produce 3/4 cup plus 1 tablespoon of egg. Similarly, for one cup of egg, either five Large, four Extra Large, six Medium, or seven Small eggs may be used. Table 16-3 shows these relationships.

Table 16-3   Guide for Using Whole Eggs of
                  Various Sizes in Recipes

Number of Large Eggs	Equivalent To: Extra Large Eggs	Medium Eggs	Small Eggs	Providing the Following Approximate Volume of Egg
1	1	1	1	3 tablespoons
2	2	2	3	¼ cup plus 2 tablespoons
3	3	4	4	½ cup plus 2 tablespoons
4	3	5	6	¾ cup plus 1 tablespoon
5	4	6	7	1 cup
6	5	7	8	1 cup plus 3 tablespoons
8	6	10	11	1½ cups plus 2 tablespoons
10	8	12	14	2 cups
12	10	14	17	2¼ cups plus 2 tablespoons

Source: Based on United States Department of Agriculture material.

Similar relationships of number of eggs to equal one cup of egg are listed in Table 16-4. These relationships are expressed in terms of how many whole eggs, or how many whites, or how many yolks are required.

Another comparison that is of significance when decisions are being made on what eggs to purchase relates price to value on the basis of weight. There are many guides that have been developed to make the calculation of these relationships easy and rapid. Tables 16-5 and 16-6 provide examples of how the comparisons are made.

Egg Prices

The prices of eggs are closely related to supply, demand, and quality. The wholesale market egg prices are established each day as a result of the demand dealers express for eggs of certain quality and size, and how that demand relates to the supply of eggs available.

The demand stays fairly constant, but prices do fluctuate over the short

Table 16-4 Approximate Number of Eggs Required to Make One Cup of Egg

Egg Size	Number of Whole Eggs	Number of Whites	Number of Yolks
Extra Large	4	6	12
Large	5	7	14
Medium	6	8	16
Small	7	10	18

Source: Based on United States Department of Agriculture material.

Table 16-5 U.S. Weight Classes for Consumer Grades of Shell Eggs

Size Or Weight Class	Minimum Net Weight Per Dozen, In Ounces	Minimum Net Weight Per 30 Dozen, In Pounds	Minimum Net Weight For Individual Eggs, At Rate Per Dozen, In Ounces
Jumbo	30	56	29
Extra Large	27	50½	26
Large	24	45	23
Medium	21	39½	20
Small	18	34	17
Pewees	15	28	—

Source: Based on United States Department of Agriculture material.

Table 16-6   Comparing the Value of Eggs on the
Basis of Weight

When Large Eggs Cost Per Dozen . . .	Subtract This Amount To Get the Comparative Value of Medium Size Eggs . . .	Subtract This Amount To Get the Comparative Value of Small Size Eggs . . .
36 to 43 cents	5 cents	10 cents
44 to 51 cents	6 cents	12 cents
52 to 59 cents	7 cents	14 cents
60 to 67 cents	8 cents	16 cents
68 to 75 cents	9 cents	18 cents

Source: Massachusetts Cooperative Extension Service.

time period, due to changes in the supply of eggs coming to market. For the year as a whole, the differences in volume of supplies, and the differences in prices which they cause, are usually the result of weather conditions and the seasonality of egg production. There are less pronounced seasonal variations now than in the past, but they still remain and have an effect on prices.

Other factors that affect the price of eggs to the foodservice operator are not related to changes in the wholesale egg market. There are costs for handling eggs on their way to market. There are delivery charges, and there are charges for other distribution services.

It is value, not just price, that determines whether the purchase of an item at a particular price is a good buying decision. The same is true for eggs. The wholesale market price is just part of the picture.

Sources of Supply

A variety of types of firms supply eggs to foodservice operations. The supplier may be a purveyor specializing in the egg business. He may be an institutional supplier who provides eggs along with other foods to foodservice establishments. He may be a poultryman who produces the eggs and sells them directly to the foodservice buyer.

Regardless of the type of supplier, foodservice buyers need to be concerned about the ability of the suppliers to meet their specifications for quality, variety, and service. Evaluate suppliers on the basis of those factors, and buy from the ones who can provide what is wanted, when it is needed, in the form and condition desired, and at a fair and reasonable price.

As in all foodservice purchasing, specifications should be used in buying eggs. Keep specifications for buying shell eggs as simple as possible, but make sure they include all the information the supplier needs. He needs to understand the needs of the operation. The specifications should also specify the conditions of delivery.

Specification Examples

Two examples will show specifications in use in purchasing eggs for foodservice establishments. Here is one:

Eggs, Fresh Whole

Massachusetts Grade A Large

Delivered twice weekly in new cases.

Not more than two days to elapse between grading and delivery.

In meeting these specifications, the purveyor would be expected to comply with the egg quality and egg size law of the Commonwealth of Massachusetts. The eggs would have to have an average minimum weight of not less than 24 ounces per dozen. However, a tolerance of not more than 4 percent of the eggs, which weigh not less than at the rate of 22 ounces per dozen is allowed. In other states, the name of the state would be substituted for Massachusetts and the egg regulations of the particular state would apply.

Here is another specification, this time requiring that the eggs meet the U.S. grades.

Eggs, Fresh Whole

U.S. Grade A Large, minimum weight of individual eggs at the rate of 24 ounces per dozen.

Delivered twice weekly in new cases.

Not more than two days to elapse between grading and delivery.

The supplier who meets this specification will be guided by the federal grade standards. Also, this specification has a narrower range in size of eggs than the other. The buyer here has specified that no eggs shall weigh at a rate less than 24 ounces per dozen.

Both of the sets of specifications also include requirements regarding delivery and time of delivery, as well as requiring that new cases be used.

U.S.D.A. Acceptance Service

Foodservice operators can purchase eggs that are graded to their own specifications and certified by a federal grader as meeting those specifications. This service is known as the U.S.D.A. Acceptance Service.

Both the purveyor and the grader should be provided copies of the specifications. The purveyor should be informed when bids are requested that inspection is a requirement in the specifications and the purveyor will pay the charges for the inspection service. After the federal grader has checked the eggs and finds that they meet the requirements of the specifications, he stamps the U.S.D.A. Acceptance stamp on the case. If the eggs meet federal grade specifications, he may also stamp the case with the federal shield and a grade letter designation. The grader stamps the invoice in the same way as the case is stamped.

U.S.D.A. Inspection Service

The United States Department of Agriculture has an Egg Products Inspection Service, and inspects a large proportion of egg products. This inspection program includes strict plant sanitation and facilities requirements. There is a continuous inspection of the processing operations. A final check is made after the products have been pasteurized, cooled, and packaged, to ensure the product's wholesomeness.

The products that are officially inspected and passed have the U.S.D.A. inspection stamp on the package.

There are also state regulations governing these products. Eggs moving in interstate commerce must now be pasteurized or otherwise treated to kill all viable Salmonella organisms.

Care and Handling of Eggs

Eggs are a perishable product, and although the shell and the arrangement of the egg inside the shell provide some help in maintaining quality, they need to be handled carefully and under the right conditions. Two factors have the most effect on changes in the quality of eggs—time and temperature. Of the two, temperature is the more important.

When eggs are stored at room temperature, quality goes down rapidly. If the eggs are kept under refrigeration, they will maintain their quality grade for days and even weeks. Eggs freeze at 28°F. The change in quality is slowed down considerably when the eggs are held below 50°F. So, most cooler units operate at a temperature that is satisfactory for short-term storage of eggs.

Figure 16-3 shows the effect of holding temperatures on egg quality. In this case, the data relate to eggs of AA quality, which were stored for 10 days at different temperatures. When the eggs were held at over 75°F., the quality went down most rapidly and to the greatest extent. The quality of the eggs that were held at 30°F. went down very little.

Protecting Egg Flavor

The shells of eggs do much to protect the egg, but they are porous, and eggs absorb foreign odors readily. These odors affect the flavor of the egg. If eggs have an objectionable flavor, it is usually the result of the eggs having been stored with certain vegetables and fruits, or having been stored in musty coolers.

251

Figure 16-3   Effect of Holding Temperature and Time on Albumen Quality

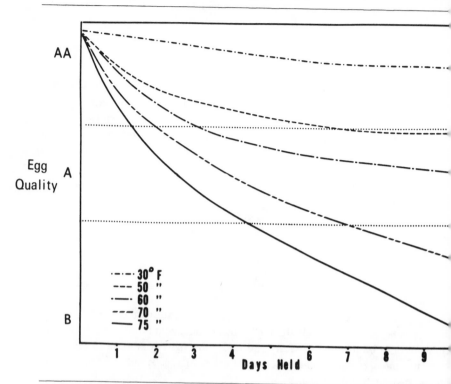

Source: Adapted from material in a publication of the Department of Poultry Science at the Ontario Agricultural College.

Humidity also has an effect on egg flavor. The quality is retained best when the eggs are held in coolers that operate at 70 to 85 degrees relative humidity. However, a humid environment does encourage mold to develop and the eggs to absorb odors. So, it is important that the coolers where eggs are stored be clean, free from odors and well ventilated.

Size and Grade of Eggs and Their Use

The food that is right for the particular use intended in the meal has much to do with how successful the meal is and how satisfied the customer is. In the use of eggs, grades and size are closely related to what use is to be made of the eggs. For some uses, top quality grade eggs are best, while for other uses eggs that fall in the lower quality grades can be perfectly satisfactory. The same is true of size. For some dishes, size is important; for other uses it is not.

Figure 16-4 lists some of the foodservice uses of eggs and relates to those uses the qualities and the reasons that certain qualities are best for certain uses and that certain sizes are best.

Shell Egg Purchasing Guide

As in the case of the purchase of other foods for use in a foodservice establishment, the buyer needs to know the product, and then apply that knowledge to how eggs are purchased. Here are some suggestions that make up a good guide for purchasing shell eggs.

Specify Grade A Eggs

This is the quality most available.

It is satisfactory for all uses.

It holds up well. Given normal care, eggs in this quality grade should remain in grade for the average amount of time eggs are held in a foodservice operation.

Specify Large or Medium Size

Usually large eggs are in best supply.

Figure 16-4   An Egg That's Right for Every Use

Uses	Quality	Reasons

Fried
Poached
Soft-cooked
	Grade AA or
	    Grade A.
	Large or
	    Medium Size.
		Egg white is firm.
		Yolk is round and usually well
		    centered.

Hard-cooked	Grade A.
	Large or
	    Medium Size.
	Not Shell-treated.
		It may be difficult to peel hard-
		    cooked eggs which have just been
		    laid or have been shell-treated.
		    Ease in peeling is associated with
		    the loss of carbon dioxide from
		    the eggs. Eggs which have been
		    stored under refrigeration for a
		    few days and which have not
		    been oiled usually peel well.

Omelets Scrambled	Grade A. Size unimportant.	Quality is satisfactory. Yolk and white blend well.

Baking and
    general
    cooking
	Grade A or
	    Grade B.
	Large or
	    Medium Size.
		Grade A is always in best supply
		    and you may not wish to inven-
		    tory multiple quality grades.
		    However, Grade B eggs are
		    perfectly satisfactory for general
		    cooking use.

They provide servings of adequate size.

They are the standard for most recipes.

At certain times of the year, Medium size may be available at advantageous prices.

Medium-sized eggs from young flocks are of excellent quality.

Specify New Cases

New cases keep to a minimum the breakage of eggs.

Clean cases keep clean eggs clean.

Clean eggs retain quality better.

Specify Delivery at Least Weekly

Quality goes down with time, and eggs should not be held too long in storage.

Frequent delivery reduces the amount of holding space needed in the foodservice establishment.

Store Eggs in a Clean and Cool Place

Clean holding places help eggs to retain their flavor.

The drop in quality is slowed if eggs are held under refrigeration.

Check the egg purchasing and egg holding practices of the operation against this list. See if the recommended practices are being followed.

Egg Products

Shell eggs are not the only form of eggs in use. Egg products are available commercially in a variety of forms that meet about all the needs for eggs in a foodservice establishment. There are liquid eggs, frozen eggs, and egg solids, which are known also as dried eggs. These forms of egg can be purchased as whole eggs, whites, yolks, or blends. Some of these products are also available in fortified form. Salted and sugared yolks are examples.

Many of the things of importance in shell eggs have similar importance for processed eggs. So, some consideration of these items is important for the person who is buying food for the foodservice operation. Again, a good knowledge of the products, their availability, grades, holding conditions, and uses is essential for efficient purchasing.

Liquid, frozen, and dried eggs have a number of advantages for foodservice operators. They:

eliminate the need to break out eggs and so save on labor there and in other handling tasks

reduce the amount of storage space for eggs

provide uniformity in quality and color

eliminate waste of eggs

reduce volume of garbage

make measurement and use of eggs easier

provide more versatility

Egg products have a wide range of uses and for foodservice operations offer much in the way of convenience. When they are processed correctly, egg products are equal in their cooking and nutritional qualities to fresh eggs.

Frozen mixtures of egg and nonfat milk can be used for scrambled eggs and omelets. There are cylinders of egg that provide both yolk and white in each slice. Offered also are combinations of omelet mixes, and many variations of egg products that provide for practically all of the needs for eggs in a foodservice operation.

Convenient Containers

Eggs traditionally have been available in 30-pound metal cans for frozen eggs, but this is too large a container for many foodservice users. So, more convenient containers are now available. Egg products are offered in 10-pound polyethylene bags in corrugated containers. They also come in 10-pound enameled steel cans; and they can be purchased in plasticized cartons of the kind used for half-gallons and gallons of milk.

Care in Handling

Egg products are an excellent place for spoilage organisms to grow. Even though the product is in top condition when it is received, it can deteriorate quickly if it is not handled correctly.

There are certain precautions that should be taken in handling and storing egg products, in order to maintain quality. Here are a few:

Store frozen eggs at 0°F. or lower. Eggs freeze at 28°F., so borderline freezer temperatures are not adequate.

Thaw frozen eggs as rapidly as possible. The maximum shelf life of thawed eggs is two days.

Store liquid eggs at 32°F.

Keep containers of liquid or frozen eggs tightly closed when not in use.

Remember that food poisoning bacteria grow at temperatures above 40°F.

Equivalency of Egg Product and Shell Eggs

The amount of egg product needed to replace specified numbers of whole eggs, egg whites, or egg yolks is shown in Tables 16-7 through 16-9.

Table 16-7 indicates the number of shell eggs that are equivalent to one pound of frozen egg product, and to one pound of dried egg product, with similar equivalencies for whites and yolks. Table 16-8 shows the amount of frozen egg product to replace one shell egg and 12 shell eggs, with similar information for the equivalencies of yolks and whites. Table 16-9 provides similar information for dried egg product to replace shell eggs.

Table 16-7   Equivalency of One Pound of Egg Product

Product (pound)	Large Sized Shell Eggs (Number)
Frozen Product	Fresh Eggs
Whole	10 Whole Eggs
Whites	16 Whites
Yolks	26 Yolks
Dried Product	Fresh Eggs
Whole	32 Whole Eggs
Whites	100 Whites
Yolks	54 Yolks

Source: U.S. Department of Agriculture material.

Table 16-8   Frozen Egg Product to Replace Specific Numbers of Eggs, Whites, and Yolks

Shell Egg Equivalent	Frozen Egg Product (Thawed)	Amount to Use
1 Egg	Whole	3 Tablespoons
12 Eggs	Whole	2¼ Cups
1 Egg	Yolks	1½ Tablespoons
12 Eggs	Yolks	1 Cup
1 Egg	Whites	2 Tablespoons
12 Eggs	Whites	1½ Cups

Source: U.S. Department of Agriculture Material.

Table 16-9   Dried Egg Product to Replace
Specific Numbers of Eggs, Whites,
and Yolks

Shell Egg Equivalent	Dried Egg Product (Sifted)	Amount to Use
1 Egg	Whole	2½ Tablespoons plus 2½ Tablespoons of Water
12 Eggs	Whole	2 Cups plus 2 Cups of Water
1 Egg	Yolks	2 Tablespoons plus 2 Teaspoons of Water
12 Eggs	Yolks	1½ Cups plus ½ Cup of Water
1 Egg	Whites	2 Teaspoons plus 2 Tablespoons of Water
12 Eggs	Whites	½ Cup plus 1½ Cups of Water

Source: U.S. Department of Agriculture Material.

Thawing Frozen Eggs

In the use of frozen egg products, it is necessary to thaw the product. Table 16-10 shows three methods in which thawing before use can be done.

Since liquids and solids have a tendency to separate when they freeze, it is a good idea to mix the product before thawing completely in order to get a uniform blend.

It is not necessary to thaw a can completely, since the dough hook on a mixer will break up small frozen clumps satisfactorily. Since the product is not thawed completely, the temperature of the liquid egg will be low.

Table 16-10   Suggested Methods, Temperatures, and
Estimated Times for Thawing

Method	Temperature	Time*
Running cold water (do not submerge can)	50–60°F	8–15 hrs.
Crush or slice frozen egg and put in water jacketed kettle or ingredient mixture.	55–60°F	2–8 hrs. Maximum depending upon grind fineness.
Cooler-refrigerator	40°F	48–72 hrs.

*Figures stated are for 30-lb. container. Ten-lb. container will require approximately 25 percent of this time.

Source: Pennsylvania State University, Cooperative Extension Service.

Summary

Knowledge of quality, size, value, and uses of each for particular needs is essential for effective foodservice purchasing of eggs. Also needed is an understanding of the egg marketing practices, grades, and quality indicators. There are quality grades for eggs with differences in the federal and state grade names, although the specifications are similar. Tolerances are allowed. Size and weight of eggs and price are closely related and are factors in purchasing.

Value, not price alone, determines good buying decisions; and specifications play a big part in getting desired value. The U.S.D.A. offers inspection and grading services.

Eggs are a perishable product and time and temperature are important factors in the loss or maintenance of quality; correct refrigeration is also necessary.

Foodservice people also use egg products such as liquid eggs, frozen eggs, and egg solids, which can be purchased as whole eggs, whites, yolks, or blends. A good knowledge of the products, availability, grades, holding conditions, and uses is necessary for efficient purchasing of egg products. Tables are available that show equivalency of egg products and shell eggs.

Questions

1.   List six things that a buyer of eggs needs to know in order to do the best egg buying job.

2.   Name the six major parts of a shell egg.

3.   In purchasing eggs, grade is an important factor. What are two other important factors?

4.   Describe the differences in shell, air cell, white, and yolk between Grades AA, A, B, and C.

5.   Explain the effect of holding temperatures and time on egg albumin quality.

6.   Give reasons why Grade AA or Grade A Large or Medium size eggs are best for frying, poaching, and soft-cooking.

7.   Describe precautions to be taken in storing and handling egg products so that quality is maintained.

17

Purchasing Dairy Products

Purchasing dairy products for a foodservice establishment involves special problems for the food buyer because of the wide variety of the products and their perishability. The buyer of dairy products needs to know the characteristics and the uses of these products, which have a place in all parts of the menu and combine with many other foods in meal production. Probably a fifth of the food purchasing budget is spent for dairy products. So, correct procedures for purchasing, handling, storing, and serving these products have a great deal to do with the success of the total foodservice operation. Correct selection and effective quality control are especially important.

Know What Is Needed

As in the purchase of any items, it is essential to know specifically what is needed, for what use, at what time, and at what location. Only through the clear definition of the needs of the operation, and the translation of those needs into the items to be purchased in a very specific way, can the purchasing be effective.

So, the first step for the person who is buying dairy products is to be sure he has the information to answer the questions on what is needed at what time, and at what place.

What specific dairy product is needed? Of what standard should it be? Then, what is available to the buyer, and what is the quality of the products that are available?

What is the use for which the product is needed? What amount is needed to satisfy that need? What specific kind and size of package or container will meet the need?

At what time will the product be needed? At what time should it be delivered? At what time should it be ordered? Since those times are all interrelated, it is important that they be scheduled so that the need can be met at the specified time.

In what way is the product to be used or adapted? Will it be served as is? Will it be an ingredient with others in the production of a meal item? How is it going to be stored until use? What refrigeration or other storage conditions will enable it to retain its quality?

Where is the product available? From what manufacturing source? From what local source? What kind of delivery situation exists?

Where can information about the product be obtained? Where can information about prices, the market, demand, supply, and similar subjects be obtained?

Many other questions could be added to that list, but these are representative of the amount and kinds of information the foodservice buyer needs when purchasing dairy products.

With that information the buyer is in a position to make wise selections, to see that the products are handled correctly, and to see that the correct dairy items are obtained for the specific uses for which they are best suited. In the process, the buyer is contributing greatly to the efficient conduct of the overall foodservice business. What and how this purchasing job is done directly affects the efficiency of cost control, labor use, waste volume, sanitation, customer satisfaction, and other aspects of the operation.

This chapter provides information to answer some of those questions that face the food buyer, and should be of much assistance in identifying and solving operations problems that relate to dairy products procurement. Table 17-1 includes much information on the amount of various dairy products to be purchased to meet foodservice needs.

Sources of Supply

Few operators encounter problems in getting the quality and amounts of dairy products that they need except in unusual circumstances. Usually, milk and cream are produced relatively close to where the operation is located, and there are local dairy companies or other kinds of distributors

Table 17-1   A Quantity Guide for Dairy Product
Purchasing

Product	Pur-chase Unit	Weight per Unit (Pounds)	Size of Serving	No. of Servings per Purch. Unit	Approx. No. of Purchase Units for 25	100
Butter (Prints)	Carton	1.00	1 Pat	72	(1)	1½
Butter (Patties)	Case	5.00	1 Pat	360	(1)	(1)
Cheddar Cheese	Pound	1.00	1 Ounce	16	1¾	6¼
Cottage Cheese	32 Ounce Carton	2.00	4 Ounces	8	3¼	12½
Process Cheese	Pound (Sliced)	1.00	1 Ounce (Slice)	16	1¾	6¼
Coffee Cream	Quart	2.13	¾ Ounce	42	(1)	2½
Whipping Cream	Quart	2.10	1¼ Tbls.	50	(1)	2
Ice Cream	Gallon	4.50	No. 12 Scoop	22-26	1	4
			No. 16 Scoop	31-35	(1)	3
			No. 20 Scoop	38-42	(1)	2½
			No. 24 Scoop	47-50	(1)	2
Ice Cream	2½ Gallon	11.25	No. 12 Scoop	55-65	(1)	2
			No. 16 Scoop	77-87	(1)	1¼
			No. 20 Scoop	95-105	(1)	1
			No. 24 Scoop	117-125	(1)	(1)
Milk	Quart	2.15	8 Ounce Glass	4	6¼	25
	Gallon	8.60	8 Ounce Glass	16	1¾	6¼
	5 Gallon Dispenser	43.00	8 Ounce Glass	80	(1)	1¼
Sherbet	Gallon	6.00	—— Same as for ice cream ——			
	2½ Gallon	15.00	—— Same as for ice cream ——			
Nonfat Dry Milk (Instant)			About 6½ cups per pound			
Nonfat Dry Milk (Regular)			About 3¼ cups per pound			
Dry Whole Milk			About 3½ cups per pound			

(1) Indicates less than one purchase unit required.

that make deliveries. The deliveries may be as frequent as every day, which is desirable considering that milk and cream are the most perishable of the dairy products.

Two other perishable dairy items—cottage cheese and ice cream—are usually available from local dairy companies or ice cream manufacturers, with deliveries once or twice a week in many areas.

Other dairy products that are somewhat less perishable include butter, cheese, and nonfat dry milk. These are usually available from more distant sources and delivery is less frequent. These products are available through jobbers, purveyors, or salesmen who sell to the foodservice industry.

Find out about the dairy company that is to supply the needed products. Visit the plant and see how they process products. Describe your needs and problems in getting specific items. Many valuable suggestions on what is available, the best selection, the needed storage conditions, and the particular uses for which a product is best suited can be obtained in this way.

Get to know the purveyors, jobbers, and salesmen who supply the other dairy products. They know much about the market, wholesale prices, market trends, changes in products, and similar things that can be of much value to the buyer.

Also, become familiar with the market reports issued by federal and state departments of agriculture and also those from private sources. These reports contain much current market information.

The Dairy Products

To purchase effectively for a foodservice establishment, the buyer needs to know a great deal about the products to be bought—their quality, grades, sizes of packages, the terms used in reference to the product in the trade and in market reports, and any other things that will help him get what is needed.

There are many federal, state, and municipal laws, rules, regulations, and definitions for dairy products—probably more than for any other group of foods. In the case of most dairy products, minimum standards of composition and identity have been established, although many of the dairy products available in commercial channels are well above the minimum standards.

Often this large amount of regulation has an effect on the prices that are paid, since products that meet certain standards cost more than those at a lower standard of quality. A premium ice cream, for example, costs more than a product made to sell at a competitive advantage. An ice cream that is flavored with natural fruits brings more money than one that is artificially flavored. This difference is important when it comes to comparing prices and developing specifications that must be met before the product will be purchased.

This chapter includes information on terms that are used, sizes of packages, grades, and product variations for the most widely used dairy products in foodservice operations.

A Lot about Milk

Fluid milk is a whole milk product that is used as a beverage and also in preparing various menu items. There are variations in the amount of butterfat that milk must have depending on the requirements of the particular state. But it usually is about 3.25 percent fat as a minimum, which is the minimum level that is recommended by the U.S. Public Health Service's "Grade A Pasteurized Milk Ordinance," used as a basis for many of the state laws. The average fluid milk on the market has a fat content from 3.5 to 3.7 percent. There are some exceptions for certain milk from Guernsey and Jersey dairy animals that average from 4.5 to 5.0 percent fat.

The terms Pasteurized, Homogenized, Standardized, and Vitamin D are used in the labeling and identification of fluid milk. Just about all milk sold today has been pasteurized to kill harmful bacteria and to maintain its quality better in storage. The product is exposed to a heat treatment for a period long enough to kill most of the microorganisms in the milk.

Public demand now is generally for homogenized milk. This is milk that has been subjected to a mechanical process in which the globules of fat are reduced in size. As a result, the milk does not have a cream layer. It is uniform from top to bottom and remains that way in storage. The homogenization process does not require the addition of anything to the milk, nor taking away anything.

Standardization refers to the process in dairies of blending and adjusting the fat content of milk of varying contents to a specific level. The milk as received from farms varies a little in fat content. Standardizing makes it possible to provide milk that has a uniform fat content from day to day.

Vitamin D milk is milk to which Vitamin D has been added. To carry that terminology, the Vitamin D content must have been increased to at least 400 U.S.P. units per quart. If Vitamin D is added, the milk must be so labeled. Sometimes other vitamins are also added. In those cases, the milk must be labeled as Vitamin Fortified Milk.

Low Fat, Fat Free, and Skim Milk

Some other fluid milks have importance on the market. In fact, they have greatly increased in popularity and demand as people have become more concerned about being overweight. These products do not have enough fat content to be considered a whole milk product. These fluid products are processed and packaged in the same way as whole milk products. The difference is in the amount of milk fat.

Nonfat, fat free, and defatted milk are terms for a product that has less than 0.1 percent of milk fat. Lowfat milk usually has between 0.5 and 2 percent of milk fat. Skim milk or skimmed milk is a product that usually has less than 0.5 percent milk fat. In some states, these products may be fortified with nonfat dry milk. If they are, then they must be labeled as fortified. There are also varia-

263

tions in the amount of fat that can be in the product of these various names, depending on the state.

Flavored Milk and Flavored Milk Drink

Another fluid milk product is produced by adding flavoring materials to milk. Chocolate flavoring is added to whole milk to produce chocolate milk. If it is added to skim milk or to a partially skimmed milk, then the resulting product is labeled chocolate drink or beverage. Strawberry, coffee, and maple flavorings are also added to milk to make similar flavored milk and milk drink products.

Buttermilk and Yogurt

Cultured buttermilk is made by adding a lactic acid-producing bacterial culture to skim or partially skimmed milk. This produces a buttermilk that is thicker than skim milk and which has a slightly acid aromatic flavor. The treatment causes a partial coagulation of the milk protein. While almost all of the commercially marketed buttermilk is cultured, there is a natural type of buttermilk that is a byproduct of the butter-making process. In some parts of the country, small butter granules are added to the buttermilk.

Another cultured product that uses specific bacteria to produce a fairly strong acid flavor and its characteristic aroma is known as yogurt. Yogurt is available in both liquid and semi-solid forms. It is flavored with fruit as well as being available in unflavored form. Also, flavoring materials such as vanilla are added to yogurt and the product is marketed as vanilla yogurt in the case of this particular flavoring.

Packaging Variety

These fluid milk beverages come in a variety of packages made of paper, plastic, and glass. One-half pint, pint, quart, one-half gallon, and gallon are the usual sizes for glass and paper containers. Plastic bottles are of gallon and half-gallon capacities.

In foodservice operations, there is wide use of refrigerated milk dispensers. Five-gallon metal cans are available for the wall-mounted or counter-height dispensers. Ten-gallon metal cans are used for the floor model dispensers that have a pumping unit.

The flexible plastic bag in a corrugated cardboard box can be used for the five-gallon-of-milk type of refrigerated dispenser. It is a nonreturnable, disposable container, in contrast to the metal can. Sometimes, however, reusable rigid, plastic containers are used instead of the corrugated cardboard box. The disposable containers are usually five- or six-gallon size.

Foodservice establishments that use large amounts of milk in preparing foods, can obtain milk in three, five, or ten-gallon metal containers. For the very small foodservice establishment, where the need for fluid milk is small, the ten-quart plastic bag-in-the-box container that will fit into a household refrigerator is a good choice.

What type and size of container is used depends on the needs and the storage facilities and dispensing facilities of the particular establishment. Also, there is the problem of disposal of paper and the single-service plastic containers; and the need for facilities for storing and handling metal and glass returnable bottles or containers.

Cream in a Variety of Forms

Cream is another dairy product that comes in a variety of forms, with the content of fat again a factor in distinguishing one from the other.

Coffee cream, half-and-half, light cream, and all-purpose cream are the dairy products normally used for coffee. All of these products provide the desired results, but there may be considerable variation in the cost, due to the different compositions. Light cream, also known as coffee cream and table cream, usually varies from 16 to 20 percent fat. The U.S. Food and Drug Administration standard for this product sets a minimum of at least 18 percent milk fat. Most state standards now include that minimum. Half-and-half is a mixture of cream and milk, and it contains from 10 to 12 percent fat with added milk solids. All-purpose cream has from 20 to 25 percent fat.

Heavy cream, extra heavy cream, and whipping cream are normally used to produce whipped cream. Under the federal standards of identity, whipping creams are divided into light and heavy. Light whipping cream must have at least 30 percent milkfat, and heavy whipping cream must have at least 36 percent milkfat. All of these products will whip to the needed consistency under the right conditions. Which is selected depends on which best meets requirements. They can all be tried and then the one that does the job best can be the standard choice.

Sour cream and sour half-and-half are two other cream products. Sour cream is made by adding lactic acid bacteria culture to light cream, to produce a cream that is smooth and thick, with at least 18 percent milkfat and a characteristic flavor. Sour half-and-half is the result of adding a lactic acid bacteria culture to the mixture of milk and cream called half-and-half.

Other Products

There is also available a product called imitation milk, which is the reconstitution of dry milk solids into a fluid form. The name comes from the fact that some laws regarding milk required that this product be labeled as imitation. If there is fat in the product that comes from other than milk, then the product is called filled milk.

Diet foods produced from milk products are also available. In addition to the liquid form there is a dry version. These diet foods usually have a high content of milk solids and are fortified with minerals, vitamins, and other food elements.

The use of cream for coffee in foodservice establishments has declined in favor of artificial dairy products that do not have any dairy products in them. There is wide use of coffee whiteners, half-and-half, and a whipping cream that has neither milk nor other dairy product content. A whipped frozen product that resembles whipped cream also falls into this same category.

Concentrated Milks

Some concentrated fluid milks, known as evaporated milk and condensed milk, can be purchased.

Evaporated milk is prepared by heating whole milk that has been homogenized under a vacuum, in order to remove half of the water content. Then, the product is sealed in cans and sterilized. Evaporated skim milk is also available.

Sweetened condensed milk is a concentrated milk to which sugar has been added. This addition of 40 to 45 percent sugar helps preserve the condensed milk. Again, about half of the water has been removed from whole milk to make this product. Although usually canned, condensed milk is available in some places in bulk.

Forms and Nomenclature of Butter

Butter is a creamy and sweet dairy product used as a spread, and also used in cooking. Most of the butter is produced in the central part of the United States and shipped to suppliers in the rest of the nation. It is usually available from purveyors who supply foodservice establishments. Many dairies that supply fluid milk and cream also distribute butter.

Butter is made from cream that has been pasteurized. The cream is churned to produce butter and buttermilk, and the buttermilk is drained off, leaving the butter to be washed, salted, and finished.

Butter is available in the form of patties, prints, and tubs. The patties are individual servings of butter that may vary from about 48 to 96 pieces per pound, depending on the size of the individual serving. The five-pound package of patties is popular with many foodservice people. Sometimes these small pieces of butter are referred to as chips, since they can be obtained on small paper or plastic chips.

Prints refers to butter that is packaged in one-quarter pound or one-pound amounts, which are individually wrapped to protect the quality. Tubs of butter are the large-sized units. The tub usually is 40 to 64 pounds and provides butter in bulk form for large users.

In selecting from among these various forms of butter, the particular needs of the establishment provide the guide as to which is best. Also, exact specifications are necessary, so that the product purchased is what is wanted and really does meet the needs.

Whipped butter is another form of this dairy product often used in food-service establishments. It is butter that has been expanded in volume by incorporating it with air. It has a softer consistency than normal butter, and it is much easier to spread at any temperature. Whipped butter usually comes in tub quantities or in packages of six or eight prints per pound.

Margarine

Margarines for foodservice operations today are designed specifically to meet varied needs: cooking, frying, baking, and table service. As an example, for table service margarines have now been developed that spread smoothly when cold.

Margarine may be made from precisely controlled mixtures of highly refined and hydrogenated vegetable oils, chiefly soybean and cotton seed. They may also contain milk solids, emulsifiers, Vitamin A (one manufacturer provides 15,000 USP units per pound), salt, artificial color, and flavoring. Margarine may also contain animal and dairy fats. Some margarines have butter blended with their other ingredients for extra richness. Operators should select the margarines developed to meet their specific needs.

Margarine for table service is available in square, paper-wrapped pats; in one-pound squares or large tins; and whipped. Triangle portion cuts are also available for areas where their use is mandated. One product has been developed from a blend that is high in polyunsaturates for use in hospitals, nursing homes, and schools to meet special diet requirements.

Cheese—300 Varieties

More than 300 varieties and types of cheese are identified in the world. Some 20 to 30 varieties are of importance here in the United States. Information about the characteristics of some of these are in Table 17-2.

Cheese is produced in a variety of sizes and shapes. Some cheese is referred to as processed cheese. When the term process or processed is used in relation to the kind of cheese, it means that the natural cheese has been melted, blended, and solidified with or without food additions. The label provides information on what has been added.

Most varieties of cheese in the United States are manufactured in this country, but others come from other areas of the world.

Natural cheese is made by separating most of the milk solids from the milk by curdling with rennet or bacterial culture or both. Then, the curd is separated from the whey by heating, stirring, and pressing. For some types of cheese, both milk and cream are used. Most cheese manufactured in the United States is made from whole milk.

267

Table 17-2   Characteristics of Some Popular Varieties of Natural Cheeses

Kind or name Place of origin	Kind of milk used in manufacture	Ripening or curing time	Flavor	Body and texture	Color	Uses
Soft, Unripened Varieties						
Cottage, plain or creamed. (Unknown)	Cow's milk skimmed; plain curd, or plain curd with cream added.	Unripened	Mild, acid	Soft, curd particles of varying size.	White to creamy white.	Salads, with fruits, vegetables, sandwiches, dips, cheesecake.
Cream, plain (U.S.A.)	Cream from cow's milk.	Unripened	Mild, acid	Soft and smooth	White	Salads, dips, sandwiches, snacks, cheesecake, desserts.
Neufchatel (Nŭ-sha-tĕl'). (France)	Cow's milk	Unripened	Mild, acid	Soft, smooth similar to cream cheese but lower in milkfat.	White	Salads, dips, sandwiches, snacks, cheesecake, desserts.
Ricotta (Rĭ-cŏ'-ta) (Italy)	Cow's milk, whole or partly skimmed, or whey from cow's milk with whole or skim milk added. In Italy whey from sheep's milk.	Unripened	Sweet, nut-like.	Soft, moist or dry	White	Appetizers, salads, snacks, lasagne, ravioli, noodles and other cooked dishes, grating, desserts.
Firm, Unripened Varieties						
Gjetost,[1] (Yĕt'ŏst). (Norway)	Whey from goat's milk or a mixture of whey from goat's and cow's milk.	Unripened	Sweetish, caramel.	Firm, buttery consistency.	Golden brown	Snacks, desserts, served with dark breads, crackers, biscuits, or muffins.
Mysost (Müs-ŏst) also called Primost (Prēm'-ŏst). (Norway)	Whey from cow's milk.	Unripened	Sweetish, caramel.	Firm, buttery consistency.	Light brown	Snacks, desserts, served with dark breads.

	Kind of Milk	Ripening or Curing Time	Flavor	Body and Texture	Color	Uses
Mozzarella (Mō-tsa-rel'la) also called Scamorza. (Italy)	Whole or partly skimmed cow's milk. In Italy, originally made from buffalo's milk.	Unripened	Delicate, mild.	Slight firm, plastic.	Creamy white	Snacks, toasted sandwiches, cheeseburgers, cooking, as in meat loaf, or topping for lasagne, pizza, and casseroles.
Soft, Ripened Varieites						
Brie (Brē) (France)	Cow's milk	4 to 8 weeks.	Mild to pungent.	Soft, smooth when ripened.	Creamy yellow interior; edible thin brown and white crust.	Appetizers, sandwiches, snacks, good with crackers and fruit, dessert.
Camembert (Kăm'ĕm-bâr). (France)	Cow's milk	4 to 8 weeks.	Mild to pungent.	Soft, smooth; very soft when fully ripened.	Creamy yellow interior; edible thin white, or gray white crust.	Appetizers, sandwiches, snacks, good with crackers, and fruit such as pears and apples, dessert.
Limburger (Belgium)	Cow's milk	4 to 8 weeks.	Highly pungent, very strong.	Soft, smooth when ripened; usually contains small irregular openings.	Creamy white interior; reddish yellow surface.	Appetizers, snacks, good with crackers, rye or other dark breads, dessert.
Semisoft, Ripened Varieties						
Bel Paese[2] (Bĕl Pä-ā'-zĕ). (Italy)	Cow's milk	6 to 8 weeks.	Mild to moderately robust.	Soft to medium firm, creamy.	Creamy yellow interior; slightly gray or brownish surface sometimes covered with yellow wax coating.	Appetizers, good with crackers, snacks, sandwiches, dessert.
(Brick) (U.S.A.)	Cow's milk	2 to 4 months	Mild to moderately sharp.	Semisoft to medium firm, elastic, numerous small mechanical openings.	Creamy yellow	Appetizers, sandwiches, snacks, dessert.

(continued)

269

Table 17-2   Continued

Kind or name Place of origin	Kind of milk used in manufacture	Ripening or curing time	Flavor	Body and texture	Color	Uses
Muenster (Mŭn'stêr). (Germany)	Cow's milk	1 to 8 weeks	Mild to mellow.	Semisoft, numerous small mechanical openings. Contains more moisture than brick.	Creamy white interior; yellow tan surface.	Appetizers, sandwiches, snacks, dessert.
Port du Salut (Por dŭ Să-lŭ'). (France)	Cow's milk	6 to 8 weeks.	Mellow to robust.	Semisoft, smooth, buttery, small openings.	Creamy yellow	Appetizers, snacks, served with raw fruit, dessert.
Firm Ripened Varieties						
Cheddar (England)	Cow's milk	1 to 12 months or more.	Mild to very sharp.	Firm, smooth, some mechanical openings.	White to medium yellow orange.	Appetizers, sandwiches, sauces, on vegetables, in hot dishes, toasted sandwiches, grating, cheeseburgers, dessert.
Colby (U.S.A.)	Cow's milk	1 to 3 months.	Mild to mellow.	Softer and more open than Cheddar.	White to medium yellow orange.	Sandwiches, snacks cheeseburgers.
Caciocavallo (Kä'chō-kä-val'lō). (Italy)	Cow's milk. In Italy, cow's milk or mixtures of sheep's, goat's and cow's milk.	3 to 12 months.	Piquant, similar to Provolone but not smoked.	Firm, lower in milkfat and moisture than Provolone.	Light or white interior; clay or tan surface.	Snacks, sandwiches, cooking, dessert; suitable for grating after prolonged curing.
Edam (Ē'dăm). (Netherlands.)	Cow's milk, partly skimmed.	2 to 3 months.	Mellow, nutlike.	Semisoft to firm, smooth; small irregularly shaped or round holes; lower milkfat than Gouda.	Creamy yellow or medium yellow orange interior; surface coated with red wax.	Appetizers, snacks, salads, sandwiches, seafood sauces, dessert.

Name	Milk	Ripening	Flavor	Body and Texture	Color	Uses
Gouda (Gou´-dä) (Netherlands)	Cow's milk, whole or partly skimmed.	2 to 6 months.	Mellow, nut-like.	Semisoft to firm, smooth; small irregularly shaped or round holes; higher milkfat than Edam.	Creamy yellow or medium yellow-orange interior; may or may not have red wax coating.	Appetizers, snacks, salads, sandwiches, seafood sauces, dessert.
Provolone (Prō-vō-lō´-nē) also smaller sizes and shapes called Provolette, Provoloncini. (Italy)	Cow's milk	2 to 12 months or more	Mellow to sharp, smoky, salty.	Firm, smooth	Light creamy interior; light brown or golden yellow surface.	Appetizers, sandwiches, snacks, souffle, macaroni and spaghetti dishes, pizza, suitable for grating when fully cured and dried.
Swiss, also called Emmentaler. (Switzerland)	Cow's milk	3 to 9 months.	Sweet, nut-like.	Firm, smooth with large round eyes.	Light yellow	Sandwiches, snacks, sauces, fondue, cheeseburgers.
Very Hard Ripened Varieties						
Parmesan (Pär´me-zän´) also called Reggiano. (Italy)	Partly skimmed cow's milk.	14 months to 2 years.	Sharp, piquant.	Very hard, granular, lower moisture and milkfat than Romano.	Creamy white	Grated for seasoning in soups or vegetables, spaghetti, ravioli, breads, popcorn, used extensively in pizza and lasagne.
Romano (Ro-mä´-nō) also called Sardo Romano Pecorino Romano. (Italy)	Cow's milk. In Italy, sheep's milk (Italian law).	5 to 12 months.	Sharp, piquant.	Very hard granular	Yellowish white interior, greenish-black surface.	Seasoning in soups, casserole dishes, ravioli, sauces, breads, suitable for grating when cured for about one year.
Säp Sagō[1] (Sap´-sagō). (Switzerland	Skimmed cow's milk.	5 months or more.	Sharp, pungent clover-like.	Very hard	Light green by addition of dried, powered clover leaves.	Grated to flavor soups, meats, macaroni, spaghetti, hot vegetables; mixed with butter makes a good spread on crackers or bread.

(continued)

271

Table 17-2   Continued

Kind or name Place of origin	Kind of milk used in manufacture	Ripening or curing time	Flavor	Body and texture	Color	Uses
				Blue-Vein Mold Ripened Varieties		
Blue, spelled Bleu on imported cheese. (France)	Cow's milk	2 to 6 months.	Tangy, peppery.	Semisoft, pasty, sometimes crumbly.	White interior, marbled or streaked with blue veins of mold.	Appetizers, salads, dips, salad dressing, sandwich spreads, good with crackers, dessert.
Gorgonzola (Gôr-gôn-zō´-là). (Italy)	Cow's milk. In Italy, cow's milk or goat's milk or mixtures of these.	3 to 12 months.	Tangy, peppery.	Semisoft, pasty, sometimes crumbly, lower moisture than Blue.	Creamy white interior, mottled or streaked with blue green veins of mold. Clay-colored surface.	Appetizers, snacks, salads, dips, sandwich spread, good with crackers, dessert.
Roquefort[1] (Rōk´-fêrt) or (Rōk-fôr´). (France).	Sheep's milk	2 to 5 months or more.	Sharp, slightly peppery.	Semisoft, pasty, sometimes crumbly.	White or creamy white interior, marbled or streaked with blue veins of mold.	Appetizers, snacks, salads, dips, sandwich spreads, good with crackers, dessert.
Stilton[1] (England).	Cow's milk	2 to 6 months.	Piquant, milder than Gorgonzola or Roquefort.	Semisoft, flaky; slightly more crumbly than Blue.	Creamy white interior, marbled or streaked with blue green veins of mold.	Appetizers, snacks, salads, dessert.

[1] Imported only.

[2] Italian trademark – licensed for manufacture in U.S.A.; also imported.

Source: United States Department of Agriculture.

Flavor, body, and texture differentiate cheese of one type from another. These characteristics are determined to a great extent by the kind of milk that is used, how the milk is curdled, and how the curd is formed, the kind of bacteria or molds that are used for ripening, how much seasoning has been added and the kinds of seasonings, and the temperature, humidity, and time to which the cheese is subjected in the ripening process.

After the cheese is formed, it is wrapped or given a protective coating, and then allowed to cure. The length of the cure depends on the kind of cheese that is made. The United States Department of Agriculture lists ripening classifications as: Unripened, Soft Ripened, Semisoft Ripened, Firm Ripened, Very Hard Ripened, and Blue-Vein Mold Ripened.

The soft unripened kinds such as cottage cheese have relatively high moisture content and do not get any additional curing or ripening. Firm unripened cheese contains very low moisture. The curing in soft-ripened cheeses progresses from the outside of the cheese toward the center. Mold or culture of bacteria or both are allowed to grow on the surface of the cheese during the curing process.

The semisoft ripened cheeses ripen from the inside as well as from the rind. A bacterial or mold culture, or both, is used. Firm ripened cheeses ripen with the assistance of a bacterial culture and ripening takes place throughout the whole cheese. Very hard ripened cheeses are cured with a bacterial culture and enzymes. The curing of the blue-vein mold ripened cheese is by use of a mold culture that grows throughout the interior of the cheese, as well as by the action of bacteria.

Cheddar; Cheese In Foodservice

Some kinds of cheese get much use in foodservice operations. Cheddar is the most important cheese produced in the United States, and it sometimes carries the name American Cheddar Cheese. It is made in a variety of sizes and shapes, ranging from one pound to one ton or more. Most popular are the 20- to 60-pound sizes, which come in both rectangular and cylindrical shapes. Table 17-3 shows some of the more popular shapes of cheddar cheese produced in the United States. These are also referred to as forms or styles of cheese.

The aging, curing, or ripening of the cheese after it has been made develops the desirable flavor, body, and texture. This aging process may take a few months for some cheeses and as much as 18 to 24 months for others.

In general, the longer the cheese is cured or aged, the stronger or sharper the flavor will be. Often, cheddar cheese is marked with designation of its age and corresponding flavor descriptions. Table 17-4 lists the length of aging and the market terminology used to describe the flavor at each of those ages.

This information is important in purchasing cheese since the price at which the cheese sells increases with the length of the aging period. Also of

Table 17-3   Common Styles of Cheddar Cheese

| | | Size of Hoop | | Approximate |
| | | Diameter | Height | Weight in |
Style	Shape	(Inches)	(Inches)	Pounds
Cheddar	Cylindrical	14½	11¼	70–78
Twins	Cylindrical	14½	5¼	32–37
Daisy	Cylindrical	13½	4¼	20–22
Longhorn	Cylindrical	6	13	12–13
Young American	Cylindrical	7	7	10–12
Junior Twins*	Cylindrical	9¾	5	11–12
		Dimensions		
Square Prints	Rectangular	14 x 11 x 3¼		20
Square Prints	Rectangular	11 x 7 x 3¼		10
Square Prints	Rectangular	11 x 3½ x 3¼		5
Square Prints	Rectangular	5¼ x 3½ x 3¼		2½

*Also known as Family Twins, Pets, or Commodores.
Source: (Reproduced from Nelson & Trust, *Judging of Dairy Products*, 4th Edition, 1965, p. 177. The Olsen Publishing Company, Milwaukee, Wisconsin.)

importance to the buyer are the needs of the foodservice establishment for strength of flavor and for ease of melting. How strong should the cheese be, and how much will it be used for melting and putting into various food combinations? Aged cheddar cheese will melt more rapidly and smoothly than a young or mild cheddar cheese, but it also has a stronger flavor.

Blue Mold Cheese   A blue mold type cheese is used frequently in foodservice establishments, especially for cheese dips or in preparing various kinds of salad dressings. Such cheeses as Roquefort, Bleu, Blue, Stilton, and Gorgonzola are in this category.

Roquefort is a cheese made in France and imported into the United States. The term *Roquefort* can apply only to a blue mold cheese made from sheep's milk in the immediate vicinity of Aveyron in southeastern France. Restricting of the term to that cheese and area is incorporated into laws and regulations.

Types of blue mold cheese made from cow's milk and imported into the United States include Stilton from England, Bleu from France, Blue from Denmark, and Gorgonzola from Italy. A domestic blue mold cheese produced in the United States is sold as Blue Cheese or Blue Mold Cheese.

Table 17-4   Age and Flavor Terminology

Age	Market Flavor Terminologies
Under six months	Mild or young
Six-nine months	Medium or mellow
Nine-twelve months	Strong, aged, or sharp
Over twelve months	Very strong or very sharp

All of these blue mold cheeses have similar characteristics. They are sold under their own names. Although sometimes they are referred to as roquefort-type cheeses, the term *Roquefort* is restricted to the product from France that is the true imported Roquefort.

Other Varieties   Foodservice establishments use many other kinds of cheese. Some are domestic varieties manufactured in the United States and others are imported kinds from a variety of countries. Included are Gouda, Camembert, Liederkranz, Limburger, and Swiss or Emmentaler.

Process Cheese   Process cheese or processed cheese is a melted pasteurized blend of natural cheese with or without added ingredients. The most commonly used process cheese is made from cheddar cheese and is labeled as pasteurized process cheddar cheese. It may be manufactured from other varieties of cheese that are similar to cheddar. The varieties are listed on the label. This is the cheese for which the term American cheese is sometimes used. Among the optional food ingredients that are added to process cheese are various types of fruits, vegetables, or meats. Process cheese comes in rectangular packages of various sizes. These are usually wrapped in foil or in a plastic film to make the package airtight.

Process cheese food is very similar to process cheese except that it is slightly softer as a result of its higher moisture content. Usually some kind of milk solids are added to the cheese that is used to make this product. There often is confusion in many people's minds about what is a process cheese and what is a process cheese food.

Process cheese spread is similar to process cheese food except that it has a higher content of moisture. Many process cheese spreads are of such consistency as to be spread with a knife. Some process cheese spreads have specially prepared fruits, vegetables, or meats added to the product. There are many other kinds of spreads, process cheese, and dips that are available for use in foodservice operations.

Careful attention to the statements of contents on the packages and even sampling of the product are good guides for those who make purchases for the foodservice establishment. In this way, there is assurance that the product being purchased will be what is needed for the particular requirements of the operation.

Nonfat Dry Milk

A dairy product widely used in foodservice is nonfat dry milk, which is produced from skim milk by the removal of water. This is a process that can be used with most dairy products to make dried versions of them. However, nonfat dry milk is the most widely used dry dairy product.

It is used in foodservice in the preparation of various foods, and used by

275

food processors in many food products. It needs to be carefully selected for the use intended. It may be graded, and it may have been exposed to a specific heat treatment. It may be either spray dried or roller dried depending on its process of manufacture, and it may be in a particular physical form.

In producing nonfat dried milk, the fluid skim milk is given heat treatments before drying. Much of the nonfat dry milk is labeled according to heat treatment, and the reference is to low, medium, or high heat nonfat dry milk. However, not all nonfat dry milk has heat treatment indicated on the label.

If the nonfat dry milk is going to be reconstituted in the foodservice establishment for use as a fluid product, a low heat product should be purchased. If it is to be used for baking, a high heat nonfat dry milk will provide the best results in the finished baked products.

There is a difference between nonfat dry milk produced with the spray dry method and the product from the roller process of manufacture. The spray dry milk may be available in any of the heat treatments. But, because of its method of manufacture, roller dried nonfat dry milk is always a high heat treatment product. The roller dried products will produce satisfactory baked goods, but they do not reconstitute readily with water.

Instant nonfat dry skim milk is a special physical form of the nonfat dry milk. A much larger particle size is a characteristic. This gives it excellent properties for becoming soluble and dissolving. It is also a low heat treatment product.

It is important that the buyer designate the particular kind of nonfat dry product desired. Again, of course, the selection should be based on specific needs.

Dry Whole Milk

Sometimes, dry whole milk is used in place of fluid whole milk in preparing various foods. Dry whole milk goes through a process similar to that of dry nonfat milk in which water in the fluid milk is removed.

It is usually available to large-scale users in moisture-proof bags of 50 pounds and 100 pounds. Smaller packages are filled under vacuum or in the presence of an inert gas to prolong the keeping qualities. These are used by many foodservice people.

Purveyors and jobbers of dairy products have dry whole milk available, and some general suppliers to the foodservice industry also offer this product.

Dry whole milk may deteriorate in storage. So it is not recommended that this product be stored over a long period. An amount for four or five weeks use should be the limit to prevent loss of quality.

Ice Cream

Ice cream is available in a wide range of flavors, takes very little preparation, and is easy to serve. As a result, it is a popular and profitable item. It is a frozen, whipped blend of dairy products, to which have been added sweetening agents, stabilizer, emulsifier, and flavoring materials.

The quality of ice cream is related to what is in it, the quality of those ingredients, the weight per gallon, and the amount and quality of the materials that are added for flavoring. Some buyers overlook some of these elements, and may make their decisions on what to buy on the basis of fat content alone.

The three designations for ice cream on the market are premium, competitive, and average. From the standpoint of composition, these would have about the following content of butterfat: premium—15 percent fat; average—12 percent fat; and competitive—10 percent fat.

As the fat content of the ice cream is increased, there is usually an increase in the amount of flavoring materials used. Also, the finished ice cream will be a little heavier product, or as it is called in the industry, there will be a lower overrun. Of course, the difference in fat content, flavoring materials, and the weight per gallon will affect the price of ice cream.

French ice cream contains a liberal amount of eggs, is generally high in fat content, and has much flavor. The French vanilla ice cream has a deeper yellow color than the regular vanilla ice cream. Most ice creams now contain no eggs, with this important exception.

Many different fancy ice creams and ice cream novelties can be purchased. They include such things as ice cream cakes, pies, nut rolls, spumoni, ice cream slices, cups, molds, sandwiches, and ice cream on a stick both coated and uncoated. These are available in many different flavors and sizes. Many come ready to serve as individually wrapped slices, cones, or cups. Ice cream wedding cakes, birthday cakes, and individual molds are in demand for parties and similar functions.

Most bulk ice cream is packaged in 2½-gallon single service paper containers. Sometimes 3-gallon and 5-gallon containers are used. The 5-gallon metal container is used mainly by ice cream manufacturers who have their own retail outlets. Ice cream is also packaged in smaller containers of gallon, half-gallon, quart, and pint sizes. If ice cream is to be dipped for preparing individual servings or sundaes, bulk ice cream will be needed.

There is a wide variety of ice cream flavors from which to choose. Some 300 flavors are named. Most ice cream companies, however, maintain a current inventory of from 20 to 30 individual flavors. Vanilla is the most popular flavor by far and the most in demand. Chocolate and strawberry are next in order of popularity.

Label Requirements

Federal regulations for labeling of ice cream apply to shipments in interstate commerce and have been adopted as the basis of some state labeling requirements. They also apply to other frozen desserts such as ice milk, sherbet, and frozen custard.

Three different labeling statements can be used. For example, vanilla ice cream may be labeled Vanilla Ice Cream, or Vanilla Flavored Ice Cream, or Artificially Flavored Ice Cream. The same classification applies to other flavors, with the appropriate name included. The particular statement of flavor category depends on what is used as flavoring material. The statements mean that for Vanilla Ice Cream only pure vanilla is used in flavoring, and for Strawberry Ice Cream only strawberries are used for flavoring, to cite two examples.

For a Vanilla Flavored Ice Cream, both pure vanilla and a fortifier such as vanillin can be used but the pure vanilla must predominate. For Strawberry Flavored Ice Cream, both strawberries and an artificial strawberry flavor can be used as long as the pure strawberries predominate. Up to 49 percent of the flavor can be artificial flavor.

For the Artificially Flavored Ice Cream, the artificial or synthetic flavor predominates and can be used with or without any pure flavors. The term "flavored" on the label in conjunction with the flavor indicates that artificial flavors are used entirely or to fortify the true flavor.

Foodservice buyers should give special attention to this classification of flavors, as price differences are related to the kind of flavoring as well as to the other factors.

Ice Milk, Sherbets, Etc.

Ice milk is a frozen product similar to ice cream but with much less fat content. Ice milk has around 4 to 6 percent fat, compared with 12 percent for average ice cream. Ice milk is flavored and packaged in much the same way as ice cream. Vanilla is the most common flavor and is used frequently in frappes and milk shakes.

Sherbets and water ices are sometimes incorrectly called milk sherbet and water sherbet. Sherbet is made from milk, fruit or fruit juice, stabilizers, and sugar. It has a high level of sugar content, about twice as high as ice cream; and it contains 1 to 2 percent milk fat. Water ice is similar to sherbet except that it does not contain any milk solids. Both products are characterized by tartness and fruit flavors. There are some dairy products in sherbets, but none at all in water ices.

Soft-Serve or Ice Cream Mix

Some foodservice operations purchase a mix and freeze their own ice cream, soft-serve products, and direct-draw milk shake. The mix needs to be of the right composition for the product that is to be produced. In some places, flavoring materials are added to the mix at freezing time. Sometimes the mix is supplied with the flavor already added.

These products are manufactured by ice cream companies or dairies, and usually come in 5-gallon or 10-gallon plastic bags in cardboard or metal containers. Occasionally, they are available in 1-gallon and ½-gallon cartons for users of smaller quantities.

Grades of Dairy Products: Butter

There are federal grades for some dairy products, but for most there are no official U.S.D.A. grades. Butter is one of the few products for which there are grades. Not all the butter produced is graded. There are advantages to the manufacturer in having his butter graded. So, much of the butter purchased by foodservice buyers does have grades. Often, the market quotations for butter also include the grade designation along with the price.

The U.S. Department of Agriculture graders test and grade samples of the butter and determine its overall quality. They compare it with the U.S. grade standards, putting major emphasis on the flavor and odor of the butter. Also considered but of less importance in the grading are body and texture, distribution of salt, and the uniformity of the color.

There are four grade designations for butter—Grade AA, Grade A, Grade B, and Grade C. These correspond with the numerical scores of 93, 92, 90, and 89. The U.S.D.A. shield is used to indicate the grade of the butter. Butter that is graded but does not have the prefix "U.S." before the grade is butter that has been graded by a state—in which case the state name should be on the grade label—or graded by the manufacturer. The federally graded butter has "U.S." before the grade designation.

Most people would find it difficult to tell the difference between the two top grades—AA and A. For use as a table spread, U.S. Grade A butter is satisfactory. The advisability of paying a premium for Grade AA is questionable. For cooking purposes, margarine might be a better price choice in some places, instead of use of Grade B butter.

Here is additional information on what each grade represents. Grade AA butter has a delicate, sweet flavor, with a highly pleasing aroma. It is made from high-quality, fresh sweet cream. It has a smooth, creamy texture and spreads well. The salt is completely dissolved and blended in just the right amount. Grade A butter has a pleasing flavor; is made from fresh cream; is fairly smooth in texture; and rates close to the top grade in the quality factors. Grade B butter may have a slightly acid flavor. It is generally made from selected sour cream; and is of much value for cooking purposes.

Grades of Cheese

Quality standards for cheddar cheese and swiss cheese are available from the U.S. Department of Agriculture. The official U.S.D.A. grades for cheddar cheese are Grade AA, Grade A, Grade B, and Grade C. As in the case of butter, the major attention in grading is on the flavor and odor. That which rates Grade AA will have a clean, pleasing, nut-like flavor, and a compact body and texture. In the lower grades, the flavor is more definite and there may be some defects in the body and texture of the cheese.

Buyers should also be familiar with the Wisconsin grading system in addition to that of U.S.D.A., since Wisconsin is the principal state for the production of cheddar cheese. Official grade classifications for Wisconsin Cheddar cheese are Wisconsin State Brand and Wisconsin Junior. A cheddar cheese that does not meet either of those grades is marked Undergrade. The Wisconsin State Brand is the highest quality under this grading system.

No exact comparison or exchange of grade classifications can be made between the U.S. Department of Agriculture and Wisconsin grading systems. However, food buyers should keep in mind that U.S. Grade AA represents the best quality under the U.S. Department of Agriculture grading system, and Wisconsin State Brand is the best quality under the Wisconsin system.

Grading of Dry Milk

There are two grades established by the U.S. Department of Agriculture for nonfat dry milk—U.S. Extra Grade and U.S. Standard. Grading is based on selected characteristics of quality. The Extra Grade is the highest quality product. Nonfat dry milk that is not graded may or may not meet the standards for the U.S. graded product.

Grading of dry whole milk is based on the quality characteristics of this product. The grades are U.S. Premium, U.S. Extra, and U.S. Standard. U.S. Premium is the highest grade.

The United States Department of Agriculture Grading Service is available to manufacturers and others and is a voluntary program, as distinguished from programs that check the wholesomeness of food and are compulsory.

Quality Approved Products

Dairy products that are not covered by a U.S. Grade Standard may be inspected and carry the Quality Approved inspection shield on the container. To have this designation, the product must be manufactured in a plant that meets the U.S. Department of Agriculture sanitary requirements for both the plant and its equipment, as well as the quality specifications for the dairy product itself. Cottage cheese and pasteurized process cheese are two products that may have the U.S.D.A. Quality Approved shield, if they are of good quality and manufactured under U.S.D.A. supervision.

Use Good Purchasing Procedures

When the purchaser determines the particular needs of the foodservice operation, he can make decisions on the specific characteristics of the dairy products that are to be purchased. Then he is in a position to develop a set of orderly purchasing procedures which will make the job easier and give the establishment tighter control of quality and costs.

Some dairy products will be bought locally on a daily basis from dairy plants. Others will need to come from purveyors or jobbers, and deliveries will be on a longer term basis such as weekly or monthly intervals.

Items in Specifications

Preparation of product specifications and their use are essential so that the correct dairy product is obtained. Specifications that help do the purchasing job most effectively are ones that:

Define the dairy product by name. The minimum composition requirements are optional, but required if the product is to be above the legal state requirements.

Specify the size and type of container in which the product is to be provided.

Specify the time and the frequency of delivery. The exact place of delivery may need to be included as well.

State the amount of product per day or the projected amount over a period of time.

Specify the U.S. Department of Agriculture grade, if the product comes under the grading regulations.

State the exact point of delivery—platform delivery or otherwise.

Specifications for Fluid Milk

Sealed bids are often used by schools and other public institutions as well as some commercial firms to determine the supplier of fluid milk needs. The sealed bids are submitted by the dairy company and are based on the specifications provided by the purchaser.

The specifications must be developed to meet the needs of the particular operation, since needs differ between one establishment or group of establishments and another.

Here is a checklist that can be of help in preparing specifications. Depending on the situations of the foodservice operations, items can be deleted from or added to this list.

type of product—homogenized milk, coffee cream, etc.

minimum fat content of the milk, if a product is wanted that is above the legal standard for the state size of individual container—half-pint, quart, 5-gallon dispenser, etc.

type of package or container—paper, glass, etc.

quantity or number of units per day

period of time to be covered, such as September 1 to December 31

dates when delivery is not needed—holidays, weekend, vacation periods, etc.

frequency of delivery—daily, twice a week, etc.

time of delivery—mornings, afternoons, between 8:00 and 10:00 A.M., etc.

place of delivery—platform, cafeteria area, in refrigerators, etc.

pick up or return of empty containers

conditions for adjusting or cancelling the order due to emergencies or changes in schedules in the case of schools

Specifications Must Be Used

It does no good to have well-prepared specifications unless they are used. Suppliers must know the specifications of the products that you want if they are to supply you what you need.

Once the specifications have been developed, ordering should be done so that there will be a continuing adequate supply of dairy products. A standing order for certain amounts may be all that is needed. Daily telephone orders are used by some establishments for milk, cream, and ice cream. Ordering may have to be done for some products so that there is a minimum amount below which the inventory does not fall, or there is a maximum amount above which it should not go. The aim is to have an adequate supply in stock at all times, but at the same time not affect quality of the product due to too long storage.

For competitive purchasing, bids should be obtained from suppliers who want to provide what the foodservice operation needs. Sealed bids are often used by public institutions. It is vital to the purchaser that the specifications be complete and clearly stated so that the supplier knows exactly what product he is to supply.

Know the Results of Purchasing

Often overlooked is the last step in an effective food purchasing procedure. Know the results. Purchasing does not end with the placing of the order. It is necessary to follow up to be sure that the products received are the products that were ordered. A continual check on the quality of the products received is essential.

Correct receiving, storing, and handling have a definite part in maintaining the quality of the dairy products purchased until they are used. All the effort and care that goes into the manufacture of a quality product can be lost by lack of attention to proper receiving, storing, and handling procedures in the foodservice establishment.

Summary

Dairy products present buying problems for foodservice operations because of the large number of products and their perishability. The specific product needed, its intended use, time it is needed, how it is to be used, availability, and sources of information are all vital for effective purchasing. Buyers also need a knowledge of terms, product quality, grades, package sizes, and the laws and regulations affecting dairy products.

Fluid milk is available in whole, low fat, fat free, and skim milk forms, and each has specific butterfat content requirements. Flavored milk, flavored milk drinks, buttermilk, and yogurt are other variations of milk. Light, heavy, coffee, half-and-half, and all-purpose cream are on the market, as are imitation and concentrated milks.

Butter is available in patties, prints, and tubs. Margarine is another product of interest to foodservice people. There are twenty to thirty varieties and types of cheese of importance in the United States; cheese is available in a number of ripening classifications. Processed cheese is a melted pasteurized blend of natural cheese with or without added ingredients.

Nonfat dry milk, dry whole milk, and ice cream are other dairy products in much use in foodservice establishments, as are ice milks, sherbet, and soft-serve or ice cream mix.

There are grades for cheese, butter, ice cream, and dry milk. Some other dairy products may be covered by a U.S.D.A. quality standard and be eligible for a quality approved marking.

Questions

1.   Define the terms, Pasteurized, Homogenized, and Standardized as applied to milk.

2.   Describe the differences between nonfat, fat free, and defatted milk.

3.   What is the difference between flavored milk and flavored milk drink, and between buttermilk and yogurt?

4.   Compare the butterfat content of coffee cream, half-and-half, light cream, and all-purpose cream.

5.   What are the three factors that differentiate cheese of one type from another type?

6.   List the U.S.D.A. ripening classifications for cheese.

7.   Why is cheese aged, cured, or ripened?

8.   Nonfat dried milk is labeled according to heat treatment. Which treatment—low heat or high heat—should be used for: (a) fluid product; (b) baking?

9.   In addition to fat content, what other factors determine the quality of ice cream?

10.   What is the difference between ice cream, ice milk, and sherbet?

11.   What are the four U.S.D.A. grade designations for butter?

12.   What are the U.S.D.A. grades for cheddar cheese?

13.   What is meant by the Quality Approved inspection shield on the dairy products container?

18

Effective Communication

Most surveys in which foodservice people list problems they face in their operations show that communication is a major, if not the most important, problem in this industry. No classification of employees is immune to communication deficiencies. In some establishments, management is the biggest offender in violating the rules of good communication. Even persons who do not specify communication as a problem describe the *symptoms* of communication problems when answering questions about what causes difficulties in their operations. It is paradoxical that communication should be an obstacle to effective operations of a foodservice establishment, when communicating with people is such a vital and major part of such operations.

Communicating is one of the most practiced acts of behavior in life. People start communicating in their earliest moments, and have continual practice all their lives. Yet, all too often it is such a continuous practice that they communicate almost automatically, with little thought to the purpose of their communication, and little concern for how they do the communicating.

Too Little Listening

Many conversations are characterized by very little listening. Often it is only enough to get the desired Yes or No answer, with almost no attention to anything else that is said. Much communication is conducted with little or no recognition of the obstacles that prevent understanding.

The fact that communication effectiveness probably averages 10 to 15 percent is often not related to the countless problems caused daily by faulty communication. In fact, many people do not recognize that they may be the cause of many problems in the business operation through their ineffective communication.

A Costly Deficiency

In the foodservice industry, where so many factors of success involve people—employees within the firm, customers, suppliers—the toll taken by ineffective communication is great. Lost sales, unhappy clientele, spoiled food, damaged equipment, frustrated management, and hostile employees are but some of the results of poor communication that occur frequently.

Even more serious is the failure to understand how communication occurs, why it is not effective, and what can be done to improve the communication efficiency of individuals and firms. Probably in no other facet of most business operations can so much be accomplished with so little cost and action as when the operation's efficiency of communication is increased.

The problem in this area is threefold. There is need to:

Recognize that communication is a problem.

Gain a better understanding of communication.

Take needed action to improve the efficiency of communication.

Watch for the Symptoms

To recognize that communication problems exist in a foodservice operation is not difficult, even though some of the signs of defective communication are similar to signs of other deficiencies in the operation. First, management must recognize that management itself may have communication deficiencies. Too often, the owner, the manager, or the supervisor has the attitude that "I need to train these workers in communication; they just don't seem to understand." Maybe the manager should be saying: "I myself need training in communication so that they are able to understand."

Then, attention should be directed to the signs that there are communication problems in the operation, such as:

spoiled food when directions are not followed and the wrong things are done

difficulty in operating equipment even though complete instructions have been given failure to understand what people are saying even though the words are commonly used ones

failure of people to do what is expected of them when they have been told what was to be done

blank looks on the faces of people when there should be expressions of understanding

complaints from customers about what they are being charged

too many misunderstandings with people

only partial carrying out of instructions

These are symptoms of trouble, symptoms of problems that exist. Of course, problems other than communication can produce similar symptoms; but check to see if the problems might be in the area of communication. Many times they are, and the real cause goes unnoticed.

One comment that is often heard is: "But I told him so. He is just too dumb. Why can't we get better help these days?" There are some obvious questions that foodservice people who make statements such as that should have asked themselves. He told him so, but did he who did the telling think at all about the ability of the person to whom he was talking to receive and understand what was meant? In many cases, no thought was given to it. Was the fault with the person who made the comment, or was the fault that of the person about whom the comment was made? In many cases, it is the fault of the originator of the comment.

So, look for symptoms of poor communication, and see if that might be what is wrong. Look behind the symptoms of problems and see if those symptoms might be a reflection of poor communication rather than other causes.

What Is Involved in Communication

It is not difficult to see why good communication is not so simple as might be expected from the frequency with which people communicate. There are many pitfalls on the road to effective communication.

One difficulty is that communication involves both the tangible and the intangible. When the supervisor, for example, decides to communicate with a member of the kitchen staff, he has an idea in his mind that he wants to convey to the staff member. His task is to get that idea into the mind of the other person. To do so requires that he transform that intangible idea in his mind into something tangible that will have a physical form and so can be transmitted to the other person. In communication, this physical form is called "the message."

To transform the intangible idea in the mind into the physical form of the message requires some complex things on the part of the person who originates the messages, who in this case is the supervisor. First of all, the supervisor must have a clear idea in his own mind of what he wants to communicate. He must have some knowledge of the subject. He must have skill in communicating so that he can construct and transmit the message in the correct way. Also, he must understand pretty well the person with whom he is communicating. Only then can he select the words, put them together in the right way, and say the things that the other person can understand exactly. This is a large order, to be sure, but it is something that must be done every time, if communication is to be most effective.

The Communication Process

It is possible to put together a visual representation of some of the steps that make up the process of communication. However, a word of warning is in order. A process is not something that arranges itself into steps that are individual and separate. It is a dynamic thing. It is not static. Everything operates at the same time. Each part affects the others. The process is undergoing continual change.

However, in order to visualize what does happen in the process of communication, the process must, in effect, be stopped so that it can be looked at and studied at a particular moment of time. Remember, though, that it is a process, and putting it into individual step-by-step sequence greatly oversimplifies the process.

Components of the Process

This particular model of the process of communication starts with the source from which the communication comes, which will be designated as the *originator.* It is in the originator that the recognition of the need to communicate arises, that the purpose of the communication is defined, and where the detail of the communication is sorted out. All of this is of an intangible nature, occurring in the mind of the originator.

The next element in the model, or step in the process, is the transformation of the intangible idea in the originator's mind into a physical form. This can be called the *translator.* There is a choice of what physical form may be selected for the transformed idea. Words, drawings, pictures, or signs can be used. The transformed idea, now in physical form, can be called the *message.* It is necessary, if communication is to take place, to move this message from the originator to the person who is to receive it. So, a *channel* must be selected; and the messages will be moved through that channel.

Figure 18-1   The Process of Communication

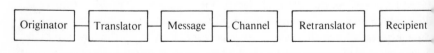

Originator — Translator — Message — Channel — Retranslator — Recipient

Figure 18-2

The Route of Idea to Message to Idea

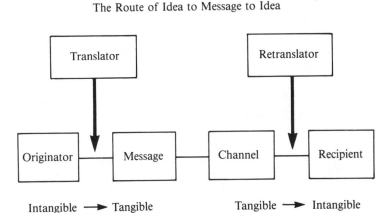

The next step becomes the reverse of the translator that changed the intangible idea into the physical form of the message. The physical form of the message must be again translated, this time by the person who is receiving the message, from its physical form to the intangible form of an idea in his brain. This element of the model can be called the *retranslator*, or simply as in the first situation, translator. Then when he accomplishes that he receives the message and becomes the *recipient*.

The model can then be put into the visual form shown in Figure 18-1. In the example cited previously, the supervisor would be the originator, and the translator. The idea he had in mind would be transformed into the message. It would move through a channel selected by the originator to the staff member who would be the retranslator and the recipient.

When the staff member replies to the supervisor, the whole thing is reversed. He then becomes the originator, translates the idea in his mind as the translator, selects the form of message, and sends it through a channel to the supervisor, who acts as the retranslator to change the physical message to an idea in his mind, and he then is the recipient.

The Process of Communication

Many people have offered models to represent the process of communication. The terms used differ. The number of elements or parts differ. Some models have many more parts. The diagrams that represent the model take many different forms. But all of these models are essentially the same, with some being merely more elaborate than others. Basically in its most simplified form the process has four parts:

ORIGINATOR   MESSAGE   CHANNEL   RECIPIENT

But, it is desirable to include the TRANSLATOR and the RETRANSLATOR in the basic model, since the function performed at these points in the process is so vital to successful communication.

The Purpose and the Audience

Two things of great importance to effective communication are the purpose of the communication and the audience to which the communication is directed. If communication is to be effective, the purpose must be known and clearly understood by the originator. Also the originator must have a good knowledge of the audience to which he directs his messages.

All communication is designed to get action of some kind. It may be information that the recipient of the message needs and that he should be able to understand, accept, and put to use. It may be directions to do a specific task; action is taken to accomplish that task. It may even be the action of the originator in reading a prepared statement to see if it sounds correct and means what he intended it to mean. The goal or the purpose is action. Whatever the purpose is, it must be clear in the mind of the originator; and the action that he wants to result from his communication efforts must be clearly defined and understood.

If the originator is to succeed in attaining his purpose and getting the action he wants, he must give much attention to the characteristics of the recipient or recipients—the audience—who are to understand the purpose and take the desired action. This means knowing a great deal about the recipient, his knowledge and abilities, the things from his heritage, and the place he has in the world that make him an individual. It means, too, that the translator must tailor his transformation of the intangible idea to its physical message form, so that the message can be retranslated from that physical message form to the intangible form of an idea in the mind of the recipient, in order that he can best receive and understand what he is to do and then be able to carry out the purpose of the communication.

The form that the message takes may be different for one recipient than it is for another. The words and whether the message should be oral or written may be different, depending upon the recipient. The purpose of the communication may well be different for different individuals and different groups. So, much knowledge about the recipients of the message, the audience, is a vital requirement if communication is to be as effective as it can be.

Figure 18-3

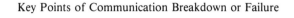

Key Points of Communication Breakdown or Failure

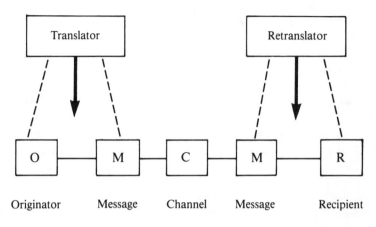

Things That Affect Communication

The things that can affect the fidelity of communication, that can contribute to inefficiency in communication, that can be the cause of personnel difficulties and troubles with production, and that can influence the success or failure of the business are numberless. There is the translation of an intangible idea to a physical message that needs to be done. There are many differences in people and their abilities and knowledge. There is need to transmit the message through one channel or another. So, it is no wonder that there are many places in the process of communication where communication efficiency is lowered or communication is completely ineffective.

These many things that affect the efficiency with which communication is conducted can be classified into several groups:

> ability and knowledge of people
>
> attitudes
>
> physical blocks
>
> people differences
>
> environmental factors

If a person does not understand how communication occurs and what is involved in one person's communicating with another, he will not be an effective communicator. If he does not have the necessary knowledge about the subject that he is communicating, he cannot communicate effectively about it. This lack of knowledge will reduce the success of his efforts.

A person's attitude toward the subject he is discussing and toward the people involved in the communication situation with him can also have serious effects on how well the communication is done. Even the communicator's attitude toward himself can reduce the effectiveness of his communication efforts.

A whole array of physical blocks can cause communication problems. Not all people see with equal ability; not all people hear equally well. The same is true for the other senses. Since all communication must take place through the senses—hearing, seeing, touching, smelling, and feeling—defects in abilities to use those senses can have a big effect. In the foodservice industry, more reliance is placed on smelling and tasting than in many other industries; and deficiencies in the ability to use these senses can have serious effects.

People differ greatly, and this factor has much influence on how well or how poorly communication is conducted.

Environmental factors also are major blocks to good communication. Communication cannot take place effectively when there is too much noise, and when the temperature, humidity, and other conditions distract people or prevent them from fulfilling their part in the communication process. The pressure of deadlines, the inadequacy of equipment and facilities, the atmosphere of the place can produce environmental problems which in turn affect the efficiency of communication that is attempted under these conditions.

It is vital that all potential blocks to good communication be recognized and considered in respect to their potential and actual impact on communication efficiency. Many times, these blocks to communication can be removed and the effectiveness of the communication greatly increased. Changing temperature levels, increasing ventilation, repairing equipment are all things that can be done. However, at other times, it is not possible to remove the blocks, and it is necessary to find ways around the blocks. What is important is that these potential reducers of communication effectiveness be identified and removed, or the communication procedure or behavior be changed to counteract the blocks before they produce their negative effects. In other words, find a way around them in advance.

Foodservice Communication Problems

For the foodservice person, there is value in considering specifically some of the communication problems commonly found in operations. The specifics may vary from one establishment to another, but the basic communication problems are the same. A major area of communication diffiulty is found in the communication that goes on between supervisors and the workers whom they supervise.

In many foodservice operations, the work force is made up of people with many different ethnic backgrounds. Language difficulties and diverse customs are contributing factors. Consider, for example, the following situation.

John Barrie is responsible for the work of twelve employees and the successful operation of a restaurant kitchen and its meal production function. He has difficulty in getting all of the people in this kitchen to understand what he communicates to them so that what he wants to get done is done correctly and on time. There always seem to be some members of his staff who do not get the full meaning of what he says. This causes production problems, personnel problems, and Mr. Barrie's puzzlement about his inability to communicate with the effectiveness that he knows is necessary if he is to carry out his responsibilities successfully. He made a list of what he thought might be the causes of his problem, and his list included the following:

Language   His group of twelve included persons who spoke three different languages; some did not speak English very well but apparently well enough to converse successfully.

Attitude   There were no indications that any of the twelve had an obstructionist attitude, although all had some feeling about not being paid enough.

Knowledge   All were experienced in kitchen operations and had served successfully in other establishments before coming to this restaurant.

Outside Interests   As nearly as he could determine, there was a wide and diverse range of their outside interests. He was aware that a majority of the group had a special interest in the local minor league baseball team during the baseball season.

The Environment   Generally, he felt that the environment in which these people worked was no better and no worse than similar kitchens in other restaurants with which he was familiar. But there was in the manager's office a list of complaints about lack of ventilation, excessive heat, and too much noise from some of these employees and from others who had preceded them.

Use of Senses   A check of the ability to see and to hear well indicated that six of the twelve had some impairment in either or both of these senses, and in two cases it was a severe impairment. He could find no appreciable difference in the employees' abilities in the use of their senses of feel, smell, and taste.

293

Figure 18-4   Blocks Which Prevent or Reduce Effectiveness of Communication

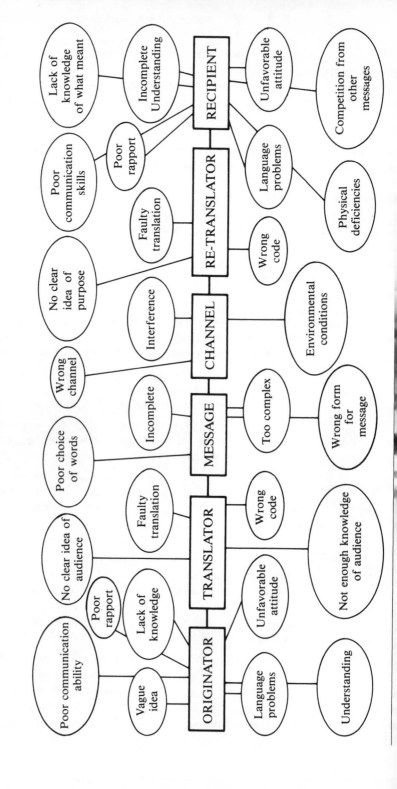

With this list in hand, John Barrie sat down and attempted to evaluate the situation. He ruled out attitude, knowledge of the job, and the environment as being major causes of his communication problem. He did this with some reluctance in the case of the environment, since he was certain that improved environmental conditions would have a positive effect on communication efficiency. But since he had not been able to do anything about getting improvements in the past, he was pessimistic about any positive results from trying again.

He decided that the basic problem in this situation was one of incomplete understanding of what was communicated. The language difficulties, the impaired hearing and seeing in the case of some of the staff, in the environmental situation that existed, probably were the blocks that he was attempting to identify.

Self-Analysis Was in Order

Then, he turned to a consideration of himself. He took pride in feeling that he had a wide choice of words, talked intelligently, and had impressed people many times with his ability to use complex words. But he wondered if here might be a problem. Maybe he was not talking the "language" that his workers understood.

He gave himself a high score on knowledge. He had much success in kitchen operations himself, knew his business thoroughly, and had a record of success as a supervisor. He could find no real fault with his attitude toward himself or his workers. Several of them were puzzlers to him and he never could understand their values, but he accepted them for what they were. His own hearing and seeing were excellent. His outside interests were much different from theirs except for a growing interest in the welfare of the local baseball team.

His conclusion was that most of the problem was with himself. He was not communicating with his workers in terms that they understood. He had neglected to consider the differences between them and had been trying to communicate in the same way with all of them. He had been constructing his messages from his own point of view without sufficient consideration of their backgrounds, their knowledge, their language problems, and what the messages they received meant to them. He had forgotten that meaning in words and messages is related to people's background and experience, and what words meant to him might be something entirely different from what they meant to those who listened to him.

So, he set his communication improvement course in the direction of making three changes. He would consider what he had to communicate from the point of view of the recipients of the messages as well as from his own. He would use different methods of communicating with members of the staff, instead of relying solely on a group meeting. He would make it a point to talk with some of the staff about the local baseball team, since this was one subject on whic they probably shared a greater common ability to communicate than on mar others.

This is but one example of what could be done to determine communic tion problems, analyze the situation, and develop a program to improve cor munication.

Employees and Customers

Another area in a foodservice operation in which good con munication is vital is in the relationship between employees and customer Often, the ineffectiveness of communication in this area is the source of pro lems that are reflected in lost customers and lowered profits.

In many operations, the attitude of those employees who contact th customer is a basic source of communication problems. The diversity of th customer group, their views and attitudes, and their needs all can be sources c problems in communication. In this area of the foodservice operation, the dela in recognizing and correcting communication difficulties immediately can hav serious financial results.

Supervisors and Management

If the goals and plans of management are to be reached, the must be effective communication between those who are managers and owne and those who see that the directions of management are carried out by worker This is a function of supervisors. Many times, management is so engrossed wit its broad view of things that it finds difficulty in understanding some of th complaints, reports, and suggestions of supervisors, who reflect the problems a the production level.

The same applies between owners who are not directly involved in th operation and the managers they employ to direct the operation. One classi example is the problem that the manager of one operation had in trying t explain to the owner that a foodservice operation could not produce the ex tremely high margin of profit that the owner was getting from some othe businesses he owned that were of an entirely different type, characterized by high profit over the original cost of the goods he purchased.

Employees and Suppliers

Another area of many communication problems is that o employees in their contacts with suppliers. Communicating the needs of th establishment for food products is a good example. The need for specifications i based on communication problems, and the specifications must be prepared ir such a way that they can be clearly and completely understood. Grades, o course, provide a common language so that the needs of the place can be communicated effectively enough so that the supplier can provide exactly what is needed.

The Route to Improved Communications

Whether one's purpose is to improve the effectiveness of his own communication, to provide training to his employees so they may improve their communication, or to identify and solve communication difficulties in the foodservice operation, here are some guides that point the way to better communication. There must be:

1. an understanding of what the communication process is, how it functions, and what keeps it from functioning effectively

2. a critical analysis of communication within the operation

3. a recognition and definition of the communication deficiencies that the analysis reveals

4. a determination to do something about the situation

5. the acquiring of needed knowledge and information so that the needed improvement may be made

6. a plan of action to make the needed changes

7. action to put into effect what is necessary to improve communication performance in all aspects of the operation

Communication Suggestions for Foodservice People

Here are ten suggestions that can lead to an improved foodservice operation:

1. Know what you want to say and be sure of what it means to you. If you are not sure of what you mean, you cannot expect other people to know what you want them to know or to do. It is hard enough to get understanding without adding handicaps.

2. Know as much as you can about your audience, their educational level, their interests, attitudes, skills, and abilities. Information of this kind can help you make what you have to say more readily understood by those with whom you are communicating.

3. Try to put yourself in the place of the person with whom you are communicating and consider what you have to

297

say as you think he would. This is hard to do, but it is well worth the effort. Relate what you have to say to things that you know are of interest or concern to your listeners.

4. Give attention to the people who are communicating with you. Being a good listener can mean a great difference in the effectiveness of communication.

5. Make communication a two-way street and not two one-way streets. If people have an opportunity to ask questions and check to see if what they heard is what is meant, communication will be much more effective.

6. Recognize the limitations of the various communication methods. Dashing off a memorandum is not the best way to communicate in all circumstances and situations.

7. Remember that many factors affect understanding by other people of what you say and write. Some factors may be more important at one time than at another time.

8. Do not try to impress people with big complicated words. Research shows that even people of high intellectual levels pay better attention and react more effectively to messages that are in shorter, simpler words. Many people do not have time to try to determine the meaning in long-word material. Make the correct choice of words. Some words are general with many different meanings. Others are specific with less chance of being misunderstood. The meaning people get from words is closely related to their experiences and the meanings they have come to associate through those experiences with the words. So, meaning differs among people.

9. Peoples' opinions are not always based on reason and logic. Often logical statements of fact do not result in their correcting their views and agreeing. Instead, they strengthen their determination to continue holding the views that they have, and they make greater efforts to find new reasons to support those views.

10. Above all, recognize your need to improve communications; want to improve your communication; and work hard at it. The foodservice industry, and other industries as well, would find communication a far less serious problem if more people were willing to admit that they are not doing a good job of communicating and really tried to do something about improving it.

Summary

The source of many foodservice problems is inefficient communication, with a high cost in lost sales, unhappy customers, spoiled food, damaged equipment, hostile employees, and frustrated managers. Many problems are caused by a lack of good communication.

The communication process, involving an originator, translater, message, channel, retranslator, and receiver, offers many places where communication efforts can go astray. The translation of an intangible idea in a person's mind, its transmission in the form of a physical message, and its retranslation into an intangible idea in the mind of another is the basis of communication; it depends on effective use of the senses, ability and knowledge of people, attitudes, physical blocks, environmental factors, and differences in people.

Much can be done to improve communication, but first must come an understanding of how communication occurs, a study of the communication situation in the foodservice operation, and a recognition that meaning is in people and related to their experience, to be elicited through the cues or signals that messages provide. The receiver of the message is the most important part of the communication process, and the reaction of the receiver is the test of communication effectiveness.

Questions

1. Describe the significance of effective communication in the successful operation of a foodservice establishment.

2. What are five symptoms of communication problems in a foodservice operation?

3. Explain how communication involves both the tangible and the intangible.

4. In diagram form, illustrate the process of communication.

5. What is the significance of purpose and audience in effective communication?

6. List five things that affect the efficiency with which communication is conducted.

7. List the blocks to good communication frequently encountered in foodservice operations.

8. Describe a program to improve communication in an operation that has been encountering communication problems.

19

Foodservice and the Computer

Scared of the computer? Don't know what it does? Avoid trying to find out? Yet, hearing a lot about it? Knowing some people are using it? Many foodservice people find themselves in the computer dilemma—knowing that computers are doing important and valuable things, but not knowing what the computer can mean to them on their jobs, and worse yet, avoiding finding out.

Many of their fears are groundless. The computer is not something to be feared and avoided. Instead, it should be understood and used where its application is of value. It is not necessary to be a computer expert or an engineer, either. A simple understanding of this electronic machine is easy to obtain and the potential of the computer in foodservice is easy to understand. This chapter offers some information to help foodservice people gain that understanding.

Used by Foodservice People

The foodservice industry has been using computers for a number of years. Corporate restaurant chains use computers to provide detailed systems for keeping track of sales, costs, payroll, and inventories. Hotels have systems that make reservations before guests arrive, monitor them while they are in the hotel, check them out, and follow up later to remind them that they are welcome back. Foodservice buying groups use the computer to determine their needs, to order, to maintain inventories, and to distribute to the members of the groups.

But, for many foodservice people, computers have been too confusing, too expensive, or too complex. Those terms could have been applied with good reason when computers first came onto the scene in 1948. They were huge, required a large staff to operate, and were very expensive. Those days are gone. There have been big changes in computers, and there have been three generations of computers in the course of this change, all the time reducing the needs for size, large staff, and large costs.

The Three Generations

Because the development has been so spectacular, a closer look at the changes is in order. The first generation of computers were large installations. They used vacuum tubes, and the other components of their circuits were generally large. They required great amounts of electrical energy and large cooling systems. Cathode ray tubes, magnetic drums, and even chemicals were used for the memory or storage function of these computers. In brief, they were very large, very expensive, and they required a large staff to operate.

Two electronic developments produced the second generation of computers. One development was the advent of the transistor, which also revolutionized the size and complexity of radios. Another was the introduction of the magnetic core as a means of storing data and instructions. The computers of this second generation had many advantages over their bulky predecessors. They occupied less space, they were lighter in weight, and they used much less power for their operation. All of these reductions also aided in reducing costs across the board. A big gain was in the speed of the computer's internal operations. These computers operated much more rapidly.

Again, developments in electronics had much to do with the appearance of the third generation of computers. One development made it possible to put many of the computer parts into one machine. More sophisticated circuits were developed and made what the computer could do much larger in scope. The problem of protecting the data stored in the cores from being lost was solved; and the storage capability of computers was extended greatly by the use of disks, data cells, and new kinds of cores. Another big development was in relating the computer to communications equipment and facilities. This opened the way to using telephone lines to feed data to and from many locations. Again with this generation, the amount of time required for internal operations was reduced; and it became possible to interrupt a program in operation to take care of a higher priority need.

Other Developments

Minicomputers, developed with the same technology that has produced small, inexpensive calculators, are relatively inexpensive, small in size, and do not require a lot of computer technical know-how to use. Also, calculators are incorporating some computer functions, in another development that promises even more widespread use of computer technology and electronic assistance.

So, instead of shying away from the computer, the trend for foodservice people is now one of getting acquainted and seeing what computers and computer technology can do in taking care of payrolls, determining orders, checking inventories, planning menus, and doing a number of other jobs in the accounting area, including keeping records, writing checks, and determining taxes.

A Basic Question

What is a computer? That is a logical question. A computer is an electronic device that has tremendous speed and total accuracy in processing data that would take humans many hours with great expenditure of energy and likely with questionable accuracy. It is, in simple terms, a high-speed processor of data. But it needs the help of human beings, because without such help it cannot do anything.

How the Computer Works

The computer is really a system made up of three units in its simplest form. These can be described as input, processing, and output. In other words, in using a computer, information is fed into the machine; the computer does with that information what it is directed to do; and the information comes out in the form needed. Thus, comes that input, processing, and output sequence.

Processing can involve any number of functions, such as adding figures, storing information for later retrieval, solving problems, making comparisons, summarizing vast amounts of data for analysis, and making decisions.

It has been stated that the computer is no better than the person who feeds it the information; and it might be added that the computer's performance is no better than the instructions it is given. For the computer to function, it needs to be instructed regarding what it is to do. It must have these instructions in a very detailed manner. They must be precise, and they must be arranged in a logical way. The computer operates in a step-by-step manner.

These instructions, written in a form that the computer can interpret, make up the program; and the person who writes the program is called a programmer. The computer may be given a program, for example, on how to handle the information needed for a foodservice establishment's payroll.

Foodservice people do not have to be programmers. There are now more and more already developed programs available for sale, which cover many of the functions of the foodservice operation. This development has been a factor in the more widespread use of the computer in foodservice businesses.

Along with the instructions, the computer needs the data or information that it is to process, following the step-by-step instructions provided to it. So, the input contains both instructions and data.

Putting Data into the Computer   Since computers have not yet progressed very far in accepting spoken human words, there must be some method of putting information into the computer. One of the most common ways of putting information into a computer system is by using punched cards. These cards have horizontal rows and columns, and holes can be punched into the cards. Printed on the cards are numbers in the row arrangement, usually with the first row being zeros and then each row increasing by one numerically until the bottom row of nine is reached. Actually, each column can be used to represent any single letter of the alphabet, any number, or any special character.

The holes are made in the cards by a keypunch, a device that is also sometimes called a data recorder. It is a device with a keyboard much like a typewriter, and the operator can punch holes in certain places on the cards. When the card has been punched, it goes into the input unit of the computer, which is called a card reader. This machine locates the holes and electronically tells the central processing unit what and where those holes are on the card. In this way, the information in the person's mind or in a report or other document is translated into holes in a card, and then retranslated into data that the computer processing unit can accept and store.

Data can be introduced in many other ways, including the typewriter, touch-tone telephone, paper tape, cathode ray tubes, and various types of readers. But, the punched card method serves to illustrate the basic steps involved.

A Three-Part Unit   There are three parts of the central processing unit. One is for storage; one is for arithmetic and logic functions; and one is for control of all other elements. The storage unit is where the instructions or program and the data are stored. It is the place to which information can be moved in and from which information can be moved out. It is also a place in which information can be moved around in different ways.

The arithmetic and logic part of the central processing unit does adding, subtracting, multiplying, and dividing. It makes comparisons. It can test things. The control unit provides the direction for the entire system and it coordinates what happens. It puts into effect the directions that are given to it in the instructions and causes the various potentials of the computer to become actualities.

There is still need, however, to get output, and this is the function of the output unit. The line printer that provides output in printed form is probably the most common form of output unit. The electronic impulses from the central processing unit select the printed characters, and at the same time activate how those characters are printed on the printout paper at speeds up to 2,000 lines per minute. Data can also be obtained from the computer by use of the cathode ray tube and by several kinds of readers.

Basically, and in its simplest terms, that is how a computer works—receiving data, processing it in accordance with a previously provided program, and providing output in the form needed—all at tremendous speed.

Foodservice Uses of the Computer

Actually, what the computer does is what the foodservice operator does by hand, at considerable requirements in time and labor cost. So, it is well to consider which of the jobs done in the foodservice operation can be turned over to the computer with savings in both time and labor, and the added benefit of greater accuracy. Being able to do that leaves more time for managers to perform their function of management.

Payroll is one job that requires much computation and eventually the preparation of checks. A computer can be programmed to do all of the processing and even to write the checks from the data fed into its input unit.

Categorized and total sales information is determined in many foodservice operations. Computerized cash registers with category keys can provide data for processing into the needed form at a fraction of the time and labor required to keep a manual listing of the items that customers select.

The problem of keeping the required records accurately is a common one in school foodservice operations, which regularly submit claims to the state school foodservice office. It is also found in other types of foodservice operations as well.

A School Foodservice Example   Programmable calculators with the necessary programs on magnetic cards can provide an answer to the school foodservice program needs, as it has in a Massachusetts city. These programs made it possible to compute and total daily servings, and to compute the various lines on the milk and reimbursement sections of the report form; to add and deduct from the items and quantities on the item inventory; and to list items, quantities, prices, and values. It also made possible adjustment of the inventory level and the listing of the total value of the inventory.

The inventory pricing program also was used. This enabled input and price changes for inventory after the prices had been entered on the magnetic program cards. Individual prices could be entered or changed, and the item price list of inventory could be obtained in printout form. Calculations can also be made on inventory items without affecting the permanent inventory.

The machine can categorize menu items, and help with costing and pricing. The bookkeeping program can keep track of all receipts and expenditures, greatly simplifying the accounting job. It also offers a double check on the work on claims, as it provides an audit trail of all the financial transactions.

The result in this school foodservice system has been a big saving in time, much greater accuracy, and the meeting of deadlines for claims through the use of these computerized calculators.

Reducing Delays   Electronic cash controls make a significant contribution to the efforts of foodservice operators to control labor costs, food costs, and inventory. The accumulation of identifiable data, the analysis of cost figures, and the capability of getting needed information quickly make it possible to arrive at better decisions more quickly.

For multi-unit foodservice organizations, this factor of less delay in getting current figures in a form for easy analysis at the company headquarters is of major importance. A combination of electronic cash control devices at the units combined with the use of telephone lines to get information to the headquarters can reduce the time lag as much as a week, or in some cases even a month.

Connecting electronic cash registers, which now have more capability, to larger computer systems offers the foodservice firm a big advantage. Data terminals tied in with a computer at another location provide an opportunity to obtain computer services without having to own and operate a computer.

A Foodservice Chain Example   An example of what can be accomplished is provided by one of the chain foodservice operations. This company was concerned because the mail was too slow in moving data from store to store and from the stores to the main office.

Management introduced a system using minicomputers tied in with telephone communication with the central unit. Each store transmits its data to the central office. There, it is recorded on disks; and after it is recorded all the registers in the units are returned to zero, ready for the next day's business.

Included are data for labor cost, breakdowns of sales, payroll, and other financial records. Available from the computer are labor cost and utilization analysis of sales and resultant adjustments to other operations and work flow over the day. The computer can also reorder items based on data on what is sold.

What the Terms Mean

To understand the computer and the discussion of it, there is need to know the meanings of some of the terms used in talking about the computer. Following are some commonly used terms.

Algorithm   series of steps defined in a logical way that represent the solution to a problem.

Arithmetic/Logic unit   part of the computer that does addition, subtraction, division, and multiplication; makes comparisons and tests.

Bit   single storage unit of a computer.

Bug   error in a computer program.

Byte   group of bits that represent a character.

Card reader   part of the computer that locates the holes in the cards and informs the central processing unit.

Character   symbol that a computer can read, store, or write.

Collating   arranging data in a sequence that has previously been determined.

Computer   high speed electronic processor of data.

Computer system   combination of input, processing, and output units of a computer.

Control unit   part of the computer that directs and coordinates the system.

Data   units of information that a computer can process or produce.

Data recorder   device for punching holes in cards that represent digits, letters, and special characters used to introduce information to the computer.

Disk   used to store data outside the computer memory.

Hardware   equipment such as the computer and its accessories, including computer circuits, printers, screens, disks, keyboards, etc.

Key punch   device for punching cards for computer use.

Line printer   output unit of a computer that provides printed information.

Machine language   combinations of plus and minus magnetized bits that make up the machine language into which the instructions in English must be translated.

Memory   computer's central control system storage area for instructions and data.

Program   instructions to the computer to perform a certain task.

Programmer   person who develops the step-by-step instructions.

Printer   output unit of the computer.

Punched card   form of putting data into the computer.

Reader   device for sensing holes in a card.

Software   programs and procedures used in getting the computer to do certain things, usually provided by the manufacturer of the computer.

Storage   where the instructions and data are stored in the computer.

Terminal   device for sending and receiving information on a communication channel, which usually has a keyboard and a display device.

A Job for the Computer To Do

Reviewing what happens when the computer is given a specific job to do will help clarify exactly what happens. There is need to add two numbers—8 and 6. Doing this simple arithmetic problem is a matter of reading one number, storing it in the brain, reading the second number, adding it to the first number stored in the brain, following the principles of addition learned previously, and stating or writing down the total of 8 and 6, or 14, which is the answer to the problem.

The computer can do this same problem, but it needs much more detail in its instructions. To add 8 and 6, it would need to read the first number and store it, read the second number and store it, move the numbers to the central processing unit and into the section of that unit that does the arithmetic and logic operations, add the two numbers, produce the answer, and provide it. This, then, is the program that the computer would be given. It must be detailed, precise, with each part in order, and all in a step-by-step sequence.

This adding of one simple number and another simple number is a simple computation, and it has a simple program. The computer, however, is capable of much more complex operations; and the programs for such operations are much more complex and detailed. But that simple arithmetic problem indicates what the computer is all about.

Get Acquainted

The purpose of this chapter is not to get into the complete computer story, but rather to acquaint the reader with what the computer is and what it can do for people in the foodservice industry. Many books and articles have been written on the computer, its applications, and the many forms of equipment that are used. Reference to these, or consultation with representatives of companies that have equipment and software to sell can provide much information and the answers to many questions.

The purpose of this chapter will be accomplished if the reader puts aside any fears of the computer, and logically sets out to find how it can be used to help in the foodservice operation to save time, labor, and provide greater accuracy in the daily operations of the business.

Look at the Situation

For foodservice people interested in purchasing a minicomputer, these are some things to keep in mind:

1. Consider the needs of your operation. Look at time, accuracy, quantity of information, and other factors to decide what you need, and even whether you need a computer.

2. What problems are you having now where handling data quickly, with less labor, and with accuracy is of great importance, but is not being done the way it should?

3. Check what is available that will meet your needs.

4.   Find a reputable manufacturer or dealer.

5.   Determine what software you will need in addition to the machines.

6.   Be sure that good servicing of the equipment will be available.

7.   Consider costs of computer versus costs of doing the work the way it is now being done; and consider what problems can be eliminated with the computer and what savings can thus be made.

Do I Need Computer Assistance?

To decide whether you should invest in computer assistance, either by purchasing equipment, leasing time in computer systems, or otherwise getting aid from a computer, check the following:

1.   Are you lost in paperwork and feel you cannot go on?

2.   Do you need data that you cannot get immediately?

3.   Do you lack information for analyzing your operation?

4.   Do you have data but no time to analyze it?

5.   Are your labor costs for paperwork mounting to heights that cannot continue?

6.   Are you always behind in your reports and your records?

7.   Do you have problems in operating the business and do not know where to locate them?

8.   Do you have difficulties in knowing what needs to be ordered?

9.   Is inventory control a disaster?

10.   Are you buried in details?

11.   Are you prevented from functioning as a manager?

If the answer is Yes to many of these questions, you ought to investigate computer assistance.

The Future

All indications are that the world will become more and more computerized as time goes on, and as the cost of computers becomes less and less. *Smaller, less expensive,* and *quicker* are the words that describe the trend. Smaller circuits speed up the processing of data and reduce costs. Storage chips of fantastically small size and large capacity have reduced the size of equipment, and have expanded storage capacity. Much faster printing speeds reduce the time required for getting output. Programming has moved from essentially numbers to something closer to English with a standard keyboard.

The development of minicomputers has only started as has the application of computer functions and capabilities to calculators, cash registers, and other machines. Programs stored in the computer, software that can be easily used, hardware that is modular, multiple use of the computer for different purposes at the same time, and even greater uses to which the computer can be put are evidences of the way things are moving.

For the foodservice industry, with its many transactions, many items, masses of data, and the need for continual analysis, the computer will become an integral part of the operation. This will be true, not only in large companies, but also in small foodservice businesses. The time is coming when individuals will have their own personal computers and will use them on a regular basis, and foodservice businesses will be computer directed.

So, for foodservice people, the choice is obvious. There is a need to forget fear of the "electronic monster," and find out what it is, how it operates, and what it can do, and determine if it is needed now. The computer is a valuable management tool that can free foodservice people from a lot of paperwork and allow them to plan ahead, instead of spending most of the time trying to catch up with the mass of paperwork.

Summary

Computers are valuable machines but scare some foodservice people and so keep them from taking advantage of this technology in their daily business operations. However, computers have been used by the foodservice industry for doing many jobs quickly that would take many hours by hand.

Computer size, staff requirements, and costs have declined steadily as three generations of computers were designed and marketed. Electronic developments made possible reduced size and cost, greater capability, and wider applications of the computer.

The computer processes data at a tremendous speed and with total accuracy, but requires human assistance for directions and for the data it processes. The computer system in its simplest representation is made up of three units— inputs, processing, and output. Instructions to the computer are called a program and are introduced to the computer by punched cards and other means. The data goes to the central processing unit, which includes the storage, the arithmetic and logic functions, and the control.

The computer can save foodservice operations great amounts of time and work in such areas as payroll, inventory, purchasing, menu determination, reporting, breaking down sales, determining labor and food costs, and preparing bills. There are many foodservice operations where computer assistance can be of much value; and the future promises more and more use of computer technology in the foodservice industry.

Questions

1.   Describe in simple terms what a computer is, and what advantages the computer can provide foodservice operations.

2.   "The computer cannot entirely replace people" is a statement frequently made. Explain why.

3.   What is a computer program?

4.   Describe one way in which data can be put into a computer.

5.   What are the functions of the central processing unit?

6.   List five jobs in a foodservice operation with which the computer can be of much value.

7.   What is machine language?

8.   What is meant by three generations of computers?

9.   What is likely to be the trend in computer development in the future?

10.   What effects would such a trend have on the foodservice industry?

Appendix A

Approximate Conversions
from Metric Measures

Symbol	When You Know	Multiply by	To Find	Symbol
		LENGTH		
mm	millimeters	0.04	inches	in
cm	centimeters	0.4	inches	in
m	meters	3.3	feet	ft
m	meters	1.1	yards	yd
km	kilometers	0.6	miles	mi
		AREA		
cm^2	square centimeters	0.16	square inches	in^2
m^2	square meters	1.2	square yards	yd^2
km^2	square kilometers	0.4	square miles	mi^2
ha	hectares (10,000 m^2)	2.5	acres	
		MASS (weight)		
g	grams	0.035	ounces	oz
kg	kilograms	2.2	pounds	lb
t	metric ton (1000 kg)	1.1	short tons	
		VOLUME		
ml	milliliters	0.03	Fluid ounces	fl oz
l	liters	2.1	pints	pt
l	liters	1.06	quarts	qt
l	liters	0.26	gallons	gal
m^3	cubic meters	35	cubic feet	ft^3
m^3	cubic meters	1.3	cubic yards	yd^3
		TEMPERATURE (exact)		
°C	Celsius temperature	9/5 (then add 32)	Fahrenheit temperature	°F

*1 in = 2.54 cm (exactly). For other exact conversions and more detailed tables, see NBS Misc. Publ. 286, Units of Weights and Measures. Price $2.25. SD Catalog No. C13 10:286.

METRIC CONVERSION CARD
Approximate Conversions to Metric Measures

Symbol	When You Know	Multiply by	To Find	Symbol
		LENGTH		
in	inches	*2.5	centimeters	cm
ft	feet	30	centimeters	cm
yd	yards	0.9	meters	m
mi	miles	1.6	kilometers	km
		AREA		
in^2	square inches	6.5	square centimeters	cm^2
ft^2	square feet	0.09	square meters	m^2
yd^2	square yards	0.8	square meters	m^2
mi^2	square miles	2.6	square kilometers	km^2
	.acres	0.4	hectares	ha
		MASS (weight)		
oz	ounces	28	grams	g
lb	pounds	0.45	kilograms	kg
	short tons (2000 lb)	0.9	metric ton	t
		VOLUME		
tsp	teaspoon	5	milliliters	ml
Tbsp	tablespoons	15	milliliters	ml
fl oz	fluid ounces	30	milliliters	ml
c	cups	0.24	liters	l
pt	pints	0.47	liters	l
qt	quarts	0.95	liters	l
gal	gallons	3.8	liters	l
ft^3	cubic feet	0.03	cubic meters	m^3
yd^3	cubic yards	0.76	cubic meters	m^3
		TEMPERATURES (exact)		
°F	Fahrenheit temperature	5/9 (after subtracting 32)	Celsius temperature	°C

Index

Acceptability of product, 184
Acceptance Service, U.S.D.A., 199, 250, 251
Acid foods, 62
Age determination
   beef animals, 206
Aging beef, 216–218
Air cell, eggs, 244
Air circulation. *See* Ventilation.
Alarm system, freezers, 49
Albumin in eggs, 252
Almanac of the Canning, Freezing, Processing Industries, 224
American cheddar cheese. *See* Cheddar.
American Hospital Association, 52
Analyses
   tools of, 141
Analysis
   as management tool, 140, 141
   break-even point, 140, 141, 145–148
   chart, 86, 87
   closing point determination, 151–153
   costs, 141, 142
   effectiveness, 148

   information needed, 141
   scatter graph, 142–145, 153, 154
   use, 148–153
Architects, 80, 87, 88
Arithmetic/Logic Unit, 305
Assets
   fixed, 115, 116
   in general, 101, 104, 113, 115, 116
   liquid, 113
   total, 115
Assumptions. *See also* Forecasting.
   affecting predictions, 127
   in break-even analysis, 148
Averages, financial, 112, 113

Bacteria
   control, 72, 73
   destruction, 65
   functions, 19
   growth, 62, 66
   in food poisoning, 62–69
   in prepared frozen foods, 71–73
   life cycle, 66

psychrophilic, 74
survival, 74
types, 73
variations in number, 73
Bacterial food poisoning
control, 66–69
definition, 62
frequency, 61
growth, 68
kinds, 62–66
occurrence, 61, 62
prevention, 61, 66–69
sources, 62–65
symptoms, 62–65
Baking
quality loss, 75
Balance sheet, 101–102, 104–106, 108
accounts, 101
in basic accounting record, 101
comparative, 105–107
content, 104, 105
example, 102
function, 101
Beef
age determination, 206
aging, 216–218
cutability, 205, 209, 210
cuts chart, 195
geographic source, 198, 199
grading, 204, 205
price changes, 202
purchasing, 187–220
market class determination, 205, 206
standardization, 196
storage, 216, 217
variety of cuts, 194
Beef, specifications
age, 197
cutting style, 197
grades, 199, 204–210
packaging, 197
pre-preparation, 197
sex condition, 197
trim style, 197
using, 197
weights, 197
Beverage sales ratio, 127, 128
Bids
in purchasing, 177, 182
Bit, 305
Blind check receiving, 4
Blocks, communication, 291, 292

Blue mold cheese, 274
Botulism, 63, 65
Brands
canned fruits and vegetables, 225; 234, 235
frozen foods, 46
Break-even analysis, 140–157
chart, 154, 156
limitations, 157
use of, 148
Break-even point
calculation, 145–147
daily, 155
definition, 140, 141
formula, 147
graphs, 142–144, 153–156
Brix measurement, 228
Budget-making
accounting, 120
involvement, 123, 124
maker, 123, 124
period, 123
responsibility, 124
starting place, 124
Budgets. *See also* Operating budget.
annual fixed, 130
as useful tool, 120
cash, 120
choice, 121
construction, 125, 126
coordinating function, 121, 122
fixed, 125–132
flexible, 132–134
for control, 121–123
maker, 123, 124
operating, 120, 122–125
operational, 119–139
period, 123
sales, 120
selection, 121
use, 134, 135
variable, 132
Butcher
disappearing, 194
test card for beef, 191, 192
Butter, 266, 267
Butterfat, 263, 264
Buttermilk, 264
Buying for use
beef, 188, 189
canned fruits and vegetables, 222, 223
Byte, 306

Candling eggs, 245
Canned foods
    as convenience food, 221
    fruits and vegetables, 221–241
    storage, 21, 22
Cans
    sizes, 238
    substitution, 239
Capital
    guide in purchasing, 169
    turnover, 112, 114
Card reader, 306
Care and handling
    eggs, 251
        at foodservice establishment, 75
        at production plant, 74, 75
        frozen prepared foods, 74, 75
Cattle cycle, 201
Central processing unit, 303
Chalaza, in eggs, 244
Channel, communication, 288–291, 294
Chart, break-even, 153–157
Cheddar, 273, 274
Cheese, 267–275
    process, 274, 275
    grades, 229, 280
    varieties, 267–275
Cleanliness
    of eating places, 67–69
    personal, 66
Closing point, 144–150
Communication
    analysis, 295, 296
    improvement, 297, 298
    problem, 292, 293, 295
    process, 288–292
    suggestions, 297, 298
    symptoms, 286, 287, 292, 293, 295
Comparison
    operating budgets, 119–121, 132–135
Comparative statements
    balance sheet, 105, 106
    profit and loss statement, 105, 107–109
    types, 104, 105
Computer
    card reader, 306
    control unit, 306
    data recorder, 303
    disk, 306
    fear of computer, 300
    generations of, 301
    hardware, 306

how it works, 302, 305
input, 302, 303
in school foodservice, 304, 305
instructions, 302
language, 306
meaning, 306
output, 302, 303
printer, 306
processing, 303
programs, 302, 306
programmer, 302
reader, 306
software, 306
storage, 306
system, 305, 306
terminal, 306
terms, 305
use by foodservice people, 300, 304, 305
use decision, 308
what it is, 302, 306
Concentrated milks, 266
Containers
    eggs, 255
    milk, 264, 265
    canned foods, 238
Contamination
    by employees, 67, 73, 74
    microbiological, 72
    prevention, 66, 67
Contract buying
    beef, 214, 215
    food, 184
Contribution margin, 146
Control
    budget, 121, 122, 135
    cost, 52
    issuing frozen foods, 50
    operating statements, 119, 120
    portion, 52
    receiving, 9–12
    storage, 17, 21–23, 26, 27
    temperature, 73–75
Cooking. See also Production.
    duration, 71
    frozen foods, 53, 54
    prepared frozen foods, 75
    tests, 175, 189, 236, 237
Cooking loss test card, 187, 188, 190, 191,
        193, 194
Cooling food
    in refrigerators, 67
    rapidly, 68

Cost calculation, 133, 134
Cost control, 52
Costs
    fixed, 141–153
    major, 78
    semi-variable, 142–153
    variable, 142–153
Cream, 265
Credit memorandum, 14
Cutability grades (beef). *See* Yield grades.
Cuts of beef, 189, 190, 196
Cutting tests, 175, 236, 237
Cyclical menus. *See* Menus.

Daily food cost summary, 93, 95–98
Daily order sheet, 214
Daily receiving report. *See* Receiving clerk's
    daily report.
Damage
    frozen food package, 47
Danger zone, 54, 67–69
Data, computer, 306
Data recorder, 303, 306
Defrosting
    fish, 52
    freezers, 50
    frozen eggs, 257
    guide, 51, 52
    methods, 51
Deliveries
    checking, 47
    distribution, 10
    frozen foods, 47
    recording, 9, 10
    temperature, 48
Delivery ticket, 2, 3
Disk, 306
Distance
    in kitchen, 79
Dollies, 19
Dry whole milk, 276

Earnings statement. *See* Profit and loss
    statement.
Eggs
    containers, 255
    dried, 254, 255
    equivalents, 256, 257
    flavor, 251, 252
    frozen, 254, 255
    grades, 245–248, 252

    handling, 255, 256
    interior arrangement, 243–245
    parts, 243–245
    prices, 248, 249
    products, 254–257
    purchasing guide, 253, 254
    quality, 245
    size and weight, 246, 252
    source of supply, 249
    storage, 24, 30
    specifications, 250
    thawing, 257
    uses, 253
Enzymes, 19
Equipment
    kitchen, 79
    location, 81, 83
    receiving, 6, 7, 14, 15
    space, 83, 84
    storage, 19–25
Equity, 101
Equivalents, eggs. *See* Eggs.
Expense budgeting, 127, 128
Expense estimate, 145
Expense forecast. *See* Forecasting.
Expenses
    budgeting, 127, 128
    employee meals, 129
    level of, 133, 134
    occupancy costs, 130
    payroll taxes, 129, 130
    salaries and wages, 129

Fabricating beef, 194, 195
Factors influencing business
    assumptions, 127
Fidelity of communication, 291, 292
Fill standards, 225, 226
Financial management objectives, 100, 101
Financial ratios, 111–118
Financial statements 99–118
    as management tool, 99, 100
    balance sheet, 100, 101
    comparisons, 101, 104–108, 117
    income statement, 100
    relationship, 104
Financial ratios. *See* Ratios.
First-in, first-out, 5
Fish
    bacteria content, 73
    cooking, 54
    defrosting, 52

effects of temperature, 57
storage life, 58
Fixed operating budgets, 124–132
annual, 130, 131
assumption, 125, 127
construction, 125, 126
forecast, 124, 125, 127
needed information, 128
sales level, 124, 125
Flexible operating budgets, 132–134
construction, 132, 133
cost calculation, 133, 134
nature of, 133
Flow of work
in kitchen, 81, 83, 84
Food
contamination, 66, 67
control, 44
cooling, 66, 67
cost, 7
handling, 29, 67
holding, 67, 68
ordering, 5, 8
perishable, 20
safety program, 72
semi-perishable, 20
storage, 24–40
Food and Drug Administration, U.S.
Department of, 225–226
Food cost determination
actual, 94
daily, 94
estimated, 94, 95
Food, direct, 10, 191–194
Food, Drug, and Cosmetics Act, 225, 227
Food poisoning. See Bacterial food
poisoning.
Food sales ratio, 80, 87
Foodservice
consultants, 80, 87
workers
changing characteristics, 164
Food Stores, 10, 91–94
Forecasting
expense, 127, 133, 134, 137
for purchasing, 188
menu relationship, 168, 188
need, 168, 169
sales, 125, 127, 128, 168, 169
Forms
frozen food issuing, 50
receiving record, 90
storeroom requisition, 90

Freezing
effects on foods, 71, 75
effects on microorganisms, 73, 74
efficiency, 49, 50
storage criteria, 48
without delay, 71
Freezer practices
air circulation, 49
rotation, 49
segregation, 49
temperature check, 49
unloading, 49
Frozen custard, 277
Frozen foods
accountability, 50
advantages, 44
brands, 46
care and handling, 71–77
control, 52, 53
cooking, 50, 51, 53, 54
delivery check, 47, 48
deterioration, 73, 74
disadvantages, 44
freezing, 67
grades, 45, 46
holding, 54
issuing, 50
ordering procedures, 45–47
pre-cooked, 67
prepared, 71–77
preparation, 50, 51
quality, 45
quantity, 45
receiving, 47, 48
refrigeration, 48
refreezing, 54, 55
responsibility, 44, 47
storage, 48–50
storage life, 48
storage temperature guide, 57–59
temperature check, 48
thawing, 51, 52
time and temperature effects, 55–59
unit size, 46
Frozen storage
practices, 32
sanitation, 50
Fruits
canned, 225
defrosting, 59
storage, 24, 26
storage life, 26
Future of computers, 308, 309

Goals for business. *See* Financial management.
Grades, including U.S.D.A. Grades
  beef, 180, 201, 204–210
  butter, 180, 279
  canned fruits and vegetables, 225
  changes, 207
  cheese, 279, 280
  dairy products, 279, 280
  dry milk, 280
  eggs, 245, 247, 280
  for purchasing, 173, 174
  frozen foods, 45, 46
  shields, 181
  use in purchasing, 173, 174
  various products, 180

Handling. *See* Care and handling.
Hand trucks, 7
Hardware, 306
Heat
  correct use, 68
  effect on bacteria, 73
Heating recommendations, 76
Holding
  cooked frozen foods, 54
  temperatures, 54
  times, 54
Homogenized milk, 263
Humidity
  control, 24
  in storage, 22, 24, 28–29
  in storerooms, 24, 26, 27
Hygiene, 67
Hygrometer, 22

Ice cream, 276, 277
Ice cream mix, 278, 279
Ice milk, 278
Identity standards, 225, 226
IMPS, 197
Income statement. *See* Profit and loss statement.
Infection, food, 62, 63, 64
Information sources, 171, 172, 204, 244
Input, 302
Inspection
  beef, 211
  eggs, 250, 251
  deliveries 1, 2
  service, 251

Institutional Meat Purchase Specifications, U.S.D.A., 189, 197
Instructions, computer, 302
Instructors, training, 159, 160
Intoxication, food, 62–64
Inventory
  frozen foods, 45
  kitchen, 94
  purchasing relationship, 169
  storage, 91, 95
  storeroom, 95–98
Inventory taking, 5
Invoice receiving, 3, 4
Invoices
  check, 47
  delivery, 2, 3
  memorandum, 10, 14
  routing, 3
  stamp, 14
  substitution, 10, 14
Issuance of food, 50, 91, 95, 98

Job, deskilling, 163
Juices
  defrosting, 51
  temperature effects, 56

Keypunch, 303, 306
Kitchen planning. *See also* Layout, Models.
  check, 86, 87
  complications, 79
  contributions, 79
  coordination, 79
  elements of, 79
  expert assistance, 80
  flow of food, 83
  flow of work, 81, 83, 84
  goal, 79
  initiation, 80
  layout, 81
  operations, 83, 84
  space, 83
Knowledge
  best use of product, 222, 223
  for food purchasing, 221, 223
  market, 222
  of establishment's need, 222

Labeling
  below standard, 227

canned fruits and vegetables, 227–229
descriptive, 229
ice cream, 277
nutritional, 229
open code, 229
Label requirements
canned fruits and vegetables, 227–229
ice cream, 277
Labor costs, 158
Ladders, 19
Layout
check, 86, 87
kitchen, 79, 81, 83, 86
preliminary, 81
Leftovers, 41, 67, 94
Liabilities, 101, 104
current, 114
total, 114
Limitations, human, 86
Line printer, 306
Locks on freezers, 48
Low-acid foods, 62
Low-fat milk, 263, 264

Machine language, 306
Maintenance, 50
Make-or-buy decisions, 190–192
Managerial functions, 121
Manual for receiving, 9
Marbling of beef, 206
Margarine, 267
Market class, beef animals, 205, 206
Market information and reports, 171–173,
    204
Massachusetts Department of Agriculture,
    250
Meaning, computer, 306
Meat
cooking, 53
cycle, 171
defrosting, 51
storage, 24, 26–28
Meat Buyers Guide to Standardized Meat
    Cuts, 189
Meat cycle, 171
Medical examinations, 66
Membranes, eggs, 241
Memorandum invoice, 10
Menu
making, 35
purchasing relationships, 168, 188
Menus, cyclical

construction, 39–40
cycles, 36–40
flexibility, 40
leftovers, 41
pattern, 36
value, 34, 35
Message, communication, 288–291, 294
Microorganisms, 72
Milk
buttermilk, 264
dry, 276, 278, 280
fat-free, 263
flavored, 264
fluid, 263, 264, 281, 282
imitation, 265, 266
skim, 263
specifications, 281
Minicomputers, 301
Mini-max purchasing, 177, 179
Models, kitchen equipment, 81, 83
Molds, 19
Motion study, 83, 85, 86

National Association of Meat Purveyors,
    189
National Live Stock and Meat Board
beef cut charts, 194–196
uniform identity program, 196, 198, 199
Net working capital ratio, 113, 114
Net worth, 101
tangible net worth, 11, 114, 115
Non-fat dry milk, 275, 276, 280
Nutritional labeling, 229

Odors, food
given off, 29, 30
absorbed, 29, 30
Ontario Agricultural College, 252
On-the-job-training, 161, 162
Operating budget, 119–139
comparison, 120, 121
coordination, 120–123
expense budgeting, 127–130
fixed, 124–126, 130–132
flexible, 132–134
for new establishment, 137, 138
function, 119, 120
maker of, 123, 124
significance, 120
types, 124, 125
use, 134, 135
variable, 124

Operating ratios, 116
Operating statement. *See* Profit and loss statement.
Operations analysis, 83–86
  chart, 86, 87
  sheet, 135–137
  use, 135, 137
Order forms, 175–177, 182, 183, 213, 214
Ordering. *See also* Purchasing.
  frozen foods, 45, 46
  procedure check, 47
  quantity, 45
  staples, 5
Order placing, 223, 224
Originator, communications, 288–291, 294
Output, 302
Overlays, kitchen, 81, 82

Packaging. *See* Containers.
Palatability, 206, 207
Par stock purchasing, 177, 178
Pasteurized milk, 263
Pattern
  cyclical menu, 36–40
Percentage analysis
  comparative, 108–110
Performance factors in
  purchasing, 174
Perfringens, 63–65
Personal involvement, 119, 121
Planning
  budget as a tool, 134
  development, 119–121
  kitchen plan, 80
  need, 134, 140
Portion control, 52, 189, 190
Pot pies
  bacterial problems, 75
Poultry
  cooking, 53
  defrosting, 51, 52
  temperature effects, 57
Prepared foods
  cooking, 51
  defrosting, 53, 54
  effects of temperature, 57
  frozen, 71–74
  storage life, 59
Price
  changes, 198
  checking, 3
  eggs, 248, 249

Printer, computer, 306
Problems, communication, 292, 295
Procedures
  defrosting foods, 51–52
  obtaining information, 119
  ordering, 45–47
  purchasing food, 212, 213
  receiving, 47, 48
  preventing contamination, 71
  sanitation, 75
Process chart, kitchen, 83
Process cheese, 275
Process, communication, 286–288
Processing plant
  sanitation practices, 72, 73
Product review, purchasing, 185
Production, 35
  sanitation practices, 72
  standardized recipes, 35
Productivity, 158
Profit, 140, 148–151
  gross, 116
  net, 115, 116
Profit and loss statement, 99, 100, 102, 105, 107–109
  accounting period, 104
  break-even analysis, 141
  comparative, 105–108
  content, 103, 104
  example, 103
  format, 103
  function, 99, 102–104
  items, 103, 104
Profit volume ratio, 148, 149–151
Program, computer, 306
Programmable calculators, 306
Protein, in food poisoning, 65
Psychrophilic bacteria, 74
Psychrometer, 22
Ptomaine, 63
Punch cards, computer, 303
Purchasing. *See also* Bids; Grades; Ordering; Specifications.
  beef, 212, 215
  bids, 177, 182
  by grade, 173, 174, 180, 181, 220, 226, 245–248
  canned fruits and vegetables, 221–241
  contract, 184
  dairy products, 259–284
  eggs, 242, 258
  food, in general, 167–186
  forecast, 168

forms, 176, 177, 182, 183
  for use, 187, 188, 218, 221-223, 252, 253, 259, 260
information sources, 171, 172
inventory, 169
knowledge, 167, 168
market, 170, 171
market reports, 171, 172
menu relationship, 168
mini-max, 177, 179
needs, 167, 259, 260
par stock, 177, 178
performance, 174
procedure, 175, 176
purveyors, 170
quality, 173
salesmen, 170, 184
seasonality, 171, 172
size, 246, 247
sources of food, 170, 249, 260, 262
specifications, 174-176
standards, 173, 174
tests, 175
weights, 173, 246, 247
Purchasing, dairy quantity guide, 261
Purchase invoice stamp, 14
Purveyors, 170, 171

Quality approved products, 280
Quality
  beef, 188, 189, 204-212
  canned fruits and vegetables, 226, 227
  checking, 3, 47, 48
  dairy products, 260-282
  eggs, 245, 246
  frozen foods, 45
  in purchasing, 173
  loss, 19, 75
  maintenance, 71
  standards, 188, 189, 226, 227, 245, 246
Quantity
  checking, 3
  frozen foods, 52
  guide, dairy products, 261
Quick ratio, 113

Racks, 19
Ratios
  contribution, 111
  current, 111, 112
  financial, 108, 110-112

interstatement, 110
limitations, 116, 117
liquidity, 111
marginal income, 142
net working capital, 111, 113, 114
operating, 108, 110
profitability, 111
profit volume, 142, 144-148
quick (acid test), 113
selection, 117, 118
solvency, 111, 114, 115
Receiving
  area, 5
  average weight chart, 8, 9
  beef, 215, 216
  canned fruits and vegetables, 240, 241
  clerk, 3-5
  control, 2, 15
  equipment, 6, 7, 19
  forms and records, 9-14, 90-93
  frozen foods, 47, 48
  importance, 1
  location, 5
  manual, 9
  meat, 215, 216
  methods, 3
  practiced evaluation, 2
  principles, 7
  procedures, 2, 7, 9, 15
  responsibility, 1, 4
  returning merchandise, 14
  space requirement, 5
  specifications, 8, 9
  substitute invoice, 10, 11
  tests, 15
Receiving clerk
  duties, 4, 5
  responsibility, 3-5
Receiving clerk's daily report, 12, 13, 91-93
Receiving record
  contents, 10
  control, 91
  forms, 91-93
  function, 9, 90
Recipes, standard, 35
Recipients, communication, 288-291, 294
Recontamination of food, 73
Reader, computer, 306
Refreezing, 54, 55
Refrigerated storage, 31, 32
  practices, 31, 32
Refrigeration
  bacteria control, 68, 69

frozen, 22
normal, 22
of beef, 216, 217
reach-in, 48–50
walk-in, 48–50
Regulation of dairy products, 263
Requisition, food, 93
Reserves for depreciation schedule, 100
Responsibility
    communication, 285, 296
    food purchasing, 167
    frozen foods, 44, 47
    storeroom, 91
    training, 158
Retained earnings schedule, 100
Re-translator, communication, 288–291
Returning merchandise, 14, 15
Roller process, 276
Roquefort cheese, 274, 275
Rotation
    in storage, 49
Rusting of cans, 240

Safety program
    necessity, 72
Sales
    gross, 116
    net, 116
Sales analysis record
    annual, 125
    daily, 125
    monthly, 125
Sales budgets, 119
Salesmen, relationships, 184, 215
Salmonella, 63, 64
Sanitation
    in freezers, 72
    in storage, 32
    practices in production, 72
    program, 61, 66, 67, 69, 72
Scales
    receiving, 6
    storage, 21
Scatter graph
    construction, 143, 144
    expenses, 142–145
    use, 142–145
Scoops, 20
Scoring factors for canned fruits and
        vegetables, 231, 233
Scoring sheets, 233, 234
Seasonality, 171–173, 202, 203

Segregation
    in storage, 49
Servicing
    refrigerators and freezers, 25, 26
Shellfish. *See* Fish.
Shells of eggs, 244, 251
Shelves and shelving, 21, 25
Sherbet, 278
Shigella, 66
Shortages, 14
Shrink tests, 175
Size
    beef, 189
    butter, 266
    canned fruits and vegetables, 237, 238
    containers, 237, 238
    eggs, 246, 247
    frozen food units, 46
Skids, 19
Soft-serve, 278, 279
Space
    workers, 84
Specifications. *See also* Beef specifications.
    beef, 196, 197, 213
    canned fruits and vegetables, 238, 239
    dairy products, 281, 282
    eggs, 250
    in purchasing, 174–176
    use, 213
    writing, 174, 175
Spoilage of food
    frozen foods, 73, 74
Spores, 63, 64
Spray dry process milk, 275, 276
Stamps
    inspection, 211
    purchase invoice, 14
Standardization of milk, 262
Standard operating procedure, 44
Standards
    identity, 225, 226
    purchasing, 173, 174
    ratios and percentages, 117, 118
Standing orders, 177
Staples, ordering, 177, 178
Staphylococcus, 62–64, 69
Storage
    arrangement, 48, 49
    beef, 215–217
    boxes, 23
    canned foods, 21, 22
    control, 90–98
    dairy products, 24, 28, 30, 31

eggs, 24, 30
equipment, 19, 23
fish, 28
forms, 87–89
frozen foods, 25, 32
fruits, 24, 26
location, 18
management, 17, 18
meats, 23, 24, 26–28
odors, 30
perishables, 20
practices, 19, 20
product requirements, 18
recommendations, 31
refrigerated, 22, 23
rotation, 49
sanitation, 32
segregation, 49
semi-perishables, 18–20
ventilation, 22
Storages
freezer, 25, 32, 48
reach-in, 23, 25, 48
refrigerated, 23, 25, 48
walk-in, 23, 25, 48
Storeroom
clerk, 91
conditions, 20
control, 91, 93
equipment, 20, 21, 25
humidity, 24
inventory, 95–97
issues, 94
location, 20, 22, 23, 25, 26
management, 17–23
practices, 19, 20
requisition, 91–94
shelving, 21, 22, 25
size, 20
space, 22, 23
temperature, 21, 22
Streptococcus, 63, 64
Style of pack, 223
Substitution invoice, 10, 11
Supply changes, beef, 202, 203
Swells, 240
Symptoms
bacterial food poisoning, 62–66
communication problems, 286, 287
Syrup density, 228

Tables, 7, 19
Taste tests, 175, 189

Templates, 81, 82
Temperature
at center, 67–69
beef storage, 216, 217
checking, 48–50
damage, 55–56
defrosting, 50–52
duration, 68
effects on food, 55–57
effects on microorganisms, 73, 75
eggs, 251, 252
holding, 54
limits, 67
prepared frozen foods, 73–75
recommended, 58, 59, 67, 68
requirements, 21, 55–57
storage, 23–31
storage life, 58, 59
storerooms, 23–28
Terminal, 306
Tests
cooking, 175
cutting, 175
profitability, 115, 116
shrink, 175
solvency, 114, 115
taste, 175
yield, 175
Thawing. See Defrosting.
Thermometer, 7, 19, 22, 23, 48
check, 49
location in storage, 49
Time
effects on frozen foods, 55–57
kitchen, 79
Toxin, 63, 64, 69
Training
application, 162
advantages, 159
cyclical menu relationship, 36
follow-up, 162
instructors, 160
kinds, 160
management role, 164, 165
methods, 160, 161
objectives, 161
on-the-job, 158, 161, 162
orientation, 158
period, 164
preparation, 161, 162
presentation, 162
Translator, communication, 288–291, 294
Transportation, beef, 200, 201

Trucks, hand, 7, 19
Turnover
  capital, 113, 114
  frozen foods, 45

Uniform identity program, National Live
    Stock and Meat Board, 198, 199
University of Massachusetts
  frozen foods research, 55
Unloading, 49
Use of produce. *See also* Cooking.
  as purchasing basis, 167–169
  eggs, 247, 252, 253
  egg products, 254, 255
U.S. Consumer Grades, eggs, 245, 246
U.S. Department of Agriculture
  acceptance service, 197, 250
  beef yields, 205, 209–211
  butter grades, 204, 205, 207–209
  canned fruit and vegetable grades, 224,
    225, 230–234
  cheese quality standards, 279, 280
  dairy products, 279, 290
  egg products inspection, 250, 251
  egg standards, 245, 246
  frozen foods, 45, 46
  fruit and vegetable grades, 224, 245,
    230–234
  inspection, 211, 212
  institutional meat specifications, 197
  livestock division, consumer and
    marketing service, 198
  market reports, 171, 204
  specifications, 197, 198, 249, 250
U.S. Department of Commerce, National
    Bureau of Standards, 235
U.S. Public Health Service
  bacteria growth, 54, 55
  Grade A Pasteurized Milk Ordinance,
    263

Variable cost percent, 150
Variable operating budget, 124
Variety, 223

Vegetables
  canned, 224, 225
  cooking, 59
  defrosting, 51
  storage, 20, 23–25
  storage life, 58
  temperature effects, 57
Ventilation
  air circulation, 49, 50
  frozen foods storage, 49, 50
  storage, 22
Vitamin D, in milk, 263

Water ice, 278
Weight
  beef, 189
  canned fruits and vegetables, drained,
    233–235
  charts, average, 9
  checking, 46, 47
  drained, 233, 234
  as factor in purchasing, 173, 174
Weight charts, 9
Western Utilization Research and Develop-
    ment Laboratory, U.S.D.A., 55
White of egg, 244, 254–259
Wholesomeness
  inspection of beef, 211, 212
Wire baskets, 7
Wisconsin grading system, dairy products,
    280
Worker characteristics, 164
Work centers, 81
Work space
  areas of reach, 85, 86
  layout, 83, 85, 86

Yeasts, 19
Yield
  beef carcasses, 205, 208, 210, 212
  grades, 205, 209–211
  tests, 188, 189
Yogurt, 264

8 8 6 1

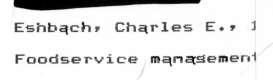